Virginia Tech
Land-Grant University

1872–1997

Virginia Tech
Land-Grant University
1872–1997

History of a School, a State, a Nation

Second Edition

Peter Wallenstein

VIRGINIA TECH.
PUBLISHING

Blacksburg, Virginia

Second Edition first published 2021 by Virginia Tech Publishing

Virginia Tech Publishing
University Libraries at Virginia Tech
560 Drillfield Drive
Blacksburg, VA 24061

Cataloging in Publication Data
Name: Wallenstein, Peter, 1944– author.
Title: Virginia Tech, Land-Grant University, 1872–1997: History of a School, a State, a Nation | Peter Wallenstein.
Description: Second Edition | Blacksburg, VA : Virginia Tech Publishing, 2021.
 | Includes bibliographical references and index.
Identifiers: ISBN: 978-1-949373-78-3 (PDF) | ISBN: 978-1-949373-79-0 (epub) |
 ISBN: 978-1-949373-77-6 (pbk) | DOI: https://doi.org/XXXXX
Subjects: 1. Virginia Polytechnic Institute and State University—Education.
 2. Virginia—History. 3. Higher Education—History. 4. Education—Government
 Policy.

In memory of my parents—
R. Carol Wallenstein and
Crandall R. Wallenstein—who
grew up urban folks but who, in
the years after World War Two,
made a rural home near a faraway
small town

For my brothers and sisters—
Ckristopher, Andrew, Kathryn,
Nancy, Mark, Holly, and Faith—all
of whom, wherever life took them,
have returned to New Hampshire

For Sookhan, who came from
halfway around the world

And for
the students, staff, and faculty
of Virginia Tech
past, present, and future

Contents

Illustrations

Preface to the First Edition

Dan Thorp and I keep very busy with our work at Virginia Tech. This might surprise anyone who accepts uncritically the notion that he generally teaches only one course, or "three hours" a week, and I usually teach only two cour-ses. But, as associate chair of the Department of History, Thorp also runs the undergraduate history program, schedules all undergraduate history classes, and advises half the undergraduates in the Western world. In addition, he writes essays, works on his next book, and serves on various committees. His "three hours" of work take anywhere from 40 to 60 hours a week to do and do right. He does right.

I teach my classes, in fact keep making up new classes to teach, and assign multiple essays to however many students I have in a class, whether 20 or 120. I direct graduate theses and independent studies, work with various department commit-tees, and give talks to high school classes and historical societies and at professional conferences. I am always at work on about 17 research projects—always coming across an idea that I wish to explore, though it may have to wait its turn until next week or next year.

Nonetheless, I stop by Dan's office almost every day, and he stops by mine often, too. This book is his fault, I think. He stopped by my office.

This particular visit came on Thursday, January 23, 1997, soon after spring semester began. The topic Thorp brought to me was Tech's upcoming 125th anniversary. A possible course on the history of Virginia Tech floated to the surface of our conversation. Rather than reject the idea—my wife knows I try to do far too much, and she reminds me from time to time that I do not have enough time—I decided to teach such a course. It should be a big class, as many as 125 students, and have no prerequisites, so that pretty much anyone who wished to take it could do so.

That was the easy part. Within days, Thorp had it on the books, scheduled to be taught beginning in August. By then I had begun thinking of what I must do to prepare to teach it. My students, all of them, would of course go out and do short research papers on some aspect of Tech's past—seek out and analyze documents, interview people who remembered the 1930s or 1950s, spend time in *The Virginia Tech* or *Collegiate Times*. They would be historians in my history course and, under my direction, write their own history.

But they would need a road map. What would I assign them, something already written, to guide them through the course? Nothing of the sort existed, nothing that remotely met the specifications I had in mind. Sure, Tech had sponsored a big book by Duncan Lyle Kinnear on the history of the school for its hundredth birthday in 1972. Much more recently, Clara Cox had taken charge of two fine books, one in 1996 celebrating the 75th anniversary of women students at Tech, the other, out at the beginning of 1997, offering wonderful photographs and outlining the major developments associated with each of Tech's presidential administrations through its first 125 years.

For my course, I wanted something else. And I needed it in six months—not just an idea, preferably not just a typescript, but a book: published (even if only in a preliminary version), illustrated and inexpensive, sitting on a shelf in the Tech bookstore. I considered an outline of how I might organize such a book, but I turned my attention back to an essay I had to mail off. Then—to test the model—I tried out a sample chapter, on the look of the world before there was a Virginia Tech. It seemed to work. I put some other things in the mail, and then I turned serious. Valentine's Day, a Friday, occasioned the beginnings of two draft chapters, one on the 1920s, one on the 1990s.

I had fun. I knew some of what I needed. I knew the major questions I wanted to explore, to expose my students and other readers to. I had ideas, information, a sense of the size of the book, the pace, the level of detail. When I turned my full attention to writing it, I found myself spurred by the pleasures of writing about my own institution, rather than deterred by the terrors of doing so. The project took on a life of its own.

I still needed a book. I found it—though, when I did, I found it had doubled in length from my original projections. (Inevitably, I have neglected many people, places, events, and topics that merit mention.) I hope you find it's a mixture of satisfying, provocative, entertaining. If you do, then I did right.

* * *

This book had a late start, but its origins go back the length of my biography. Before I first came to Blacksburg, in 1983, I had already taught at Sarah Lawrence College, at the University of Toronto, and with the University of Maryland on military posts overseas—in Korea, Japan, and Guam. Thus, I had taught small classes and large ones, in little schools and big ones, private schools and public institutions, whether a teaching college or a research university, in North America and Asia. I had wonderful colleagues and great students at each place.

I brought all those experiences with me when I moved to Virginia to teach at Tech. I had previously lived in Virginia, but it was the Tidewater, not the mountains, and I was too young to remember—it was my first home, my Dad was in the military during World War II, and not long after that we moved to New Hampshire. By way of detours long and many, I eventually moved south more than half the length of the Appalachian Trail.

Many of the people and buildings mentioned in this book came and went long before my arrival at Tech. But I have had offices in McBryde and Major Williams and have lived at Foxridge and out North Main Street. Many of my colleagues in the history department arrived at Tech at just about the time I began teaching at Sarah Lawrence in 1970, so they have taught here as long as Tech has been a university.

For a decade now I have taught the history of Virginia, and for much of that time the subject has given me more fresh topics that I can investigate. I teach Virginia history; I write Virginia history; I teach at Tech. Deciding to teach a class on the history of Virginia Tech was a natural; so was deciding to write a book on that history. Long before it occurred to me to write this book, I was preparing for when I would.

I intend this book for far more people than will take my class, for I have multiple audiences in mind. I am writing for historians, educators, anyone interested in the development of higher education in America. I have in mind all my students from over the years—including the ones who said things like, "Doc, when are you going to write your book on the history of Virginia?" I intend it for all the students at Virginia Tech, past, present, and future—and for their families, who might want to know more about the place their sons, daughters, brothers, sisters, or grandchildren have gone off to. It is also for the faculty and staff at Virginia Tech—again past, present, and future—some of whom no doubt know portions of the story better than I do but who doubtless also have misconceptions or unanswered questions.

This book is also for my parents, for R. Carol Wallenstein and in memory of Crandall R. Wallenstein. It is for my brothers and sisters: Ckristopher, Andrew, Kathryn, Nancy, Mark, Holly, and Faith; and it is for Sookhan.

* * *

No history is written without help from researchers and writers who came before. Certainly this is true of a work that relies on studies of many institutions and many states to chart points of

reference and sketch other histories. Along my main story line,
I have relied heavily in places on Duncan Lyle Kinnear's pioneering book on the history of Virginia Tech, and Clara Cox's
more recent work has lightened my load and lighted my way,
too.

I have had the fortune to have in my classes over the years
various students who, historians in their own right, have told
portions of the story that appears in this book. Chief among
them is Anthony Deel, whose master's thesis I directed some
years ago on the early years of racial desegregation in Virginia's institutions of higher education. Among my undergraduates—particularly those who worked with me as I grew better
about shepherding them toward original research in Virginia
history—some whose work then helped me in my work here are
Jennifer Alderson, Michael Phelps, and Wendy Wickham.

Various people—Tech faculty, administrators, and alumni—
have shared with me, and thus with my readers, perceptions
and recollections of various aspects of Tech's history. Some have
inspired one story or another with things they have said over
the years. Tom Adriance, had he lived, could have enriched
some portions of the later chapters. Jack Dudley and Barbara
Cowles in University Honors urged me on.

Other people, too, helped in important ways. My hasty
writing benefited much from Byrgen Finkelman's keen eye and
red pencil. Sookhan and Hugh Campbell also read chapters
and improved the final product by their comments on style or
substance. I have swapped materials with Elaine Carter as she
developed the history of black women at Tech. In the closing
weeks, Cordel Faulk chased down some final things—newspaper stories, enrollment figures. Mary C. Holliman provided me
a good press that could meet my impossible deadline, and Laura Wilson worked wonders in formatting the text for printing.

People in Media Services, PhotoGraphic Services, Special
Collections, and University Relations provided essential help in

my obtaining most of the illustrations. Jack Dudley in University Honors helped with money to cover the costs of reproducing those illustrations, as did Bert Moyer from the history department's Johnston–Lucinian Fund.

* * *

Some of my students at Tech contributed to this history. Many more will no doubt contribute to another printing or subsequent edition, one that reveals new stories or that remedies shortcomings in old ones, and I will continue to work with this project. I have not solved to my satisfaction all the mysteries I have encountered.

That brings me to note an invitation to my readers: Some of you will say, as you peruse a page: Yes, that's exactly right, that's the way I remember it. As likely as not, however, you will have occasion at some point to shake your head and say: No, that's not right. Or you may think: If only the author had told a related story, as I recall it.

When you have any of those responses, please feel free to let the author know. Email me at pwallens@vt.edu or write to me at the Department of History, Virginia Tech, Blacksburg, Virginia 24061. Perhaps a subsequent printing can accommodate changes.

All such eventualities have the potential of making this book a continuing, open-ended project, and an interactive one, one in which the people of Tech continue to participate. That is what I hope for.

Peter Wallenstein
Blacksburg, Virginia
June 1997

Preface to the Second Edition

In late 2017, Virginia Tech president Timothy D. Sands appointed a Council on Virginia Tech History, to be led by Vice provost Menah Pratt-Clarke and chaired by theatre arts professor Robert Leonard. During the next few months, the Council developed an ambitious menu of projects. It set its own agenda, but its work would also, to some extent, mesh with a soon-to-be-formed steering committee to oversee planning for the university's official 150th anniversary in 2022.

The Council set out to explore the history of the place, its people, and its programs. Our charge, as I quickly came to see it, was first to assess Virginia Tech's current landscape, and then press on to develop a robust sense of how the present had emerged from the past, all of this with an eye to the future. What might—or rather what should, what would we like to see—Tech become? So, the historical work was intended, in part, to stretch out and fill in the boundaries of knowledge about the school's past and, at the same time, press toward desired change, as past met future. The Council's work has often emphasized developing a greater understanding of what we've called "hidden stories."

Among the wide range of projects soon undertaken by the Council was a new history of Virginia Tech, to be written by me as history professor and Council member. My intention is to construct the new book on the foundation established in *Virginia Tech, Land-Grant University, 1872–1997*, which I wrote in 1997 to mark the university's 125th anniversary. I had long referred to that book as "the little orange book," or "Orange," and I referred to the proposed new book as "Maroon," an informal title soon adopted by the rest of the Council.

All Council members read Orange as their first item of business. From the very beginning, therefore, the 1997 book informed, and at times inspired, the Council's work going forward. Maroon will revisit and expand on the history presented in Orange while also extending the period under exploration through the first two decades of the twenty-first century.

Along the way, an idea emerged to bring out an intermediate book project, a new edition of the 1997 book, or "Orange 2.0." That new edition would enable me to bring Orange back into print, while permitting some touching up of the original: light editing throughout and, as the revisions unfolded, extensive renovation in places, particularly in the chapter on the 1950s. The most substantial changes are the addition of this lengthy new preface.

In substance, it remains much the same book—in its approach and structure and pace, with many passages, especially in the early chapters, altered little if at all. I have eliminated scattered infelicities of fact or phrasing that had made their way into the original, and my understanding of many matters has definitely evolved. On the whole, Orange has worn well, especially for a book quickly written. But the narrative in Orange 2.0 is certainly improved, and various images are new.

With the publication of this new edition, Orange 2.0 is supplanting Orange 1.0. The remainder of this new preface highlights some of the changes in emphasis or detail I have made to this revised edition—or that I will include in Maroon.

Addressing Readers' Recommendations

In the years since Orange appeared in August 1997, various readers have taken me up on my invitation to point out shortcomings they saw in the original.

Among the early entries from discerning readers, Louis Trigg, class of 1950, clearly remembered Rohran Tung, a native of China who had graduated in his class and appeared in my book. Why, though, he asked, had I highlighted Rohran but neglected her sister Shiran? Once I knew to look for Shiran, I found her; she had graduated the year before.

Later, I located and corresponded with both Shiran and Rohran. Each had gone on to another institution, in both cases land-grant schools, to obtain a master's degree. Each had married and settled in America, and, many years after their time at VPI, the two were living a short distance from each other. They had shifted their homes from South China to Southern California but had studied at VPI along the way.

Some concerns came not directly to me but, rather, through university archivist Tamara J. Kennelly. From one of the six pioneer black women of 1966—Linda Adams Hoyle, class of 1968—I heard that she definitely did not come to Blacksburg as a transfer student, as I had stated. Rather, she had simply moved to the main campus after completing her lower-division work at a branch campus of VPI near her hometown, Covington. That school, the first edition of today's Dabney S. Lancaster Community College, in Clifton Forge, had opened in 1964, just in time for her to start her college classes there.

In a book I co-authored in 2004 with Warren Strother—a study of President T. Marshall Hahn's transforming presidency of VPI during the 1960s—I was able to correct that misstatement. Not only was she Tech's first black female graduate, Linda Adams was very likely the first female African American ever to enroll at any campus of VPI.

In that later book I was also able to address a concern raised by another of the students who, like Linda Adams, came to Blacksburg in one of the first two classes for which African Americans were actually recruited to VPI, free—unlike their predecessors of the 1950s—to live in campus housing and to pursue any academic major that the school offered. This was

Dr. James D. Watkins, class of 1971 and a founding member of a VPI chapter of a black fraternity, Groove Phi Groove. With an off-campus rented house at what is now 302 Jackson Street, Groove Phi Groove promptly became a hugely important part of campus life for black students, who had generally found their chosen college to be academically rewarding but socially uncomfortable.

In early 2018, I heard from someone who had, online, come across one of my early writings on Virginia Tech. Gigi Lee-aphon—daughter of Cato Lee, class of 1927, the third ethnic Chinese young man to enroll at VPI, the second to graduate, the first to spend four years at the school—contacted me and then visited campus to see where her father's footsteps might have taken him. She visited, for example, Barracks No. 1, the building that acquired the name Lane Hall years after his footsteps took him back to Asia. She had recently published a book on her father and his family. Now the story of his time at VPI can be told within a far richer context as to how he made his way from Thailand to China to Hong Kong to Canada to New York to western Virginia, and then how, when he returned to Thailand, he took with him his training in mechanical engineering and his experiences in the Corps of Cadets.

These are among the many reconsiderations that I have partly addressed in this new edition of Orange and plan to incorporate more fully into Mar-oon. New materials make it clear that the readily available documentary evidence can go a great distance in recreating the past—but only so far. To construct a full and accurate story, one needs, where possible, to listen to the individuals who actually lived the lives under discussion.

New Evidence, New Understandings

Elaine Dowe Carter grew up in Montgomery County, but after graduating from the all-black Christiansburg Institute in 1948 she left the region. Returning in the 1990s, she enrolled as what she called "Tech's oldest graduate student" and catalyzed an effort—the "Black Women at Virginia Tech Oral History Proj-ect"—to recover the stories of the pioneer black female students who arrived in Blacksburg in 1966, among them Linda Adams, who accomplished at that time what Elaine Carter could not when beginning college eighteen years earlier. Joining in the project was the recently hired university archivist, Tamara Kennelly.

In March 1996 Elaine Carter interviewed Dr. Linda Edmonds Turner, class of 1970. At roughly the same time, Tamara Kennelly interviewed Marguerite Harper Scott and Jacquelyn Butler Blackwell. That project led to similar interviews with the two other surviving members of the 1966 cohort ("Freddi" Hairston, later Dr. LaVerne Higgins, and Linda Adams Hoyle) as well as with some pioneer black men of the 1950s. More such interviews followed, and the resulting tapes and transcripts shed invaluable light on several rich chapters of Tech's history between the 1950s and the 1970s.

Irving Peddrew's interview revealed that he had applied to VPI in 1953 only because Mrs. Elizabeth Hines, a teacher at Phenix High School, on the campus of Hampton Institute, had advised him in the spring of his senior year that "they are beginning to take our people at their schools," or words to that effect, and that he would be an ideal candidate to push the process along.

That clue from Peddrew widened my inquiry regarding the process that brought the first African American students to a segregated college—how critical it was to be nurtured and encouraged by black teachers in the segregated schools to think in those terms. Lindsay Cherry, who enrolled at VPI the next year, together with two of his classmates from Norfolk's Booker T. Washington High School, tells a similar story about his teachers, in particular physics teacher John Perry—the prime mover in sending the trio to VPI in 1954—and math teacher James Johnson.

Peddrew's observation eventually led to my realization that, indeed, Mrs. Hines would have known about people like the first black doctoral student at the University of Virginia (Walter N. Ridley enrolled in 1950 and finished his Ed.D. in 1953) and the first black students permitted to enroll at the College of William and Mary (Edward A. Travis, for one, entered the law school in 1951 and graduated in 1954). Not only were they in the news, they both came from local families. In fact, as I discovered, the Hines family and the Ridley family were related. As for Mr. Perry and his efforts in 1954, he would have known about Irving Peddrew's enrollment at VPI in 1953. So the process in Virginia of race and change in higher education continued to unfold, or rather specific individuals saw to it that the momentum continued.

The men of 1954 opened for me yet another vista for understanding the process of desegregation. Ever since the 1920s, the Norfolk-based Lincoln Foundation (now Lincoln–Lane) has pursued a mission of dispensing scholarship funds to enable financially challenged youths from Tidewater Virginia to attend college. Aware that perhaps none among his trio of prospective VPI students would be financially able to enroll even if accepted, John Perry successfully urged the men of the foundation to expand their constituency and provide aid to his three graduating seniors at Booker T. Washington High.

Interviews and conversations also brought to light another dimension of the process of desegregating VPI—the critical importance of the elderly black couple who supplied a home for the first eight black students, none of whom was permitted to live on campus. Lindsay Cherry has highlighted this feature in his statement that Janie and William Hoge "offered love, compassion, and guidance to the young trailblazers, who were in search of a better life, for themselves and for others."

Recovering and Revising Other Stories

"Skipper"—the cannon that goes ka-boom each time Tech scores a touchdown at Lane Stadium—how did it come to be?

Two key figures behind it—Alton "Butch" Harper and Homer "Sonny" Hickam, both class of 1964—each, at the turn of the century, offered an account of how some cadets wondered: How come VMI had a cannon to fire, and VPI did not? And could the Blacksburg team come up with its own firepower, so it could better take on its chief rival of that time, the team from Lexington, at their annual Thanksgiving Day game at the old Victory Stadium in Roanoke? The answer came in November 1963, and many years later the backstory came to light.

As one result of my 1997 book, Warren Strother invited me to help him bring to conclusion a dual biography of President Hahn and Virginia Tech, focusing on the dozen years the two intersected. Inclined, as with Orange, to be friendly enough, but determined not to write an "authorized" history, I held Hahn at arm's length on the project until it was about done. Then I ran it by him, and he had a few corrections or suggestions. For example, he asked, "Don't you think there ought to be [a short stand-alone section] on Peggy?" "Sure," I agreed. He of course would know far better than I how to present the first lady of VPI during his presidency, as well as what he wanted to emphasize. "Tell you what," I said. "You draft it, and be sure to put in quotation marks the language you want to be attributed to you." So he did.

Virginia Tech's first Gay Awareness Week took place in January 1979, its events including the first "Denim Day" at Virginia Tech. Nancy Kelly, class of 1980, was a leader as the Gay Student Alliance served notice to the entire campus that some community members were gay or lesbian. By calling for students to wear denim on the Wednesday of that week, the Gay Student Alliance required people to consider how their clothing for the day might get them taken—or not—for being gay or an ally.

In April 2019, dozens of people, from the 1970s to the present, among them Nancy Kelly, attended a "Denim Day Do-Over" on the Tech campus. They gathered in the new Moss Arts Center for photos to mark the event and contributed to a

"Denim Day at Virginia Tech 40th Anniversary Oral History Collection." While giving renewed visibility to the events of four decades earlier, they offered a historical reconstruction of those events—and a means for present students to pay a visit to the world of the late 1970s. At the time of their gathering in 2019, people at the reunion could visit the LGBTQ+ Resource Center, which had recently opened in Squires Student Center.

Years ago, when helping to create a poster representing early "international students" for the then-Multicultural Center in Squires (across the corridor from the Black Cultural Center), I came across a small number of students from Latin America. All were men—that is, before Carmen Venegas, who graduated in electrical engineering, class of 1938. The first Latina to attend VPI, she had come to Virginia from Costa Rica, and she went on to help design planes that in turn helped the United States win World War Two. Newspaper stories about her in the 1940s, while speaking of her background, mentioned that she was writing a book titled "My Papa." Eventually I tracked down her daughter, Karen Livesay, who has an array of such materials from her mother. El Centro, a Hispanic and Latino Center, opened in Squires in 2016.

When Tim Sands became president of Virginia Tech in 2014, he and his wife, Dr. Laura Sands, were soon hearing fascinating stories, especially from old-timers. And they wondered whether those experiences had ever been recorded, so they could be preserved. These concerns led to a new enterprise, "VT Stories," which, under the direction of English professor Katrina Powell, produced an ever-growing collection of accounts of life at Tech (and beyond) over the past six decades and more. Interviewees include two notable graduates in engineering from the last years before Tech became a university: Matthew M. "Matt" Winston Sr., class of 1959, and Mary Virginia "Prim" Jones, class of 1962.

Tech's Earliest Years

Tech's earliest years, too, are being reconsidered. Thanks to the book *More Than a Fraction*, it is possible to know far more than ever before about the black majority who lived on Solitude plantation. The Solitude property was already part of the new land-grant college's campus when classes began in October 1872, and the house itself has long been the oldest surviving structure on campus (ever since the original Preston and Olin Building burned down more than a century ago). The book's author, Dr. Kerri Moseley-Hobbs, is herself descended from the Fractions, one of the enslaved families living and working on the place in the 1850s and 1860s.

In the years since publication of Orange in 1997, the work of Virginia Tech writer Clara B. Cox has substantially enhanced our knowledge of the institution's founding. Tech's predecessor school was already becoming a college by 1869, she found, under the name Preston and Olin Institute. And it was not, she discovered, in dire financial straits in 1872 when it gave itself over to become Virginia Agricultural and Mechanical College.

Cox's resourceful review of the evidence has confirmed that William Addison "Add" Caldwell was the first student to enroll at VAMC. More than that, her work demonstrates that indeed he already had a scholarship in hand, as one of the "state students" (one from each district in the House of Delegates), when he arrived at the new school's front door on the afternoon of October 1, 1872.

And she has challenged the timeline that dates Virginia Tech's origins to 1872. Without question, the Virginia legislature established a land-grant institution at Blacksburg in March of that year. But the beginning can just as readily be traced back to the founding of its predecessor school, as a number of institutions do (among them Longwood University and the University of Tennessee). Classes at the Olin and Preston Institute began in 1851; the legislature granted the school a charter under that name in 1854; a large building to house it opened in 1855. The school obtained a subsequent charter, in January 1869, as the Preston and Olin Institute. Under that name, it was granted land-grant money in 1872 under certain conditions, among them adopting a new identity as Virginia Agricultural and Mechanical College.

Even as Orange came off the press in 1997, I had in mind possibly writing a follow-up book, Maroon. That new history would supply a fuller account of the school's history, would date the beginnings to 1854, and would therefore mark the 150th anniversary in 2004, just seven years later. In short, although I did not follow through at that time, Maroon began taking shape in my mind long before any discussion of a book marking Tech's sesquicentennial in 2022.

Lineage of Land and People

An alternative approach to Virginia Tech's early years can extend the story all the way back to the 1750s, not just the 1850s. Lucy Lee Lancaster, who enrolled at VPI in 1921 in the first cohort of female students, sat down for an interview six decades later, in which she supplied some extraordinary clues to the history of her family since colonial times—and of the area around what would eventually become the village of Blacksburg and later the home of Virginia Tech.

She spoke of her father, William Lancaster, as having enrolled at Virginia Agricultural and Mechanical College in 1872, in the new land-grant school's very first cohort of cadets. More than that, speaking of her earliest forebears in the New River Valley, she recounted that Casper Barger—who had been born in one of the German states in 1708 and had immigrated to Pennsylvania in 1738—had bought land (in the amount of 507 acres) at Drapers Meadows in 1754 and then visited it during the next summer to prepare to move the extended Barger family there from the Shenandoah Valley. Accompanying him, it appears, were Philip Barger the elder (Casper's father) and 13-year-old Philip the younger (Casper's son). Casper Barger was visiting at the Ingles place next door on the July day that a band of Native warriors happened to converge there as well.

The attack is conventionally characterized as the "Drapers Meadows Massacre." It took place in the early stages of the struggle known as the French and Indian War, during which hundreds of white settlers in western Virginia were killed, or taken captive, by Indians who were determined to try to turn back the tide of settlement. For some years, in fact, the Native resistance proved effective, and the territory remained contested into the era of the American Revolution.

At least one member of the Barger party survived, the not-quite-14-year-old Philip the younger, who made his way northwards back to the family home in the Shenandoah Valley. Not until the early 1770s, as the heir of Casper Barger, did he finally come to reside on the land that his father had intended to be the family's home years earlier. Around 1801, very late in his life, he constructed the tiny first edition of what would later become the house at Solitude.

Use of the King James Bible's "begats" of the Old Testament book of Genesis, or of the New Testament book of Matthew, can track the story directly from Philip Barger to William Lancaster and then on to Lucy Lee herself. Philip Barger (born in 1741) begat Catherine (1782), whose son John Barger Helm (1805) begat Arabella (1830). She married Josiah Lancaster, and their firstborn, in 1857, they named William.

As for the original land, purchased by Casper Barger at Drapers Meadows in 1754, in the years after 1800 it changed hands several times among members of the Barger family and the neighboring Prestons. In the 1850s, Robert Taylor Preston (who by then had inherited it from his father, James Patton Preston) gave his home—known then and now as Solitude—its modern configuration. When William Lancaster's classes began in October 1872, VAMC had just recently purchased the Solitude plantation from Robert Preston as a farm for the campus.

Lucy Lee Lancaster pointed me toward the 1750s. There I found Philip Barger the younger as well as the two older family members she identified, Philip the elder as well as Casper. In 1755, the 13-year-old German-speaking would-be settler Philip Barger was not much younger than his great-great-grandson William Lancaster would be when beginning classes at VAMC at the age of 15, or for that matter Philip Barger's great-great-great-granddaughter Lucy Lee Lancaster, who began at VPI in 1921 at the age of 16, soon joined by her younger sister, Arabella. The saga of Philip Barger the younger opens new ways to understand the history of the place that has become Virginia Tech.

Updating the Pylons

When Orange appeared in 1997, one Pylon listed 36 former Virginia Tech students who had died in the military during the Vietnam War era, a quarter-century and more earlier. But even something so permanent as the Pylons can come to appear incomplete, and over the next quarter-century the roster grew. By late 2017, nine names had been added to the Pylon that listed men from the 1960s and early 1970s, and soon a new name was blasted onto the cenotaph titled "Medal of Honor Alumni." The most recent two men added, both killed in action in Vietnam, embodied extraordinary actions in a time of war. And both satisfied the Board of Visitors' criterion, established in 2018, that a student must have finished at least one year as a Tech student to qualify for inclusion.

Luther James "Jim" Doss Jr. arrived at VPI in 1966 looking to major in engineering. But he married during his sophomore year and took time away to work. Then, drafted, he was sent to

Vietnam. An Army Ranger, he was killed in combat in April 1970. In 2017, his fraternity brother Dana Hesse (class of 1986) discovered that Brother Doss's name was missing from the Pylon—and went to work to remedy that, a task accomplished that November. Doss's son reflected at the time about his dad, "I think he thought, 'if I'm going to be a soldier, I'm going to be the best damn soldier I can be.'"

Another former Tech student, 1st Lt. Gary Lee Miller, died in combat in February 1969. As a young man from Alleghany County, in 1965–1966 he attended the local branch of VPI, what soon became Dabney S. Lancaster Community College. That school had long since honored Miller in two significant ways as a local hero, but the connection to Tech came to light only recently. In November 2020, Miller's name was added on the Cenotaph, bringing to eight the number of names there of former Tech students awarded the Congressional Medal of Honor. When his name gets added also to the Vietnam War era Pylon, the number of names there will have grown by 10 to 46.

Student Research and the History of Virginia Tech

Each time I have taught the "History of Virginia Tech" class—three times back in 1997–1998 and then several times more recently—students have researched some aspect of that history on a topic each has chosen. The book on Marshall Hahn's presidency relied upon and cited numerous papers from the early classes, all of them preserved in compilations and thus still readily accessible in Special Collections and University Archives. Maroon will reflect the more recent work as well.

In one of the early papers, Shane Beamer wrote about his father's playing days at the then-new Lane Stadium and how those experiences subsequently shaped his approach as head coach. Christopher Johnston and William Charbonneau developed a prodigious project on the Rockefeller Foundation scholarships that VPI used with considerable success for a few years beginning in 1966 to go out, often to what were still all-black high schools, and actually recruit black undergraduates. Other students, animated by their own experiences and commitments as Tech undergraduates, have written on the history of theatre arts at Tech, for example, or the great early football player Hunter Carpenter, the YMCA, the German Club, aviation, women engineers, the computer science department, the Marching Virginians, or the Stadium Woods controversy.

Each of these students' work embodies undergraduate research at a research university. Each has contributed something of substance toward a better understanding of their university's past and present. Along the way, each has pulled together the key ingredients of a good historical research paper: ideas, facts, and words or, to use bigger words, the conceptual, empirical, and rhetorical elements of historical research and writing. Each has confronted key questions like: What do I want to know? Where to look for it? What exactly to do with it?

And each has learned the lyrics to a teaching song of mine that begins with "just cuz it's wrote down don't mean it's true." (Other lines are "just cuz it's true don't mean it's relevant"; "just cuz it's relevant don't make it interesting"; and also "just cuz it's true don't mean it's wrote down.")

Graduate students, too, have enriched this history. In 1997, I highlighted Anthony Blaine Deel's crucial contributions excavating the beginnings of racial desegregation not only at Tech but also at other state-supported schools in Virginia. In the years since 1997, Leslie Ogg Williams wrote a master's thesis far more fully developing the history of the first half-century of female enrollment, and Saranette D. Miles did one on the life and career of the redoubtable Laura Jane Harper.

Never "All-Male" or "All-White"

Beyond the more visible constituencies—students and faculty—
Virginia Tech never was an all-male institution, nor was it ever
all-white. From its origins, both men and women—and both
black and white—played significant support roles.

Across the years, white women filled essential roles as administrative assistants and department secretaries. By 1903, when
Mary G. Lacy became VPI's first professional librarian, the
academic work of faculty and students alike, all of them male,
might depend on a woman's knowledge and assistance. Women
also helped keep the campus healthy; Anna G. Hannas, for
example, supervised the infirmary from 1906 to 1945. Cora
Jean Crawford (subsequently Jean Crawford Glassett) served as
secretary to all three presidents of the 1910s and 1920s (Barringer, Eggleston, and Burruss) both before and after the enrollment of the first female students.

Andrew Oliver was employed as a janitor at VAMC from its
beginnings in 1872. The 1880 U.S. census expressly identified
him as "Janitor VA+MC," a job he had held from back when
the school was Preston and Olin Institute. He, his wife, Fannie
Vaughn Oliver, and at least one of their young children, Andrew
Oliver Jr.—all of them having been born nearby into slavery—
worked at the Preston and Olin Building in the 1870s. After an
additional building (eventually it would be named Henderson
Hall) was constructed for the president's home and office, they
worked there as well, and, in the days before telephones and
email, young Andrew conveyed messages from one campus
building to another.

From the 1870s, black residents of Blacksburg and the surrounding area always played important support roles in the life
of the campus, even if neither they nor their children or grandchildren, at least into the 1950s, could ever enroll for classes, let
alone teach there. Among these contributors to the life of the
institution—and to the well-being of its official participants—

some were maids in faculty households, such as Sallie Countz and Mary Kyle in the home of Professor James H. Lane, as captured by the 1880 census.

Some were custodial staff in campus buildings, including Andrew and Fannie Oliver in the 1870s and Gordon Trigg Mills in the 1910s and 1920s. Others were laundresses who looked after cadets' uniforms, as well as Preston Mays, who worked as an orderly in the infirmary, and Nash Tyler, football team trainer. Others among the many black workers on an "all-white" campus were barbers to the cadets, among them Alonzo Freeman and John Sears early in the twentieth century, Fred Caldwell and then Charles A. Johnson later on.

Janie Hoge, as reported in the 1940 census, worked as a chamber maid at the Faculty Center (later called Donaldson Brown; still later, the Graduate Life Center). She and her husband, William Hoge, also ran a small boarding house on East Clay Street, located on what is now a vacant lot adjacent to the First Baptist Church. Beginning in 1953, when the first African American to enroll at VPI, Irving Peddrew, came to Blacksburg, the couple looked after Tech's pioneer black students. During a period of seven years between 1953 and 1960, the Hoges boarded all eight black students, as many as four at a time. During those years, when VPI remained segregated but had begun to enroll a very few black students, not only did those students have to major in engineering in order to attend classes, they were barred from living in the barracks.

The couple offered not only a room but also three meals a day, laundry for their uniforms, and a welcome respite from a campus that was often hostile, or at best indifferent to their presence. The Hoges also introduced the pioneer black students to the wider black community in the town and the surrounding area. As one of those pioneers, Lindsay Cherry, has stressed, and as others including Irving Peddrew have agreed, the Hoges were absolutely central to the success of the dual experiment, by the institution to enroll a few black cadets, by the students themselves who embarked on the initial steps toward desegregation.

It is easy to say that Tech was an all-male institution, and certainly this was true in terms of its student enrollment for roughly its first half-century. It is also easy to say that, regarding the students, the school was perhaps all-white before the 1920s and categorically non-African American into the 1950s. But the institution always had a female presence and always had an African American presence.

Finally, the presence of Cato Lee in the 1920s and of Rohran and Shiran Tung in the 1940s points up how racial segregation worked in Virginia during VPI's second half-century. Persons of color, as they might be described in the twenty-first century, could enroll in any academic program and also live in campus housing—provided they were not African American, i.e., people regarded as having African ancestry from any of the forty-eight states.

Black Virginians could never enroll, even with a raft of racial restrictions, until after all three of these ethnic Chinese students had graduated and gone on to their adult lives, whether back in Asia or still in the United States. In practice, the line separating people on one side of the racial binary from those on the other was between black (as in African American) and nonblack (everyone else), rather than white and nonwhite.

Red and Black in the Making of Virginia Tech

The background to VAMC reflects the complicated history of Virginia Tech and its relationship to settler colonialism, racial capitalism, and national expansion. Native land and black labor combined to make the university possible.

A "land acknowledgment," increasingly called upon in recognizing Tech's location, has evolved in several forms. A short version currently says it this way: "Tutelo/Monacan people are the traditional custodians of this land." A longer version says it like this: "We acknowledge the Tutelo/Monacan people, who are the traditional custodians of the land on which we work and live, and recognize their continuing connection to the land, water, and air that Virginia Tech consumes. We pay respect to the Tutelo/Monacan Nations, and to their elders past, present, and emerging."

Such acknowledgments effectively get at the local history— yet, from a wider perspective, Tech's history actually exists in a national context stretching from the Atlantic Coast states to the Pacific Coast. Thus, the story very much includes Native peoples from west of the Mississippi River as well as from east of it. Taking shape at present is an upgraded land acknowledgment that expressly points toward the Trans-Mississippi West without which there would be no land-grant system of higher education at all, quite aside from any example in western Virginia of such an institution.

In March 2020, the magazine *High Country News* published the results of a prodigious two-year investigation into the financial underpinnings of what it called "land-grab universities." A collection of stories together declared a bold thesis: "Expropriated Indigenous land is the foundation of the land-grant university system." *High Country News* thereby highlighted what I had briefly described in Orange as the means by which the federal government acquired "public lands," mostly in the Trans-Mississippi West, that it then made available to states to finance their portions of the land-grant system.

Virginia illustrates the report's central thesis. Virginia's land-grant scrip land was located, just about all of it, west of the Mississippi River—to some considerable extent, for example, in Arkansas, Oregon, Wisconsin, and Wyoming; in even greater amounts in Colorado, Kansas, Minnesota, Montana, Nebraska, Utah, and South Dakota; and most of all in California.

I suggested in Orange that, had Tech's students actually been attending classes on the land that originally financed their

institution, they might have had to make their way, during
fifteen-minute class breaks, "from Nebraska to North Dakota."
Those were plausible choices in 1997, but in the current edition
I have modified the language more appropriately to "from California to Colorado."

Another initiative that has gained ground since the publication of Orange is "Universities Studying Slavery." Tech might
seem to have no meaningful connection to issues of the sort
being addressed there, since as a land-grant school it took shape
some years after general emancipation. Yet, in the absence of
the Preston and Olin Institute in the early 1870s, there could
have been no assignment to that school, under a new name and
a new administration, of any portion of Virginia's share of land-
grant money.

That predecessor school, established in the early 1850s, so
two decades earlier, brought an academy for white boys to
Montgomery County, just up the hill from the town of Blacksburg's original sixteen squares. In part, the school's name
honored William Ballard Preston, who came from a prominent
family that had a tremendous impact on educational enterprises
in several southern states and certainly in the Blacksburg area.

The Prestons had the economic capacity as well as the cultural ethos to play such leadership roles. William Ballard Preston
and one of his two brothers, Robert Taylor Preston, each served
as a trustee of the new academy. And each brought considerable
wealth to back its development. As revealed in the U.S. census
for 1850, 49 enslaved people lived on Ballard Preston's estate,
Smithfield Plantation, and another 24 lived on Robert Preston's
place, Solitude. Those numbers grew during the 1850s.

The Prestons lived their lives in a world in which enslave-
ment brought both social prominence and considerable com-
fort to some people, but at the cost of great misery and relentless toil to others. The many amenities available to local whites
included schooling, something legally barred for all black
Virginians. Far more people of African origin lived at Smith-

field and Solitude than did people of European origin. People of African origin who came to Virginia during the preceding century—and their children, grandchildren, and great-grand-children—generated the wealth that made local academies for white children possible. They also performed some of the labor that went directly into construction of the Preston and Olin Building, the structure that made possible a land-grant college in Montgomery County.

Reconstituting the Past

Publication of Orange led quickly to an entirely unanticipated outcome, one that demonstrated how the study of the past can be not only illuminating but also consequential, both exhila-rating and disturbing, transformational as well as revealing. In the fall semester of 1997, one team of students in the "History of Virginia Tech" class, while exploring old yearbooks as one set of sources, made a startling discovery in the 1896 edition of the *Bugle*. Claudius Lee was pictured on a page with a student organization called the "K.K.K." His office, evidently equivalent to president of the group, was "father of terror." This discovery, having inadvertently opened an unwelcome door to the past, turned out to be far from the only such glimpse of VPI in the years around 1900.

Lee had gone on to a career of teaching electrical engineer-ing at VPI, and in 1968 a large residence building was named Lee Hall in his honor. Long story short, the discovery in Octo-ber 1997 led to national press coverage and a controversy that roiled parts of three successive university presidencies. In the long aftermath, the residence hall Peddrew–Yates was dedicated in 2003, honoring Irving Peddrew, the first black student to enr-oll, and Dr. Charlie Yates, the first to graduate. And in summer 2020 Lee Hall was renamed to honor Janie Elizabeth Patterson Hoge and William Harris Hoge Sr., the couple who provided an off-campus home for the first black students. When students returned to Tech in August 2020, hundreds of them moved into the newly-designated Hoge Hall as their campus home. In a companion change, Barringer Hall gained a new name honoring James Leslie Whitehurst Jr., class of 1963, who had broken through multiple barriers to black students' full participation in campus life.

A milestone that went unnoticed in the 1997 edition of Orange related to the presence of Native American students on campus. Helen Maynor Scheirbeck earned an Ed.D. in 1980 with a dissertation titled "Education: Public Policy and the American Indian." An understudied force in late-twentieth century American life, she was a Lumbee Indian from eastern North Carolina who played critical roles in Native schooling, from Head Start to higher education, throughout America for decades beginning in the 1960s. Her studies at Tech gave Dr. Scheirbeck advanced training in public policy as well as a credential that itself no doubt facilitated her continuing work.

As Virginia Tech approached its official 150th anniversary, one of the new cultural centers in Squires Student Center was the American Indian and Indigenous Community Center. And among the new student groups was Native at Virginia Tech (Native@VT), with membership not only from the state of Virginia but, appropriately enough, from across the country, including the Trans-Mississippi West.

Hoge Hall and Native at Virginia Tech both powerfully connect Virginia Tech's past with its present and its future.

Contingencies

The Virginia Tech of the twenty-first century has an ever-lengthening history, the very beginnings of which were a matter of a most improbable collection of contingencies. The conclusion of a protracted struggle in the eighteenth century between Natives and whites over colonial settlement in the reg-ion led to the successful establishment of Smithfield Plantation and the town of Blacksburg. Had black slavery not emerged in western Virginia in the nineteenth century, then far less wealth would have become available to direct toward the Olin and Preston Institute in the 1850s. Without the Preston and Olin Institute, there never could have been a Virginia Agricultural and Mechanical College—at Blacksburg, that is—in 1872.

Moreover, if there had been no Louisiana Purchase from France in 1803, and no subsequent war with Mexico in the 1840s, plus no relentless displacement of the many Indigenous peoples throughout the western territories, then the federal government would have had no "public lands" that it could direct in 1862 to the establishment of a constellation of land-grant institutions. And therefore, once again, no Virginia Tech.

Beyond all of that, if Virginia's secession and joining the Confederate States of America in 1861 had not been turned back in an enormous military struggle, then no land-grant money apportioned by the U.S. Congress could have been awarded to Virginia. Thus again, no Virginia Tech. As it was, Congress had to enact additional legislation through the 1860s to extend the deadline for Virginia and other recent Confederate states to accept the offer of land-grant money (see Appendix B). Moreover, had the Virginia General Assembly adopted VMI or UVA—or both together, or some other arrangement—then, again, no Virginia Tech.

All of those contingencies—local and national—had to line up in the nineteenth century for there to be a twenty-first century Virginia Tech. They all had to line up to create even the possibility of the experiences or contributions at VPI of Addison Caldwell, Andrew Oliver, Hunter Carpenter, Mary G. Lacy, Lucy Lee Lancaster, Cato Lee, Rohran Tung, Irving Peddrew, Janie Hoge, Charles A. Johnson, Homer Hickam, T. Marshall Hahn Jr., Linda Adams, Nancy Kelly, Elaine Dowe Carter, Clara B. Cox, Helen Maynor Scheirbeck, or anyone else mentioned in this preface.

Individuals and Institutions

Those individuals, and a great many others, have made the institution what it was and what it is. This book takes a dual approach, as it emphasizes not just the larger institutional history and its changing contexts but also, very much, people who have been part of that history, who have contributed to shaping it, and, at the same time, who represent the historical experiences of various constituent groups.

People associated with Tech have followed various paths to the place. Some have spent their college years at the school. Some remained their entire work lives there, others just portions, whether early, middle, or late. Some faculty arrived fresh out of their doctoral programs, whether they moved on or stayed. Some of Tech's administrators for one period or another changed schools a number of times but circulated within the land-grant system.

Tech has its own history, a not particularly linear phenomenon dependent both on a vast collection of personalities and on periodic changes in policy and political environments. At the same time, its history is a case study within the land-grant system's dozens of institutions—at least one in every state—thus capable of illuminating far more than the experiences shaping one school in one state.

Further Acknowledgments

This edition of Orange has been given substantial assists in various quarters. During its production, conversations with Bob Leonard, Menah Pratt-Clarke, Hugh Campbell, Lindsay Cherry, and Irving Peddrew have been particularly important. The bibliography, substantially enlarged from 1997, highlights key primary sources and lists a broad range of (mostly) secondary sources. At Virginia Tech Publishing, Peter Potter, publishing director, urged such a volume, and Robert Browder and Caitlin Bean, digital publishing specialists, did wondrous work bringing it to pass. As in 1997 (though some visuals have been dropped and others added), most of the images come from what has since been rebranded Special Collections and University Archives.

The photograph of William Henry Ruffner comes from the Virginia Historical Society, those of William Mahone and John Mercer Langston from the Library of Congress.

The high school graduation photograph of Irving Peddrew, which first came to my attention many years ago via the Black Cultural Center, was taken in 1953 by (the then) Hampton Institute's legendary photographer Reuben V. Burrell.

The painting of President Hahn, done by Everett Raymond Kinstler in the early 1970s at the National Arts Club in New York City, is a gift from Robert B. Pamplin, father and son, and hangs in the president's boardroom in Burruss Hall.

Prologue (1997)
Virginia Tech — Is That Near VPI?

The town of Blacksburg is home to a big school with a long name, Virginia Polytechnic Institute and State University. Both the town and the institution were ever so much smaller 125 years ago. The town consisted of the original "Sixteen Squares," so the new land-grant school was *at* Blacksburg, or very *near* Blacksburg, but scarcely *in* Blacksburg. As for the new land-grant institution, it took more than 20 years for its enrollment to reach 300 or its number of graduates in a single year to reach 10.

Most people know the school as VPI or Virginia Tech—nicknames that date from 1896, when the institution changed names from Virginia Agricultural and Mechanical College to Virginia Agricultural and Mechanical College and Polytechnic Institute. Before 1896, a school cheer went:

> Rip Rah Ree!
> Va., Va., Vee!
> Virginia, Virginia!
> A.M.C.

With the change of formal name, students produced a new cheer that began:

> Hoki, Hoki, Hoki Hy!
> Tech! Tech! V.P.I.!

Tech adopted a shorter name, Virginia Polytechnic Institute, in 1944 and a longer one again in 1970, Virginia Polytechnic Institute and State University. Still it continues to be known as VPI or, ever more so, Virginia Tech.

Despite all the good things for which Virginia Tech is and has been known, the school name often spells confusion. Nametags themselves induce uncertainty and elicit questions. "You teach at Virginia Tech," one professor will say to another at a conference. "Is that anywhere near VPI?" A student goes to a conference, wears a name tag identifying her as from VPI&SU, and is asked: "Oh, you come from VPI—but what is that other school—what does SU stand for?" And newspaper writers conjure up such contrivances as "Virginia Technical College."

Some years ago a newly-appointed faculty member, driving south with his family on I-81 through the Shenandoah Valley toward his new place of employment and listening to the radio, heard a story about the new Miss America, Kylene Barker (class of 1978), having studied at Virginia Tech. When his wife observed that the story was about his new employer, he rebutted that, no, he was going to be teaching at VPI. Then again, she was the one who, as the car approached Lexington, thought they must already be in Kentucky.

* * *

Some people at Virginia Polytechnic Institute and State University mourn that their school is not called Virginia State University. The long history of higher education in Virginia led down a road that found another school—another land-grant university—bearing that name. This book retraces that long road and recounts the story of Virginia Tech's first 125 years.

Introduction (1997)

For Virginia Tech's 100th anniversary, in 1972, Duncan Lyle Kinnear, a long-time member of the Tech faculty, wrote a 500-page history of the school. He confessed that, on many topics, his big book was too brief to do justice to its topic. I have undertaken the foolhardy task of writing, for the 125th anniversary, a far shorter book.

This book seeks to do both less and more than the centennial volume. It is more selective, less encyclopedic or comprehensive. Yet it examines Tech's past in a broader historical context, and it tells more than Kinnear did about some crucial dimensions of the university's history. I think of it as a case study in the social and political history of higher education—in the United States in general and in Virginia in particular.

The subject of this book is the history of Virginia Tech. Telling the story right, in my view, however, requires me to monitor developments in Virginia's other institutions of higher education, especially state-supported schools. From time to time, readers will see what was happening at the University of Virginia, Virginia Military Institute, William and Mary, Virginia State, or another institution. Moreover, to assess the path that Virginia Tech took through the past invites comparison with developments in other states' land-grant schools—Texas A&M, Maryland, Mississippi State, and other schools in the South, the North, or the West.

Federal Legislation, National and Regional Patterns, Institutional Particularities

Many histories of institutions of higher education are organized by presidential administrations. Such books work from the plausible premise that the major figures in an institution's history are its top administrators. In keeping with the broader perspective presented here, though, I emphasize federal legislation as the category of activity that most clearly frames the development of higher education in Virginia, the South, and the nation.

The Morrill Act of 1862 established the basis for the land-grant schools in every state. The Old Dominion established Virginia Tech ten years later, in 1872. Thus 1997 marks Tech's 125th anniversary year.

Between the 1880s and the 1910s, Congress passed a collection of acts that imposed new responsibilities, created new opportunities, and supplied more resources. The Hatch Act of 1887 broadened the activities of the land-grant schools by establishing a national system of agricultural research programs connected to them, and the Smith-Lever Act of 1914 went farther in creating an extension program. Thus the land-grant mission, which at first focused on instruction, later added research and extension or service. Between these two acts, the Second Morrill Act, in 1890, substantially increased the annual support that land-grant schools received from federal funds. It also directed that, in states that excluded black residents from one land-grant school, an alternative school must be supported, so the benefits of the land-grant system would go to black citizens as well as white ones.

Federal legislation from the Great Depression, World War Two, the Cold War, and the Great Society also shaped the growth of Virginia Tech. In the 1930s, New Deal legislation helped finance construction of many buildings on the Tech campus. The G.I. Bill in 1944, much like the 1862 law that launched the land-grant colleges, contributed mightily to democratizing Americans' access to higher education. The National Defense Education Act of 1958 was a key American response, in the context of the Cold War, to the Soviet Union's successful launch of Sputnik One into orbit around Earth. Various acts in 1963, 1964, or 1965 provided still substantially greater federal funding for higher education. The Civil Rights Act of 1964 and the Educational Amendments of 1972 curtailed the permissible range of discrimination by any state or by any public institution on grounds of race or gender.

When I ask readers to look at developments in other states, it is to supply a comparative context for a better understanding of the developments at Tech—whether they were typical, unusual, even unique—and to see how other states and other schools dealt with these same inducements and mandates from the federal government.

Decade by Decade

Though I have not arranged this book by Tech's presidential administrations, I nonetheless offer a chronological treatment. I have divided the past century and a half into fifteen ten-year periods. Each chapter takes a brief tour through the major developments of a single decade. Each develops a leading theme or topic that signals the significance of that decade—ten years in the history of Tech, ten years in the history of public higher education in the United States. Often, of course, discussions of developments in a given decade require reference to origins in an earlier time or suggest implications for a later time.

The chapters vary as to proportions that focus on Virginia Tech, statewide developments in Virginia, regionwide developments in the South, or nationwide developments in America. The first two chapters address the question "What Is a Land-Grant College?" and assess higher education, in Virginia and elsewhere, before there was a Virginia Tech. Later chapters tell of "The First Women Students" in the 1920s or recount the story of "The First Black Students" in the 1950s.

Virginia history is often thought to display harmony and continuity. Yet I have been fascinated by the degree of conflict and change that make up the Old Dominion's past. My book often highlights the political conflict that has swirled around and fundamentally shaped and reshaped the history of higher education in Virginia.

This book offers a brief history of one public institution of higher education in America. The history of Virginia Tech serves as a lens through which to examine the workings of society and politics, of education and opportunity, of democracy itself—the history of Virginia Tech, the history of Virginia, the history of the United States.

Chapter 1
The Emergence of America's Land-Grant Colleges

Justin S. Morrill, father of the land-grant college system

Justin S. Morrill of Vermont won election to Congress in 1854 at the age of 44. His father, a blacksmith, attended school for only a matter of weeks and regretted his "deprivation." Morrill himself wished to attend college but ended his formal education at age 15 to became a storekeeper in Strafford, his hometown.

Morrill spent 43 years in the U.S. Congress, from 1855 until his death in 1898, six terms in the House of Representatives and five-plus in the Senate. From the 1850s to the 1890s, he campaigned for federal money to support a practical higher education for Americans. The emerging world of science and technology in the second half of the nineteenth century, it seemed to him, rendered training on the farm and in the shop outmoded and insufficient for farmers and mechanics alike.

The Morrill Land-Grant College Act of 1862, which launched a national system of land-grant colleges, is his greatest monument. But what is a land-grant college? How did this federal support operate? And how did higher education

in Virginia and across America change with the advent of the
land-grant system?

Opportunity and Education

For a very long time now, a college education has generally
seemed essential in politics or the professions. Between the
1790s and the 1860s, by contrast, even most U.S. presidents
had no college degree. George Washington never went to
college. Nor did Abraham Lincoln. Some combination of
intelligence, industry, ambition, character, and luck propelled
each, even with little or no formal higher education, toward the
presidency of the United States.

Only half the presidents completed college who served
between the 1790s, the first decade under the U.S. Constitution,
and the 1860s, the decade that produced the Morrill Land-Grant
College Act. Thomas Jefferson and James Monroe attended
William and Mary but neither earned a degree. William Henry
Harrison attended Hampden-Sydney College, class of 1793,
for a time. Each is sometimes called an alumnus of his school,
but that does not mean he completed the requirements for a
degree.

Through the 1830s, the only presidents to have earned
degrees were John Adams (Harvard, 1755), his son John
Quincy Adams (Harvard, 1787), and James Madison
(Princeton, 1771). The presidents of the 1830s, Andrew
Jackson and Martin Van Buren, never enrolled in a college
course. The 1840s supplied two consecutive presidents with
degrees, John Tyler (William and Mary, 1807) and James K.
Polk (University of North Carolina, 1818), but they established
no new pattern. Neither president who served in 1850 attended
college: Zachary Taylor studied with private tutors on his family's Kentucky plantation, and Millard Fillmore, who succeeded
to the presidency when Taylor died, had scant schooling. The
two men elected in the 1850s had earned degrees—Franklin

Pierce graduated from Bowdoin College (1824), and James Buchanan from Dickinson College (1809)—yet neither president who served in 1865, Abraham Lincoln or Andrew Johnson, ever went to college.

Still, a college education, like many other privileges that the nineteenth century supplied some Americans, was widely perceived as a considerable advantage, both by people who benefited from it and by people who could not. The mere fact that most presidents spent at least some time in college, and that they were nearly as likely as not to have completed a degree, indicates that, even in the first half of the nineteenth century, college study had a high correlation with political advancement. Among other white men—let alone anyone else—it was a rare experience.

After 1865, virtually every U.S. president had gone to college, and after 1920 only Harry Truman obtained the presidency without some kind of undergraduate degree. One of the signal events that marks the dividing line of the 1860s—separating the time when many presidents never attended college and the time when most presidents finished college—is the Morrill Land-Grant Act of 1862. The Morrill Act did not cause the shift, but it does supply a symbolic marker.

Congressman Morrill, the West, and an American Education

Vermont's Congressman Justin S. Morrill yearned to see the federal lands of the West foster agricultural and technical education throughout the nation. He saw the public lands as a national resource. As those lands were bought up—converted from public domain to private farms—the proceeds, Morrill argued, should go into a great common fund that would benefit Americans in every state across the nation.

Western lands had long funded American social and material progress. The Northwest Ordinance of 1787 stipulated that, in each township in what became Ohio and Illinois, a piece of land would be set aside the rent from which might finance a local school. The sale of federal land in the 1830s provided the national government a vast treasury surplus that was distributed to the states, many of which then used the money to finance education and transportation.

The states themselves, in many cases, used public land within their territories as a source of money to finance such improvements. Such money supplied the funds, for example, that made it possible for Horace Mann to build his famous school system in Massachusetts. Western states used their public land, as Texas did, to finance all kinds of improvements.

In 1862, Morrill's vision became reality. The national government took advantage of the fiscal bonanza from western lands to accomplish, without taxation, a great public work. Congress passed the Morrill Land-Grant Act, designed to promote a practical education for the common people of America, particularly the farmers and mechanics. This book tracks the unfolding story of how that act of Congress altered the educational landscape for all Americans.

The Morrill Land-Grant College Act

Morrill first tried to secure passage of what he called his "College Land Bill" in December 1857. It made its way to passage in February 1959, only to have President James Buchanan, a Democrat, veto it on the grounds that education was a state matter, not a federal responsibility, and Congress had no right to give away the nation's lands. Obtaining a majority in each house of Congress had taken long and difficult work, as southerners worried about states' rights and westerners sought to reserve the benefits of western lands for themselves. Morrill saw only futility in seeking passage again before a change of administration.

In the winter and spring of 1861–1862, by contrast, eleven southern states had seceded, Congress therefore contained far fewer southerners, and his bill gained easy passage. With a Republican in the White House, the last political obstacle to its enactment vanished. President Abraham Lincoln signed it into law on July 2, 1862.

The Morrill Act signaled major changes in public life in America in the 1860s. Moreover, the timing of the bill's passage pointed up the disparate resources of the United States and the Confederate States as they warred with each other. In the Confederacy, schools closed down. Male teachers and students went off to fight; buildings were taken over for use as military hospitals; and funds, public and private alike, were diverted to pay for the war. In the North, most schools stayed open, and the United States embarked on a huge new initiative to support higher education through the Morrill Land-Grant College Act.

Congressman Morrill's failed attempt to secure passage of a land-grant bill supplied the model for his successful effort. Under the 1859 bill, each state would have been given 20,000 acres of land for each vote in the electoral college—for each of its members of the U.S. Senate and U.S. House of Representatives. The 1862 bill increased the acreage to 30,000 per member of Congress. Thus whatever amount of money might have been realized under the failed version should now increase by half.

The Morrill Act is well worth quoting. Any state that accepted the money must direct it to the "endowment, support, and maintenance of at least one college where the leading object shall be, without excluding other scientific and classical studies, and including military tactics, to teach such branches of learning as are related to agriculture and the mechanic arts, in such manner as the legislatures of the States may respectively prescribe, in order to promote the liberal and practical education of the industrial classes in the several pursuits and professions in life." The military provision, not present in the 1857–1859 bill, entered the 1861–1862 bill in the context of the Civil War and a realization that officer training ought to be fostered.

The language proved highly indeterminate. The wording that all land-grant colleges must "teach such branches of learning as are related to agriculture and the mechanic arts" had sufficient clarity. From the very beginning of implementation, however, people could and did argue about the attention "other scientific and classical studies" should get.

More important, the phrase "including military tactics" was variously construed as mandating, or at least permitting, a thorough military regimen; simply requiring that an optional military course be offered; or something in between.

Harbingers of Agricultural and Mechanical Education

Morrill's land-grant act did not fall from the sky unheralded. When Congress made federal funds available for agricultural and mechanical education, the idea of such education—though not necessarily of federal funds to underwrite it—had already been discussed widely and favorably.

In Virginia at about mid-century, Governor John Floyd urged the state's two public institutions of higher education, Virginia Military Institute and the University of Virginia, to establish professorships in agricultural chemistry. The Virginia State Agricultural Society pushed for a professorship of agriculture at either VMI or UVA.

Other proposals by Virginians, too, looked to a future different from the past. Another governor of the 1850s, Henry A. Wise, included agricultural and mechanical education in an education system that he anticipated would go beyond even what Thomas Jefferson had long ago promoted. Agricultural reformer Edmund Ruffin published an essay in 1853 on

"Agricultural Education" that called for a combination of manual labor, agricultural experimentation, military organization, and state support. None of these plans by Virginians went into effect in the 1850s, but, when discussions concerning an agricultural college resumed after the Civil War, they had a history.

Similar support for agricultural education surfaced in other states in both the North and the South. In 1854, Pennsylvania chartered the Farmers' High School, forerunner of Pennsylvania State University, and Dr. William Terrell endowed a professorship in agriculture at the University of Georgia. In 1855, Michigan established a public agricultural school, the foundation for Michigan State University. In 1856, Maryland chartered the Maryland Agricultural College, an early incarnation of the University of Maryland. And in 1858, the Iowa legislature established the first edition of Iowa State.

When Congress acted in 1862, every state had some history to build on. Some, like Virginia, had a state university, but others, like the New England states in the East, as well as Texas and California in the West, had none. Everywhere there had been proposals that the state play some role in supporting agricultural education. Central to the fiscal history of the nation and the states in the first half of the nineteenth century, moreover, was a reliance on public land to finance general benefits like education.

Jonathan Baldwin Turner of Illinois propounded some of the ideas that fused to form the land-grant system. In the 1850s he wondered why higher education focused its benefits on so few people, the future professionals of America. He declared that "workers need education just as much" as "teachers." Without formal training, he worried, "our best farmers and mechanics" would only gradually learn from experience and "come to know, at forty, what they might have been taught in six months at twenty."

Several conventions of farmers and others in Illinois in the 1850s called for public expenditures for such schooling. They urged Congress to dedicate "public lands for each State in the Union for the appropriate endowment of universities for the liberal education of the industrial classes in their several pursuits."

As enacted in 1862, the land-grant system merged these several ideas. It combined a mechanical component with the agricultural, supplied some broad guidelines and financial support from the federal government, and prodded states to take a more active role while leaving them substantial discretion as to how to do it. A people's education became a more central part of the agenda of the nation and the states. The consequences flowed out, from then to now.

What Is a Land-Grant College?

Many people, even at Virginia Tech—faculty, staff, and students—wonder from time to time what it means that the school is a land-grant institution. The typical notion appears to be that, long ago, the state of Virginia owned some land in Blacksburg, the state granted the land to a school, and a university emerged on that land.

That notion is wrong on three counts. One, the land was granted by the federal government to the state of Virginia, not from the state to the college. Two, the land that fostered the growth of a school came in the form of land scrip—paper representing a certain acreage, land to be claimed and then sold for an endowment. The endowment supplied an annuity, not a location. And three, by the 1850s and 1860s, most public land, whether state or federal, was in the West, not the East. The land scrip conveyed control of land from various sites throughout the Great Plains, so beyond the Mississippi River, even all the way to the Pacific Coast. President Thomas Jefferson had bought much of that land for the nation from France, in the Louisiana Purchase of 1803, and much more came from

Mexico after a war in the 1840s with that nation. The United States subsequently obtained that land yet again—by conquest, by treaty, by hook or by crook—this time from the aboriginal occupants, the Native peoples of the American West.

Like Virginia, most states were granted land far outside their own boundaries, so they could hardly situate a college on that land. Moreover, the land was widely scattered; one thinks of students making their way across campus between classes with only ten or fifteen minutes to get from California to Colorado.

Like most other states, Virginia obtained its land scrip, sold it, and invested the cash in a fund. Each state distributed the interest from its fund to such institutions as they designated land-grant schools under the terms of the Morrill Act. Congress created the program, and the states selected the schools it would benefit.

Key Provisions

The Morrill Act was structured to induce states to provide financial support for instruction in agriculture and the mechanical arts. Only institutions teaching these subjects could qualify for the endowment. The act outlined how each state would convert its grant of land to cash, invest the proceeds at a minimum return of 5 percent, and apply the annual proceeds to the support of one or more colleges at which courses would be taught in applied science—agriculture and the mechanical arts.

Furthermore, federal money had to be used primarily to pay for actual instruction. The money could not all go to the purchase of land, though each state's legislature could permit as much as 10 percent of it to be spent for "the purchase of lands for sites or experimental farms." Nor could any of it go the construction of buildings: "No portion of said fund, nor the interest thereon, shall be applied, directly or indirectly, under any pretense whatever, to the purchase, erection, preservation, or repair of any building or buildings."

Congress intended that the states do something to come up with matching resources. The ban on spending much of the Morrill money on real estate meant that a legislature might likely choose to put the federal funds to work at an established institution, one that already had some land and buildings.

Within these guidelines, each state had broad discretion, not only as to whether to accept the offer, but as to how to put the money to work. The money might go to a single school or be divided among several. It might go to a private institution or a public one, an established school or a new one. Agriculture might be the major subject of study, or it might be one among many. Each state must decide. As we have seen, each state had some history to build on.

What Some States Did

The benefits of the 1862 Morrill Act could not apply to any state "while in a condition of rebellion or insurrection against the government of the United States." Thus Virginia and its sister states in the Confederacy could not take advantage of the federal money until they had returned to the Union.

The states that remained in the Union through the Civil War had immediate access to the Morrill Act's benefits. Most states wasted little time before applying for their money, though each had to wait until its legislature was in session, and some states deadlocked for a time over how to proceed.

Most states did not start from scratch in establishing their land-grant schools. In Morrill's home state of Vermont, the legislature chartered an agricultural college, and Morrill himself became a trustee, but no satisfactory local bid emerged that would supply land and buildings, so the legislature attached it to an existing school, as the University of Vermont and State Agricultural College.

Several distinct approaches emerged. Most eastern states had no public university, and a number of them designated existing private institutions as their land-grant schools, or they created land-grant units that they attached to those schools. Rhode Island gave its share to Brown University (1863), Connecticut its to Yale College (1863), and New Hampshire its to Dartmouth College (1866). Maryland directed its Morrill Act money to the Agricultural College (1865), while New Jersey favored Rutgers College (1864).

Other states adapted existing institutions, public or private, as public land-grant schools. The University of Wisconsin at Madison, a public school founded in 1848 in compliance with the new state's first constitution, became a land-grant school in 1866. What is now Michigan State University opened for classes in 1857 as the Agricultural College of the State of Michigan, a public institution, and obtained designation as land-grant school in 1863. Kansas State University started out as Bluemont Central College, a private school, but in 1863 it became the Kansas State Agricultural College. California accepted an offer in 1868 made by the College of California, a private school in Berkeley, of its buildings and 160 acres of land in return for a pledge to establish a "complete university" in its place.

Still other states used the endowment to help establish new schools. The new state of West Virginia founded a school in 1867 at Morgantown. Also in 1867, Illinois established a new institution, now the University of Illinois at Urbana–Champaign; Jonathan Baldwin Turner, having campaigned for such a school, helped lay the cornerstone.

Maine, where farmers had long been calling for an agricultural college, proceeded under the Morrill Act to create one, but no decision as to curriculum or location proved easy. Bowdoin College sought the money, but so did two other private colleges, Bates and Waterville (soon renamed Colby). Maine accepted the scrip in 1863, sold it, detailed the nature of a new college to be established, but then sank into indecision. In 1866, after the town of Orono offered a central location as well as financial support—$14,000 and a farm—the state settled on Orono. The legislature supplied $10,000 toward construction of a dormitory and a laboratory. Classes began at last in September1868. The first six students graduated in 1872, the same year that the first female student enrolled. Maine State College—a land-grant school, a coeducational institution, a start on a new state university—was under way.

The Indiana legislature wrangled for four years before settling on a new institution. Among the many proposals that eventually died, one would have divided the Morrill Act money among four denominational schools. In 1869, a businessman named John Purdue broke the legislative logjam when he offered $150,000 to launch a land-grant school, provided it was established in Tippecanoe County, he was named a life member of the board of trustees, and the school was irrevocably named Purdue University. Classes began five years later, in 1874, with 39 students. The first class might have been larger, but all eight female applicants were rejected. The following year, the school reversed that policy and admitted women.

New York might have given the Morrill Act money to a small private school—briefly did, in fact—or divided it among a number of clamoring colleges. Two men, however, dreamed of a great educational institution, and they carried that dream as elected members to the New York legislature in 1864. Ezra Cornell and Andrew Dickson White coalesced their political and educational efforts. Cornell offered to bankroll a huge endowment supplemental to the Morrill money, and he supplied a farm near Ithaca for the institution. Cornell University took legal shape in 1865, and classes began in 1868. The first two buildings were named after Justin S. Morrill and Andrew D. White. No student was to be rejected on grounds of either race or gender.

Nor did these varied actions exhaust the states' options. In 1863, Massachusetts divided its money between two schools. One-third went to the Massachusetts Institute of Technology, a private school chartered only in 1861. MIT did not begin instruction until 1865, so it was hardly a functioning institution when its charter was amended to make it a land-grant school. The other two-thirds of the annual proceeds went to a new public institution to be established at Amherst, the Massachusetts State College of Agriculture, later the University of Massachusetts.

Not all decisions proved permanent, and even some that held did so in the face of strong efforts to undo them. Some states initially directed their land-grant money to an existing school but subsequently lifted the designation and the funds and launched new institutions. Connecticut lifted the money from Yale's Sheffield School in 1891 and gave it to a new institution, Connecticut Agricultural College, which later became the University of Connecticut. New Hampshire diverted the money in 1893 from Dartmouth to a new school at Durham, at about the same time Rhode Island shifted the funds and the designation from Brown to a new school at Kingston.

The States of the Former Confederacy

The states in the Union, wrestling their way to resolution regarding the disposition of their land-grant money, provided a variety of models for implementing the Morrill Act. The states in the Confederacy, even after the Civil War ended, faced a variety of obstacles to claiming the benefits of the Act. Congress amended the 1862 measure several times to give states, especially in the recent Confederacy, more time to act, but even then they had only until 1872. As will be discussed in the next two chapters, Virginia followed its own path from the passage of the Morrill Act in 1862 to the establishment of the first edition of Virginia Tech as a land-grant school in 1872.

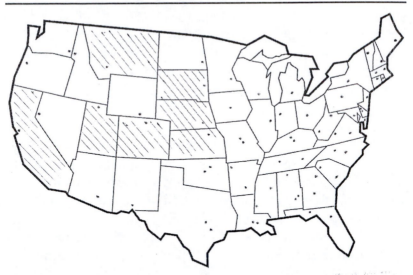

U.S. land-grant institutions as of 1950. Slanted lines indicate where considerable western lands came from that originally funded Virginia's two land-grant schools.

References

Bishop, *Cornell*, 1–179.

Calcott, *University of Maryland*, 131–52.

Carey, *Kansas State University*, 3–37.

Hyman, *American Singularity*, 35–61.

Kinnear, *The First 100 Years*, 1–11.

Kinnear, "History of Agricultural Education in Virginia," 109–63.

Lee and Ahtone, "Land-Grab Universities."

Parker, *Justin Smith Morrill*, 1–62, 259–84.

Rainsford, *Congress and Higher Education*, 29–99.

Ross, *Democracy's College*, 1–112.

Sawyer, "Evolution of the Morrill Act of 1862."

Smith, *University of Maine*, 1–40.

Topping, *History of Purdue University*, 78, 84, 88.

Wallenstein, *From Slave South to New South*, 23–31.

Wallenstein, "Morrill Land-Grant College Act of 1862," 82–91.

Wallenstein, "Reintegrating the American Past."

Chapter 2
Virginia and the Morrill Land-Grant College Act

Francis H. Smith became principal and professor at the Virginia Military Institute at its founding in Lexington in 1839, and he remained as superintendent for fifty years, until his retirement in 1889. He proved a central figure in the history of state-supported higher education in Virginia from the 1840s through the 1880s, and he reflected major developments in the state's history during those years.

Francis H. Smith,
first superintendent of VMI

Virginia seceded from the Union in 1861, and the Civil War began in earnest. VMI continued to train soldiers. One of the school's instructors gained immortal fame as "Stonewall" Jackson, and the cadets fought in the Battle of New Market. After the end of the war, Superintendent Smith put up a spirited though fruitless fight to obtain Virginia's share of the Morrill Act money for his institution.

To appreciate the events of the late 1860s and early 1870s in which Smith was embroiled, it is necessary to know all the major players in the bid for the Morrill Act money. To gauge the kinds of changes that occurred in higher education in Virginia after the Civil War, one must have some idea of the situation that prevailed before then.

Higher Education for a Few White Men

In the 1850s, Virginia had two public institutions of higher education. The University of Virginia was established in 1819 and began operations in 1825. It could thus celebrate a twenty-fifth anniversary in 1844 or 1850. It consisted of a college, a law school, and a medical school. This combination of a publicly-supported liberal arts school and a law school could also be found at the University of Georgia.

The Old Dominion's other public school was Virginia Military Institute, established in 1839 at Lexington, in the Shenandoah Valley. Its curriculum, which emphasized engineering and military training, reflected founder Claudius Crozet's experience at the United States Military Academy at West Point and, before that, at the Ecole Polytechnique in France. This combination, too, was not unusual then. Three state-supported schools in the South in 1860 that resembled VMI were The Citadel in South Carolina, the Georgia Military Institute, and the Louisiana State Seminary of Learning and Military Academy.

VMI before the Civil War had a size that is nearly impossible to imagine a century and a half later. Through its first twenty years, a total of 1,084 cadets enrolled and 354 graduated. One-fourth of the enrolled students—32 most years until the number rose to 40 in 1857—were "state cadets," so-called to distinguish them from paying cadets because they paid no tuition. In return for free tuition, state cadets contracted to teach in the Virginia schools for at least two years after graduation. The state covered part of their costs by subsidizing VMI with a modest stipend of $1,500 from the state Literary Fund. Quite aside from producing soldiers and engineers, then, VMI trained teachers.

Small as UVA was, it was larger than VMI. It grew through the 1850s to the point that, with enrollment reaching 600, it roughly matched Harvard College and Yale College in size. While student fees supplied most of professors' remuneration, the state supplied an annuity of $15,000. In return for that stipend, UVA offered free tuition for 32 students—one from each senatorial district—beginning in 1845. That number rose to 50 in 1853. By the 1850s, "state students" at UVA, like the "state cadets" at VMI, had to agree to teach in Virginia for at least two years upon graduation.

The exchange of benefits—institutions training teachers in return for support from the state treasury—worked to each party's advantage. The colleges gained a reliable source of income. Students could obtain a subsidized education. The state and its citizens secured trained teachers. In the later nineteenth century, this relationship continued at UVA and VMI, and it gained wider application as other public institutions of higher education emerged. Private schools differed.

Private Schools

Most secondary schools as well as post-secondary ones in antebellum Virginia were private institutions. The College of William and Mary, tucked away in Williamsburg, the colonial capital, was one of them. That college, the first in the South and the second in the English colonies after Harvard College, had been in operation since 1693, but it failed to match in the nineteenth century its importance in the eighteenth. Similarly, the new state government failed to match the colonial assembly's support for the college.

Thus, nineteenth-century William and Mary was a private school. From time to time, to be sure, it sought state support. In 1809, Governor John Tyler (the future president) called for state support for the school, even for making it a state institution, but the legislature ignored his advice. Virginia's lawyers and politicians of the late colonial era typically trained at William and Mary, but those of the nineteenth century attended the University of Virginia.

Just outside the village of Blacksburg, the Olin and Preston Institute was established as a Methodist school in the early 1850s. The school carried the names of Stephen Olin, a Methodist minister who had served for a while as president of Randolph-Macon College, and William Ballard Preston, a native of Montgomery County who had served as a state legislator, a member of the U.S. Congress, and President Zachary Taylor's secretary of the navy. The Olin and Preston Institute began operations in 1851, obtained a charter in 1854, and by the next year had constructed an impressive new building. Some years later, the school's trustees put in a bid for Virginia's share of the land-grant money.

Other private schools for white men in Virginia included Washington College; like VMI, it was in Lexington. In addition, there were several important church-affiliated schools: Richmond College (Baptist), at that time in Powhatan County; Hampden-Sydney College (Presbyterian), in Prince Edward County; Randolph-Macon College (Methodist), at that time in Mecklenburg County; and Emory and Henry College (also Methodist), in southwestern Virginia.

No member of the faculty of any of these schools in the 1850s—VMI, UVA, or the private institutions—had a Ph.D. Some had the only advanced degree then widely available, a master's. Yale College awarded America's first Ph.D. in 1861. This action laid the groundwork for the idea of a university where research, pure or applied, constituted a significant faculty activity and where virtually all regular faculty had earned doctorates. The future would not be like the past.

Preston and Olin, Virginia Tech's original building

Race, Sex, and Higher Education in Antebellum Virginia

In other respects, too, the past is a foreign land. VMI and UVA enrolled only white men. Few white men attended either school. No one else could attend.

White women could seek at least secondary schooling at a number of private institutions. Among these were the schools that eventually became Hollins College and Mary Baldwin College. Both began operations in 1842. The first, near Roanoke, operated under various names—Valley Union Seminary, Female Seminary at Botetourt Springs, Hollins Institute—before becoming Hollins College in 1910.

The other, at Staunton, began as Augusta Female Seminary. Mary Baldwin, a student at the school as early as 1843, took charge of it as principal in 1863 and led it to national prominence long before her death in 1897. The school's name became Mary Baldwin Seminary under a legislative act in 1895 that authorized it to grant degrees, and in 1923 it became a four-year college and took on its modern name.

Both schools endured financial struggles in the early years. Yet both supplied valuable schooling for hundreds of white women in Virginia during a long period when no state funds supported any public institution of higher education that they might attend.

In Montgomery County, the future home of Virginia Tech, opportunities arose also for secondary or collegiate education for young white women. The state legislature incorporated the Blacksburg Female Academy in 1840, and by 1852 a Presbyterian-affiliated school, the Montgomery Female College, began operations in Christiansburg.

As for black Virginians, advanced schooling in the Old Dominion was out of the question, let alone at a public institution. A state law banned any school whatever, private or public, for black Virginians, slave or free. In 1854 Margaret Douglass, a white woman, went to jail for a month for conducting an elementary school for free black children in Norfolk.

Some black Virginians, among them John Mercer Langston, escaped the Old Dominion's racial restrictions. Born free in 1829 to a white father and a black and Native mother in Louisa County, Langston moved in 1834 with his two older brothers to Ohio after their parents died. There, free of the restrictions he would have faced in Virginia, he attended Oberlin College, a private institution, where he graduated in 1849. Ohio displayed its own racism, but Oberlin contrasted sharply from anything to be found in Virginia. Not only could black youngsters go to school, even to college, but Oberlin, though mostly white and male, enrolled students without regard to race or sex.

In the 1860s, when slavery ended in Virginia, elementary schools for black children sprouted across the landscape, and even some higher education became available. By 1890 the state supported one institution of higher education for African Americans, both men and women, as well as one for white women. Both schools are discussed in chapter 4.

Higher Education across America in the 1850s

The Virginia model was clearly not universal in American higher education. And yet, in many respects, Virginia was not all that different from other states, North or South. Few, if any, public institutions of higher education existed in any state, and few people, regardless of race or sex, attended them. Virginia had UVA near Charlottesville and VMI in Lexington; Georgia had Franklin College in Athens and the Georgia Military Institute north of Atlanta; and South Carolina had The Citadel in Charleston and South Carolina College in Columbia. Each enrolled few students, all of them, like their instructors, white and male.

Coeducation might be an innovation that Oberlin College could get away with, but it was an anomaly in the 1850s. Yet change was on its way. In 1855 the University of Iowa became the first state university to admit women as well as men. Another school—also in the North, also in the West, the University of Wisconsin—followed suit in 1863. Iowa's action clearly preceded enactment of the Morrill Land-Grant Act, but, as much as any single influence, the land-grant colleges promoted the idea of collegiate coeducation.

Somewhere between coeducation and no education lay intermediate ground where women attended schools exclusively female, just as men attended schools exclusively male. The state of Georgia chartered Wesleyan Female College in Macon in 1836, the same year that Massachusetts chartered Mount Holyoke Seminary. These schools were private. They might obtain such benefits as exemption from taxes on their land and buildings, but the state offered no direct financial support. Schools for men were more plentiful. They were more likely to obtain public financial support, and they typically offered a fuller curriculum.

Women citizens had a growing, but very limited, range of opportunities for higher education. The inequity did not go unnoticed or unchallenged. Keenly aware of the restrictions on females, a group of reformers met in 1848 in Seneca Falls, New York, to protest women's universal exclusion from such opportunities as voting rights and officeholding, the practice of law and medicine, and the schooling that might better prepare them for such professions. Each of their demands would eventually be realized, but not for many years.

Outside the South, black men and black women, like white women, had some opportunities for higher education in mid-nineteenth-century America, though those opportunities were particularly scant for black residents. Even in the South— especially in the South—the 1860s would bring a widening of opportunity.

Early Postwar Virginia

Virginians paid no mind to the Morrill Act during 1862 or 1863, nor was the money yet available to them. Beginning in 1864, an occasional Virginian urged that action be taken, though not for another eight years would the state take final action. Virginians found themselves divided by political party, region of the state, race, religious denomination, and loyalty to one or another existing institution. Moreover, the federal government had things to say about developments in the Old Dominion.

With Virginia in the Confederacy, its state government in Richmond could hardly accept the offer of land-grant funds from the government against which it was warring. But was Virginia in the Confederacy? Virginians loyal to the United States and opposed to secession had organized a rival government in 1861. This rival government, operating out of western Virginia, had subsequently approved the separate-state movement of West Virginia. It then moved east and took up residence in 1863 in northern Virginia at Alexandria, across the Potomac River from Washington, D.C. There, though controlling little Virginia territory, it acted as the legitimate government of the state. It framed a new state constitution in 1864, declared it in operation, and by that means proclaimed the end of slavery throughout Virginia.

When the war ended in April 1865 with Confederate defeat and surrender, the president of the United States proclaimed this rump government to be the legitimate—though only provisional—government of all Virginia. The state government changed its seat for a third time, from Alexandria to Richmond, as the loyalist government sought to secure and display wider legitimacy by returning to the historic capital city.

Virginia's First Postwar Legislative Session

A new session of the legislature convened in December 1865, at which Governor Francis H. Pierpont advised legislators that the loyal Virginia legislature had, in February 1864, notified the federal government of its wish to participate in the Morrill Land-Grant College program—though it had done nothing more. Virginia did not yet have the land scrip, nor had it determined what school should receive the land-grant money.

Governor Pierpont spoke of Virginia's need for a "polytechnic school for the education of her young men." Referring to the Land-Grant Act's requirements, he observed that "doubtless a number of institutions of learning in the state will be willing to add the agricultural and military features required by this act to their institutions." Pierpont considered Virginia Military Institute the strongest candidate, but only if the school left Lexington and moved to Richmond.

Most legislators were surprised to learn of the Morrill Act. They had not known about the act, the fund, the means of procuring a portion of it, or the kind of institution required to satisfy the terms of the act. In the House of Delegates, the Committee on Schools and Colleges had 500 copies of the Morrill Act printed, so legislators and others could ponder the terms of the federal government's offer.

VMI came ready to act, even ready to move. VMI Superintendent Francis H. Smith had already prepared a petition for Virginia's share of the fund. He had done the groundwork for creating an agricultural college even before the war, and his institution could surely teach military tactics. Given the Union soldiers' destruction of VMI buildings in 1864, the Institute offered to move to Richmond to start over.

Yet the legislature found itself unable at that time to accept the offer and designate VMI as Virginia's land-grant school. One reason was that other schools soon accepted Governor Pierpont's implied invitation to apply for the funds. In early 1866, during that same legislative session, two private institutions, Washington College and Roanoke College, each requested a portion of Virginia's Morrill Act funds. Legislators were divided over where the land-grant money should go.

Ruffner, Sutherlin, and a Second Effort

A year later, during the 1866–1867 session, Governor Pierpont again addressed the question, but this time he urged that the College of William and Mary—if it moved to Richmond—be designated Virginia's land-grant school. The demand for a Richmond location receded, and the field of candidates grew. VMI, Washington College, William and Mary, and Roanoke College all remained hopeful, and petitions for at least part of the money also came from Richmond College, Hampden-Sydney College, and the University of Virginia.

William Henry Ruffner, who hailed from Lexington and had long sought a new type of agricultural education for Virginians, advised a committee of the legislature in late 1866 to establish a new institution rather than designate any existing school as Virginia's land-grant institution. Ruffner came no stranger to the quest nor to the leading contenders for the land-grant money. As a resident of Lexington, he had close relations with people at both Washington College and VMI. His father had served as president of Washington College, and Ruffner had served as chaplain at UVA. Ruffner knew all three schools very well, but that freed him from too great a sentimental attachment to any one of them. He believed none of them to be an ideal place to take on the land-grant mission or, therefore, to be an appropriate recipient of the land-grant money.

Another key player in the developing history of the debates over the land-grant funds was William T. Sutherlin. He, too, argued that "the federal endowment . . . should be appropriated to a new educational enterprise designed to secure practical benefits to the masses."

The legislature took no action in 1866, nor could it. In 1870, when debate resumed, and in 1872, when it concluded, political conditions differed vastly from those between 1865 and 1867. Between 1870 and 1872, Ruffner and Sutherlin argued again for a new school. The legislature acted at last, and Ruffner and Sutherlin had their way.

Reconstruction

Uncertainty and contention in the Virginia legislature delayed Virginia's designation of a land-grant college. A greater reason for delay stemmed from the political turbulence of the postwar years, as the federal government itself brought a divided mind to far more difficult questions.

At just about the time that Governor Pierpont first advised the Richmond legislature of its responsibilities regarding the Morrill money, Congress was refusing to seat the men selected for either the House or the Senate from any former Confederate state. If Congress did not recognize the current governments of those states, it would not consider them ready to implement the terms of the Morrill Act.

By the time the next legislative session met, and Pierpont had shifted his suggestion from VMI to William and Mary, Congress was moving ahead to change the complexion of the postwar world. Already, during 1866, Congress had passed, over President Andrew Johnson's veto, two major pieces of legislation addressing education and the law in the postwar South. One, the Freedmen's Bureau Bill, extended the life and expanded the authority of the organization that was doing much to promote elementary education among black southerners— including helping launch the Christiansburg Institute in early 1867.

The other, the Civil Rights Act of 1866, specified certain rights of African Americans regardless of where they lived or whether they used to be free or slave. Uncertain that the Civil Rights Act would survive a constitutional challenge in the federal courts or, for that matter, a challenge in a future Congress that Democrats might control, Congressional Republicans sought to place its major features in a Fourteenth Amendment to the U.S. Constitution. At the same time, the Fourteenth Amendment addressed the other major question that the end of slavery had raised.

Under the Constitution's Three-Fifths Clause, slaves counted for three-fifths of what they would have if they had been free, and since representation in Congress depends on population, they added to white southerners' political power. After slavery, black southerners counted full value, not three-fifths, and thus, unless they could vote their own representation, white southern Democrats would return to national politics with even more power than they had enjoyed in the 1850s.

Republican leaders found absolutely unacceptable the prospect their wartime enemies might secure additional power as a consequence of being defeated in their bid for independence. One U.S. senator, Roscoe Conkling of New York, demanded to know: "Shall the death of slavery add two-fifths to the entire power which slavery had when slavery was living?"

Another, John Sherman of Ohio, wrote his brother, the Civil War general, "Who shall exercise this [additional] political power? Shall the rebels do so?" At another time, he thundered, "But one thing I know, . . . that never by my consent shall these rebels gain by the war increased political power and come back here to wield that power in some other form against the safety and integrity of the country."

Congressional Republicans devised a means to fix the problem. The Fourteenth Amendment provided that, to the extent that black men were denied the right to vote their own representation, a state's representation in Congress would be reduced. This provision might do nothing to empower black southerners, but it would alleviate northern Republicans' fear of too much Democratic power in the House of Representatives and in the electoral college.

Among the eleven former Confederate states, only Tennessee accepted the terms of the Fourteenth Amendment and ratified it. In the months ahead, Congress took an alternative approach to securing its objectives. It superseded the provisional governments of the other ten former Confederate states and began anew the process of creating state governments.

Reconstructing Politics and Education in Virginia

In March 1867, Congress suspended the civil government in each of the ten states, including Virginia. Under federal direction, elections were called to elect delegates to another state constitutional government. Black men and white men alike participated in the elections. Of the 105 delegates elected to the Virginia convention, 68 were Republicans, 24 of them African American. The convention met in Richmond with instructions to specify black men's constitutional right to vote.

The convention lasted from December 1867 to April 1868. In defining political rights, the proposed new Virginia state constitution recognized black men's right to vote and hold office. In outlining a system of public schools that the legislature must create, the constitution provided for a state superintendent of schools whom the legislature would appoint to a four-year term, and it called for the establishment of "normal" schools for teacher training. The new state system of public schools must provide space for the children of both races, white and black, but the constitution did not specify whether the schools were to be integrated or segregated. In July 1869, after long delays, Virginians went to the polls, ratified the new constitution, and elected a new governor and a new legislature.

The legislature convened that October. It addressed Congress's demands by ratifying the Fourteenth Amendment (and the Fifteenth, which removed race as a legal basis for any state to deny voting rights), and then it waited for Congress to declare that Virginia had met the conditions for full political restoration. Congress did so in January 1870. In Washington, D.C., Virginians were permitted once again to take their seats in the U.S. House and Senate. At last, Virginia qualified for its share of the Morrill Act money. In Richmond, legislators returned to work. Decisions on what to do about a land-grant college awaited them.

The 1870 Virginia Legislature

When the legislature met again, it did so under political conditions very different from those of 1865 through 1867. A Republican, Gilbert C. Walker, had been elected governor of the Old Dominion. Democrats outnumbered Republicans in the new session of the legislature, but there were large numbers of both, and the Republicans included a number of black legislators—six of the 43 senators as well as 23 of the 140 members of the House of Delegates. Under the new state constitution, black men could vote and hold office, and the legislature must act—and did act—to create a public school system to accommodate the children of both races, though the new law creating the system mandated that black and white children have separate schools. So the new system would be segregated from day one.

Regarding the Morrill Act fund, however, like the earlier sessions, the 1870 legislature found itself paralyzed. Twenty-four different existing institutions laid claim to all or part of the land-grant money. Governor Walker called for dividing the proceeds between one school for whites and another for blacks. Able only to take a first step, the legislature directed the state auditor to secure Virginia's share of the land scrip.

Legislators left it to a later session to select a school, or perhaps more than one, as a land-grant institution. After that, such details as the school's organization and curriculum must be determined. Only then could one know what a land-grant school would look like in Virginia.

References

Bruce, *University of Virginia*, 3: 3, 8–15.

Buck, *Development of Public Schools in Virginia*, 25–64.

Cheek and Cheek, *John Mercer Langston*, 11–118.

Couper, *One Hundred Years at V.M.I.*, 1: 93–94, 352–53; 3: 114–16, 232–37; 4: 7–9.

Givens, *Christiansburg*, 70–75.

Godson et al., *College of William and Mary*, 1: 165–290.

Heatwole, *History of Education in Virginia*, 280–91.

Hofstadter and Hardy, *Development of Higher Education*, 1–134.

Hunter and Dooley, *Claudius Crozet*, 1–30, 125–33.

Kinnear, *The First 100 Years*, 11–29.

Lowe, *Republicans and Reconstruction in Virginia*, 121–82.

Pacheco, "Margaret Douglass."

Rudolph, *American College and University*, 125–28, 269–72, 307–28, 332–36.

Wise, *Drawing out the Man*, 3–33.

William Henry Ruffner, state school superintendent, and a member of VAMC's first Board of Visitors (Virginia Historical Society)

William Addison Caldwell, the first VAMC student

Chapter 3
1870s: Virginia Agricultural and Mechanical College

The Virginia Tech campus has no building named for William Henry Ruffner, though each year since 1977 the Board of Visitors has identified someone to honor with the William H. Ruffner Medal for particularly distinguished service to the university. Yet no figure from post-Civil War Virginia did more to foster public schools in general or the Virginia Agricultural and Mechanical College in particular. The 1870 legislature established a public school system, as we saw in chapter 2, and it selected Ruffner as the first state superintendent of schools, a position he held through three four-year terms. He embarked on a decade of heroic work to put the new system into place, and that was by no means all.

By the late 1860s, most states had already addressed the issue of what to do with their land-grant money. States that had been in the Confederacy still faced that question. In 1872 Virginia settled the great questions necessary to launch a land-grant school for white residents. Ruffner contributed much to the discourse that concluded, against great odds, with the legislature selecting Blacksburg as the site for such a college. As state school superintendent, he took a place on the new institution's Board of Visitors, and in that capacity he played a central role in shaping its curriculum and selecting a president and a faculty.

War of the Colleges

During 1870, 1871, and into 1872, the legislature spent many days of animated oratory and frenetic maneuvering in an effort to determine what institution or institutions would receive the Morrill Act endowment. A summary of those proceedings will illuminate the alternatives considered, the roads not taken, and the reasons the great debate concluded the way it did. Most roads led somewhere else, but eventually the legislature headed down a path that led to Blacksburg.

Legislators in the 1870–1871 session argued on and on about the land-grant money. Some observers even suggested that the benefits could not be worth the costs. No decision seemed in sight when the *Richmond Dispatch* headlined yet another story on the inconclusive action "War of the Colleges."

Neither UVA nor VMI was able to secure sufficient support. Nor was Washington College, just then changing its name to Washington and Lee University to honor Robert E. Lee, its postwar president who had recently died. Sentiment seemed to shift toward establishing a new school or adapting an existing private school to a new purpose.

Meantime, during the winter of 1870–1871, Dr. Harvey Black and the other trustees of a small private school near Blacksburg came to a decision of their own. As writer Clara Cox has discovered, the school was not—as long thought—in dire financial straits, so it was not desperately seeking a means of survival. And it was already making the transition from academy to college. Regardless, its leaders avidly joined the competition in the legislature for a share of the land-grant proceeds.

A change of name from the Olin and Preston Institute to the Preston and Olin Institute satisfied a legal fiction designed to clear the title to this formerly Methodist academy. Free to give the school away, its trustees sought to obtain a share of Virginia's Morrill Act money by offering to let the state take it over and give it a new life as a land-grant college.

The legislators went home without reaching a conclusion. Congress had extended to ten years (see Appendix B) the length of time states had to act under the 1862 Morrill formula, but the ten-year limit was fast approaching.

When the next session convened in December 1871, Governor Gilbert C. Walker reminded legislators that they had to take some action. So far, they had not even sold the land scrip and invested the proceeds. As a consequence, the state was squandering the opportunity of earning annual interest. Do at least that much, he implored. As for what action should follow, he stressed that the endowment should be split, with one portion going to a school that black Virginians might attend.

In February 1872 legislators took the first two steps. They passed a bill authorizing the State Board of Education to sell the scrip and, following the language of the Morrill Act, invest the proceeds in "safe bonds or stocks" paying at least 5 percent interest. The money was ready, but it needed a home.

A Dark Horse Candidate Emerges

Debate continued. William H. Ruffner and William T. Sutherlin continued to push for a separate school, unconnected with any existing candidate, whether UVA, VMI, or Washington and Lee. Sutherlin, who had represented Pittsylvania County at the Secession Convention in 1861, was a Danville businessman. As a spokesman for the State Agricultural Society, Sutherlin had urged legislators the year before to establish a new school, one that would grow into whatever Virginians might find they needed, a "purely agricultural and mechanical" institution at first, yet "a nucleus around which the accretions of time would gather a really great institution."

Sutherlin gained election to the House of Delegates in 1871 and showed up in Richmond that fall as a legislator himself. In a long speech in January, he reviewed the recent history of Virginia's efforts to reach a decision, and he warned Virginians in general and his fellow legislators in particular that, if they failed to apply the money to its intended use, the federal government might forfeit their claim on the fund. Decide now, he urged, and decide right. Good as VMI and UVA were at what they did, he said, they should each continue to fulfill their current mission and not twist themselves around to qualify for money that would help them do something else. Put the money to work, he advised, in an institution designed specifically to emphasize the kind of training called for under the Morrill Act.

A resolution began to emerge. Republicans, for their part, met in caucus and committed themselves to oppose both VMI and UVA, the two public schools vying for the fund. The Republicans, Sutherlin, and various newspapers swung their support to a separate school to be designated the land-grant institution if the city or county in which it was located bid sufficiently for it. The land-grant fund, by itself, would supply scant support, but, if supplemented by local donations, it might foster an effective institution.

Meanwhile, the Preston and Olin trustees mobilized strong local support. The Preston family signed on. So did Waller Staples, a Montgomery County politician currently sitting on the state supreme court in Richmond. Assurances came from someone, though it is not clear just whom, that the county would come up with $20,000 to help launch the new school, perhaps by financing the construction of one or more additional buildings.

Senator John E. Penn of Patrick County, whose district included Montgomery County, came forward to make a case for taking over Preston and Olin. Like Sutherlin, he urged that the fund go to a school in which the agricultural and mechanical function would be paramount, not secondary, dominant, not subordinate. When a bill in the Senate proposed to give one-third of the proceeds to Hampton Normal and Industrial Institute and the remainder to UVA and VMI, he offered an amendment. Strike VMI and UVA, he urged, and substitute a blank to be filled in later with some school that would adopt the name and program of Virginia Agricultural and Mechanical College.

All the while that supporters of the Preston and Olin Institute were, like their counterparts at other white schools seeking to garner at least a share of the fund, spokesmen for black Virginians also had an eye on the pot. White legislators cared little where the black share went, just as black legislators cared little where the white share went. Members of each group had emphatic wishes regarding the portion that might go to its race.

Samuel Chapman Armstrong, a wartime general in the U.S. Army, served shortly after the war as an agent of the Freedmen's Bureau and played a central role in establishing the school at Hampton. Armstrong, as superintendent at the Hampton Normal and Agricultural Institute, and R. W. Hughes, a trustee of the school, wrote strong letters to the appropriate committee chairmen in the legislature on behalf of Hampton. Both wanted to be sure, first, that blacks secured a portion of the fund and, second, that Hampton was a recipient.

Both, in fact, wanted Hampton to obtain the entire portion set aside for black education. Hughes stressed that, since five-twelfths of all Virginians were black, that was the fraction that should go to Hampton. Supporters of Hampton secured most of what they wanted. The great debate in the Virginia legislature related to the disposition of the white portion, not the black share—and not whether there should be a black portion as well a white one.

The phrase "separate but equal" came only later, but the reality emerged soon after the death of slavery. Many people, white and black, perceived that the federal mandate, under the conditions prevailing after the end of the war, did not permit complete exclusion of black Virginians from the benefits of the Morrill Act. Beyond that consideration, white legislators assumed that black Virginians, if they could benefit from the fund at a black institution, could not as readily argue that they should be permitted to enroll at a white one.

Virginia Agricultural and Mechanical College

In March 1872, with the session drawing toward a close and no action having yet been taken by either house, the Senate attempted to act. Acting as a committee of the whole, the Senate decided to allocate one-third of the proceeds to blacks and two-thirds to whites. Then, having determined that the black share would go to Hampton, it polled the individual senators' various choices for the white share. These included UVA and VMI as well as the Preston and Olin Institute. They also included Richmond College, Roanoke College, Emory and Henry College, Randolph-Macon College, and Hampden-Sydney College. They even included a school at Fredericksburg and the New Market Polytechnic Institute.

Senators agreed to hold as many ballots as necessary to give a majority to one combination, Hampton for the black share of the funds and one or more among the contenders for the white share. On each ballot, the combination receiving the least support would be dropped. It took only three ballots for the Preston and Olin Institute to win the support of a majority. A combination that paired VMI and UVA for the white portion came in a distant second.

The committee of the whole returned to order as the Senate, which then adopted the combination of Hampton Institute and the Preston and Olin Institute. Integral to the bill was the provision that Senator Penn had proposed requiring the winning school for the white share to give up its previous identity and become the Virginia Agricultural and Mechanical College.

With Senate action, half the legislature had decided; half the task was accomplished. The House, too, managed to come to a final decision, though initial proceedings there seemed far from promising. There, Montgomery County's new representative, Gabriel C. Wharton (though a VMI graduate, class of 1847), like Senator Penn, supported the Preston and Olin Institute.

First the House decided the fraction that would go to each race. Black legislators were still pushing for a five-twelfths share, but the House settled on one-third.

Next came the question of where to direct the two-thirds for whites. After an unpromising beginning, a delegate from Orange County, W. R. Taliaferro, withdrew Hampden-Sydney College as a contender. Rockbridge County's William T. Poague did the same regarding VMI, but he went further and endorsed Preston and Olin. In similar fashion, Albemarle County's J. C. Hill withdrew UVA and endorsed the Montgomery County school. Roanoke County's G. B. Fitzgerald, rising to speak for all the established private colleges, not only for Roanoke College, urged that all schools be dropped except the two—the schools at Hampton and Blacksburg—that had won endorsement in the Senate.

The House agreed and approved the measure. Virginia's Morrill Act endowment would be divided, with one-third of the proceeds going to a black school, Hampton Institute, and two-thirds going to a white school. The Preston and Olin Institute became Virginia Agricultural and Mechanical College. (See Appendix B.)

Governor Walker signed the measure into law on March 19, 1872. In that sense, Virginia Tech turned 125 years old on March 19, 1997. (If one chose to date the origins of Virginia Tech to the founding of the Olin and Preston Institute in the 1850s, then the school was already fast approaching its 150th anniversary even as it celebrated its 125th.) Much remained to be done to launch the new school—or the new incarnation of the old school.

The bill establishing Virginia Agricultural and Mechanical College provided for free tuition for as many students as there were members of the House of Delegates. As a member of the new school's Board of Visitors, Ruffner preferred that any Virginia student be admitted tuition-free, but the school's finances hardly permitted such a practice. The board set tuition and fees at $40 per year. Lodging, meals, and uniforms cost more.

Virginia's Other Land-Grant School

The Blacksburg campus never was the only school to receive Virginia's land-grant money. In line with the Virginia legislature's decision of 1872, Hampton Normal and Agricultural Institute continued to receive black Virginians' share of land-grant money until 1920, when the legislature designated another school the black land-grant institution. Today that school is known as Virginia State University.

In some ways, the two land-grant schools, the private Hampton Normal and Agricultural Institute and the public Virginia Agricultural and Mechanical College, resembled each other. Each was a recent development and had a modest infrastructure. Hampton Institute dated only from 1868, three years into the new regime that permitted the formal instruction of black Virginians. And the Preston and Olin Institute had begun college-level instruction at about the same time.

Hampton Institute differed from the Blacksburg school in admitting young women as well as young men. The greatest difference, of course, rested on the racial identity of the people who could enroll at the two schools. VAMC, as the legislature had intended from the beginning, was for white men. Hampton was for black Virginians, women as well as men.

Developments in Other Southern States

Virginia's achievements are best evaluated with some reference to the performance of other states of the former Confederacy. Several gave their allotment to existing public universities, an option that Virginia rejected and that some other states undid later. Georgia donated its fund to the University of Georgia, an existing public institution, where it remained. At first, North Carolina gave its Morrill Act money to the University of North Carolina, but in 1887 it established a new land-grant school instead, the North Carolina College of Agriculture and Mechanic Arts, now North Carolina State University.

Tennessee, alone among the eleven states of the former Confederacy, ratified the Fourteenth Amendment without delay and compulsion. As a consequence, its members of Congress gained early readmission, and in early 1867 Congress approved Tennessee's obtaining its share of the land-grant funds. The same Republican leanings that permitted ratification and early readmission led to a legislative decision to put the land-grant funds to work in East Tennessee, the area of the state that had displayed strong Unionist attitudes and behavior during the Civil War. By 1869, the Tennessee legislature had settled upon an established school in Knoxville, East Tennessee University, as the state's sole land-grant school. When Democrats returned to power in 1870, they tried but failed to undo that settlement, and in 1879 the school became the University of Tennessee. The Volunteer State subsequently fumbled through various resolutions to the question of where black Tennesseans might benefit from the Morrill money.

The view from Mississippi—majority black, cash poor, but relatively free of physical destruction from the war—offers another perspective. In 1871, the Republican-controlled Mississippi legislature designated two land-grant schools, one for black students and one for whites. An established public school, the University of Mississippi—Ole Miss—received two-fifths of Mississippi's land-grant funds. A new public school, the nation's first black land-grant college, Alcorn University, received the other three-fifths. At Ole Miss, no students showed up for the agricultural and mechanical program in 1872, a grand total of five students came in 1873, and only three the next year. The program disintegrated. So by 1876, Mississippi was down to one land-grant program, the one for black students—black men, that is, until 1895, when black women also gained admission.

The 1877 legislature proved unable to remedy the deficiency, but the 1878 body began anew. Again there would be two schools, one black and one white, but each would get half the proceeds from the Morrill fund. The legislature

reconstituted Alcorn University as Alcorn Agricultural
and Mechanical College, and it established a new school,
Mississippi Agricultural and Mechanical College.

From some twenty contenders, the board of trustees
selected Starkville as the home of Mississippi A&M.
Construction began in summer 1879, and the 1880 legislature
helped out by actually appropriating some money. Rushing
along, school authorities determined to open the school's doors
in October 1880, though the buildings remained incomplete
and doors had not been installed. On opening day, 160 students
showed up, and as many more arrived in the months ahead.
So many came with so little preparation that they flooded
the prep department (much as they had at Ole Miss when
that school reopened in 1865), but that is what it was for. By
the early 1880s, the school that would become Mississippi
State University had begun operations for keeps, and what
would become Alcorn State University was well under way.
Mississippi's land-grant operations eventually resembled
Virginia's, but the two states took different paths to get there.

Texas supplied another variation. The Texas legislature
had called for establishment of a University of Texas in 1858,
but no such institution emerged until the 1880s. The 1866
legislature accepted the provisions of the Morrill Act, but the
ragged course of national politics slowed progress, as did the
fractious nature of Texas politics. The Morrill Act money, it
was decided, would not go to the state university, which in any
case did not yet exist. Among three potential locations, Brazos
County and the City of Bryan made a bid that the legislature
accepted in 1871. A Republican majority in the 1871 legislative session appropriated funds for land and construction, as
did a Democratic majority in 1873. Texas Agricultural and
Mechanical College opened its doors in October 1876, the
first public institution of higher education in Texas. The nature
of the school veered in various directions over the next few
decades. Each set of decisions opened another set of questions,
but some things, once decided, remained settled.

VAMC: A President, a Faculty, and a Curriculum

In Virginia, the legislature settled on Blacksburg; it empowered the governor (subject to Senate confirmation) to select a Board of Visitors; and the board selected a president and a faculty.

Virginia avoided the false steps taken in such states as Mississippi and North Carolina, but, as in Texas, the way nonetheless proved difficult. The Board of Visitors met in Montgomery County in July 1872 and again in August to launch the new school. Among the board members, three were Joseph Reid Anderson, owner of the Tredegar Iron Works in Richmond; Dr. Harvey Black of Montgomery County, who served as the first rector; and William T. Sutherlin. Others were leaders of the Virginia State Agricultural Society.

Yet another member of the board of trustees, an ex officio member as state school superintendent, was William Henry Ruffner. Ruffner brought to his new task a broad knowledge of what other states were doing, a profound commitment to do all that could be done, and a considerable ability to shape the proceedings. Yet he did not always get his way. In notes he kept of developments, he wrote in disgust at one point about his colleagues' criteria for faculty for the new school. "They all had to be Virginians, Democrats, and Confederate veterans," he noted, yet "a previous technical education and practice was not deemed at all important."

Who should serve as president? Various candidates stepped forward, each with substantial support. Two were local educators, and two were scions of eastern families. Thomas Conrad, former principal of the Preston and Olin Institute, enjoyed the support of many local people and Methodists. Charles Martin, almost as local but a Presbyterian, was principal of the Christiansburg Female Academy and a graduate of Hampden-Sydney College. General Lunsford L. Lomax, an 1856 graduate of West Point, had gone with his state rather than his country in 1861 and had thus been a Confederate officer when the Morrill Act became law. The fourth candidate, Charles Landon Carter Minor, had received an M.A. from UVA in 1858 and had served briefly as president of the Maryland Agricultural College.

In a close contest between Minor and Martin, the board chose Charles L. C. Minor as president, but each of the others played a prominent role in the new school's early years. Martin joined the first faculty, and Conrad and Lomax both served as president in the 1880s. In fact, one or another among the three main contenders aside from Martin—Minor, Conrad, and Lomax—would preside at the Blacksburg land-grant school for most of its first twenty years.

The board had settled on a curriculum, though it made some changes before appointing the faculty to teach it. Charles Martin would teach English language and literature plus ancient languages. Gray Carroll, a UVA graduate, would be responsible for mathematics and modern languages. James H. Lane, a graduate of VMI, would teach natural philosophy and chemistry and direct so much of a military component as might be adopted. As for an instructor in agriculture and mechanics, the board postponed making a decision until winter, as though such an appointment were optional under the Morrill Act. Then it split the position, appointing John W. C. Davis and M. G. Ellzey, and picked J. Seddon Harvie as farm manager.

As the private Preston and Olin Institute underwent conversion into a state Agricultural and Mechanical College, many people associated with the school in its previous incarnation—local people, particularly the faculty and supporters of the former Institute, as well as Methodists throughout the state—were chagrined to see how thoroughly they had been, in Ruffner's words, "swept away." Thomas Conrad, miffed at the direction the college was taking—and at his absence from the directorship—became editor of the *Montgomery Messenger*, and from that perch he blasted the board's efforts and moaned that the only human "relic" of the old Institute was the new school's janitor—Conrad did not further identify him, but it was Andrew Oliver, a man enslaved nearby until just a few years earlier.

The faculty of Virginia Agricultural and Mechanical College (1878)

VAMC started off with five acres and a single building. With three stories and a footprint of about 40 feet by 100, that structure contained a chapel, three classrooms, and 24 lodging rooms, for as many cadets as could fit in them. Needing a farm, the school bought one in 1872 from Robert Taylor Preston—owner of "Solitude," former Confederate officer, and brother of William Ballard Preston, the owner of "Smithfield" who had died in 1862 while serving in the Confederate Senate. So by the time classes began, VAMC had a second substantial building as well as 250 acres of land, though the farm lay a short hike away from the school's principal building. The next year the Board of Visitors acquired another eighty acres, including the land that lay between the school and the farm, from the Black family.

When the new school opened its front door on October 1, 1872, the president and faculty—much like their counterparts at other new land-grant schools across America—peered anxiously out to see if any students might come trudging up the walk. The first to do so, that very day, was William Addison Caldwell, a sixteen-year-old who had walked in from Craig County. Before the month was over, 42 more young men joined him, and, before the year was out, the student population reached 132.

"Add" Caldwell arrived with a state scholarship in hand. That is, he arrived at VAMC as a "state student"—his county school board, itself a recent development, had selected him to attend tuition-free, even with a free room as long as space held out. And so did many others among the young men who drifted in as the weeks went by, as the crops were brought in, as word reached distant precincts, and as decisions were made as to scholarship recipients.

From the first term of classes at VAMC, students came from across Virginia, even if proportionally more came from west of the Blue Ridge. The availability of scholarships, one for each district in the Virginia House of Delegates, gave the new school a statewide constituency from the very beginning.

The Preston and Olin Institute conveyed a single building to the Virginia Agricultural and Mechanical College, one never designed to house all the equipment and supply all the classrooms for 132 young men studying English, French, drawing, chemistry, and a variety of other courses. Money remained scarce, and Ruffner wrote: "What a pity it would be to see this promising . . . school checked in its usefulness for the want of necessary buildings!"

Indeed, in 1874 the legislature appropriated funds for new buildings. In August 1875, at the school's first graduation exercises, the cornerstone was laid for the First Academic Building, which was ready for classes in October 1876. The Second Academic Building was completed in early 1877. State funds also covered construction of a home for the president (it would later be named Henderson Hall) and three houses for families of faculty members. The old Preston and Olin Institute took on something of the appearance of an "academical village," to use Thomas Jefferson's term for the early University of Virginia. Virginia's agricultural and mechanical school was well on its way, though the road ahead would sometimes prove as bumpy as a nineteenth-century Montgomery County byway.

The First Decade

The Virginia legislature faced a din of competing demands for the state's share of the land-grant funds, and in the end it awarded two-thirds of the annual proceeds to a dark horse candidate, Montgomery County. Black legislators successfully pushed for the other third to go to Hampton Institute. By 1880, Virginians of both races, and at both ends of the state, were studying at facilities of the sort, more or less, that Congressman Morrill had contemplated in the early years after he left Vermont to go to the nation's capital.

For a time, the VAMC student population grew. Board members and faculty members alike continued their search for a means to carry out their mandate to provide students a practical education. One commencement speaker told his audience in 1877 that, if the school was "an experiment in our state," it was also an "assured success." Such assurance was hardly warranted.

Turmoil swirled about the college in the late 1870s and early 1880s, as the next chapter will show. It surfaced in quarrels over the degree to which the institution should be organized along military lines—whether it should function more like VMI, with all students living on campus and under military regulations. The question arose in part over differences in interpreting the land-grant mandate. It also arose as a consequence of great problems in maintaining student discipline.

The first decade of Virginia Agricultural and Mechanical College supplied enough uncertainty to leave doubts about its future course. Would it survive? If it did, would it operate more like the Virginia Military Institute, more like the University of Virginia, or in some other fashion? Each decade offered its own clues as the institution continued to develop.

References

Bettersworth, *Centennial History of Mississippi State*, 1–30.

Cochran, "Virginia Agricultural and Mechanical College," 13–105.

Cox, "Early Years of Virginia Polytechnic Institute and State University, Part II."

Cox, "William Addison Caldwell."

Dethloff, *Texas A&M University*, 1: 3–153.

Engs, *Black Hampton, Virginia, 1861–1890*, 139–60.

Fraser, "William Henry Ruffner."

Fraser, "William Henry Ruffner and the Establishment of Virginia's Public School System."

Hughes and Armstrong, *Congressional Land Scrip*.

Kinnear, *The First 100 Years*, 29–101.

Kinnear, "History of Agricultural Education in Virginia," 199–238.

Montgomery et al., *History of the University of Tennessee*, 65–86, 96, 101–5.

Robertson, *Historical Data Book*, 36–40.

Sansing, *History of Higher Education in Mississippi*, 55–68.

Stadtmueller, "Pursuit of Land Grant Status."

Chapter 4

1880s: State Funds for Black Students and White Women

John Mercer Langston, president, Virginia Normal and Collegiate Institute, 1885–1887

John Mercer Langston left Virginia as a child in the 1840s and moved to Ohio. There he enjoyed a much broader definition of black freedom than Virginia offered. He graduated from Oberlin College, became a lawyer, taught school, and gained election to public office. During the Civil War, he recruited black soldiers for the Union Army.

After the war, he established and headed the law department at Howard University, one of the black institutions of higher education—along with Fisk University, Atlanta University, and Hampton Institute—that originated in the late 1860s. He tried to make Howard a school for both races and both sexes, much like Oberlin, except that Howard was predominantly black, Oberlin largely white. He then served for seven years as a U.S. diplomat in Haiti.

*William Mahone, U.S. Senator
and Readjuster leader*

In the 1880s, Langston returned to his native state and served for two years as president of a new public institution for the higher education of black Virginians at Petersburg.

William Mahone appeared a mere wisp of a man with a long white beard, but he towered over Virginia politics in the 1880s, when he served in the U.S. Senate. A graduate of the Virginia Military Institute, he served the Confederacy as a general. After the Civil War, he became a leader in the railroad industry in Virginia. Whatever other hats he wore in his illustrious career, he led a group in the late 1870s and early 1880s—they called themselves Readjusters—that transformed the political and educational landscape in the Old Dominion.

From the vantage point of the 1850s and 1860s, John Mercer Langston and William Mahone seemed the most unlikely of allies, but allies of a sort they became in the 1880s.

Virginia history's central theme of the 1880s was political turbulence associated with race, education, and public finance. Readjusters and Democrats took turns running the state and selecting VAMC's Board of Visitors. For Virginia as a whole, the extraordinary political conflict framed developments that strengthened elementary schooling and renovated higher education. Reaching into Virginia Agricultural and Mechanical College, the conflict resulted in the termination of several presidencies there.

The Readjuster Revolution

State School Superintendent William Henry Ruffner's efforts to build up a school system in the 1870s lost steam in the later years of the decade. The Virginia economy suffered from economic depression, and Virginia politicians made fateful decisions about what to fund and what to let slide. In education, growth faded into decay, optimism into pessimism.

Virginia suffered under an enormous public debt in the 1870s. Not a product of the war years or of Reconstruction, the debt had originated before the war, and it resulted from investments in railroads, canals, and other transportation improvements. The war did not create the debt, but it interrupted payments on the debt for several years while unpaid interest mounted, and it savaged the wealth that might have paid it down. The debt had grown, while the ability to service it had shrunk.

After the war, virtually everyone in Virginia was cash poor. When evaluating the operations of their state government, residents found taxes high but benefits scant. The "Funders"— Democrats who insisted on paying the public debt in full, even if doing so left nothing for the new public schools— diverted money from the schools to service the debt. The 1870 constitution directed that the new system be developed gradually with a "full introduction" by 1876, and one might have assumed that expenditures would, at worst, plateau at that level, not slope back down. Instead, the number of public schools in Virginia, never robust, fell from 3,442 for whites and 1,230 for blacks in 1877 to barely half that in 1879: 1,816 for whites and 675 for blacks.

As a consequence, Funders faced opposition throughout the state. White voters in western Virginia, like black voters in the eastern part of the state, called themselves Readjusters. Readjusters demanded a fiscal "readjustment"—a reduction in debt service and an increase in spending on schools. Moreover, black Virginians called for a state institution of higher education that they might attend. Hence a biracial coalition of Readjusters challenged the Funders for control of the state.

Historians often say that Reconstruction ended in 1877. By that, they mean that Republicans controlled all eleven states of the former Confederacy for some period between 1867 and 1877 but not later. Yet the definition and timeline apply poorly to Virginia (and not necessarily well elsewhere); Virginians had no idea Reconstruction ended in 1877. Republicans controlled the constitutional convention of 1867–1868, and they elected the first governor under the new charter, but they did not control the legislature. In one sense, therefore, "Reconstruction" never came to Virginia, or it ended before 1870.

In another sense, however, Reconstruction came to Virginia only after 1877. Virginians participated in the 1880s in as vibrant an example of biracial reform politics as the nineteenth-century South ever produced.

The Readjusters and the Schools

The Readjusters, a biracial and bipartisan alliance, defeated the Funders. They took control of both houses of the state legislature in the 1879 elections, retained control there and won the governorship in 1881, and thus controlled the state's fiscal affairs for a time in the early 1880s. While in power, they scaled back the debt, as they had said they would. They reduced debt service by more than half. They cut property tax rates by one-fifth, yet the reduction in interest payments permitted a substantial treasury surplus that they channeled into education.

Reversing the sharp decline in the late 1870s in state spending on public schools, the Readjusters brought the elementary schools to a stronger position than at any previous time. As early as 1880–1881, Virginia had more public schools than ever before, more for black students and more for whites. Those schools needed teachers. To educate more teachers for black schools, the Readjuster legislature established a school near Petersburg for black men and black women. To prepare teachers for white schools, the legislature subsequently established a school in Farmville for white women and, before the decade was over, supplied funds for the College of William and Mary to train white men.

During the 1880s, in short, Virginia embarked on a crusade to spend more state money on schools—more money on elementary schools and on higher education alike. Even more important for the history of higher education in Virginia, the state undertook to support institutions for black men, black women, and white women, three groups of Virginians that had never before obtained benefits from state spending on higher education. VAMC itself did not secure additional funding during the Readjuster interlude, but it obtained significant new construction funds in 1888, as well as new federal funds.

"Normal" Schools

The Virginia constitution of 1869 directed the legislature, "as soon as practicable," to establish "normal schools" (a name that was used for schools to train teachers). Yet the legislature turned out to be busy through the 1870s. Not only did it fail to find much money to promote the state's new "system" of public schools, it managed to ignore school superintendent William Henry Ruffner's campaign to secure one or more state-supported normal schools.

After the legislature enacted the 1870 law establishing a system of public schools, modest encouragement soon followed for teachers' professional development. The State Board of Education called for teacher institutes to be held every year beginning in 1872. Thereafter, training sessions took place, sometimes for a day or two, sometimes for a week, and sometimes, as "Summer Normal Institutes," for a month or longer. These sessions helped upgrade teachers' effectiveness, but they hardly matched what might be done in an entire year or two at a teachers' college.

A proposal in 1874 for a normal school went nowhere. In 1879 the legislature considered the question of establishing such a school. A state senator introduced a resolution pointing out the legislature's constitutional obligation to establish a normal school and, going further, he urged consideration of "how far such schools might be made use of in promoting the higher education of women generally."

Ruffner weighed back into the discussion. He declared that Virginia had three ways it could address the educational needs of white Virginia women as well as the professional training of white Virginia teachers. It could promote coeducation in current state institutions (at VAMC or UVA), establish a Female State College, or launch normal schools. He preferred the normal schools. Again, the legislature did not act.

The Readjusters, wishing to appoint their own man, removed Ruffner in 1882 as Superintendent of Public Instruction. They replaced him with Richard R. Farr, a three-term member of the House of Delegates from Fairfax County who served for the next four-year term. Farr found Virginia's teachers ill-trained and in short supply. He continued Ruffner's fight for normal schools and urged such training for black teachers and white teachers alike. Tallying the state's teachers and the places they had trained, he reported that Virginia's only normal school, the private one for black teachers at Hampton, had supplied 174 teachers. Among the remainder of the 5,078 teachers on his roster, only 45 had studied at UVA, 30 at Virginia Agricultural and Mechanical College, and 13 at VMI.

The growth in elementary schools in Virginia—first in the early 1870s and then in the early 1880s—created a great demand for teachers and, therefore, for schools to train teachers. To prepare teachers for black schools, the Readjusters established a institution near Petersburg. To prepare teachers for white schools, the legislature subsequently established a school in Farmville for white women and, before the decade ended, began to provide funds for William and Mary to train white men. These efforts to train teachers each merit discussion.

Virginia Normal and Collegiate Institute

The Readjuster legislature established Virginia Normal and Collegiate Institute, a public school for the higher education of black Virginians. The nation's first fully state-supported school for the higher education of African Americans, it was also the Old Dominion's first institution designed specifically to train teachers, as well as the first state-supported coeducational institution. The new school was located in Chesterfield County, just outside Petersburg in the heart of Southside Virginia, in as central a place as might have been found for black Virginians.

For land, buildings, and other start-up expenses, the legislature appropriated $100,000 from the proceeds of the sale of the state's holdings in the Atlantic, Mississippi, and Ohio Railroad. It also provided $20,000 in annual support. Before the school could go to work, it had to defeat a court challenge, brought by die-hard Funders, against the appropriation.

As Readjusters redeemed their promise to black voters to establish such an institution, a black legislator strove successfully to give the new school its particular shape. Alfred William Harris was born in Virginia in 1854, the year Justin Morrill first gained election to Congress. The new educational opportunities that the 1860s brought African Americans led to Harris's earning a law degree from Howard University and setting himself up as an attorney in Dinwiddie County. There he gained election to four terms in the Virginia House of Delegates, where he served from 1881 to 1888—a good example of the Readjuster insurgency.

The legislature specified that African Americans would control the new institution; the faculty would be black, as would six of the seven members of the board of visitors. It also directed the school to offer a collegiate course as well as a three-year normal program for training teachers. Much as Virginia Agricultural and Mechanical College and the College of William and Mary both found it necessary to offer secondary courses to prepare students for more advanced study, Virginia

Normal and Collegiate Institute maintained a preparatory program.

Like VAMC and VMI, the new school distinguished between "pay students" and "state students." As many as 50 state students might enroll each year; they paid no tuition provided they contracted to teach for at least two years after completing their studies. The board of visitors appointed such students, who had to be between the ages of sixteen and twenty five and of "good moral character." To assure geographical distribution, state students were apportioned on the same basis as the legislature's upper house, one from each of the 40 Senate districts and the other 10 at-large. The legislature subsequently increased the number of state students to 200, two for each district in the House of Delegates, and directed school superintendents to select them.

The school began operations in October 1883 with 62 students, a number that rose to 131 before the end of the year—numbers that resembled those at Virginia Agricultural and Mechanical College when it opened in 1872. Alfred William Harris served on the new school's first board of visitors and thus—like William Henry Ruffner at VAMC—continued actively to shape the institution's faculty and curriculum. The first two officers in charge of the school were called principals, and neither lasted long in his post, but, in late 1885, Harris and his colleagues selected John Mercer Langston as the school's first president. Langston therefore headed the school when it graduated its first class of teachers, four men and four women, in June 1886.

A Monument to the Readjusters

The Readjusters set tremendous change in motion. Yet, weakened by extreme racial tensions in the electorate—deliberately inflamed by Democratic leadership—they lost the legislative elections in 1883, and they lost the governorship in 1885. No longer calling themselves Funders, the regular Democrats took power, and they kept it into the 1960s. Though the Readjusters vanished from power, however, their fiscal innovations persisted.

So, having regained control of the legislature in 1883 and of the governorship in 1885, the Democrats recognized not only the debt settlement but also the enhanced spending on elementary schools, as well as the establishment and annual funding of Virginia Normal and Collegiate Institute. Yet they changed the composition of the school's board of visitors to majority white and Democratic. Frustrated by what he saw as hostile intervention from the new board, President Langston left the school in late 1887 and then ran for Congress the next year from his political base in Southside Virginia. And he won. His victory was disputed and his seating delayed until September 1890, but he served for part of one term in the U.S. House of Representatives, the only black congressman from Virginia until more than 100 years later.

Democrats reduced Virginia Normal and Collegiate Institute's annuity to $15,000 in 1888, but the school continued its work—its collegiate curriculum as well as its normal program—long after the Readjusters fell from power. A public institution for the higher education of black men and black women, it stood as a monument to that brief time in Virginia history when a biracial coalition took power and transformed the way in which the public business was done. The new president, James Hugo Johnston, presided from 1888 until 1914. From among the new school's graduates in the 1880s and 1890s came many of the people who became the teachers in Virginia's black elementary schools. From among them, too, came a number of the people who became lawyers and other professionals in the world that emerged in Virginia after the end of slavery.

Farmville

The Readjuster revolution had transformed the educational and fiscal environment. The rapid rise in state money going into elementary schools, white schools and black schools alike, generated an acute need for—and an obvious shortage of— teachers to staff the new schools. No doubt the establishment of a school to train black teachers encouraged white Democratic legislators to think more favorably about providing similar facilities for white Virginians. Moreover, readjustment of the Old Dominion's finances turned loose some money that might be put to such a use. The legislature quickly established a teachers' school for white women.

In 1884 the legislature created the State Female Normal School in Farmville and gave it $5,000 for equipment and $10,000 in annual support. The institution did not start from scratch, for the legislature required Farmville, in order to secure the new college, to deed the property of the Farmville Female College to the state; otherwise the legislature offered to see that another community, one that conveyed "suitable grounds and buildings," obtain the school. The former state superintendent of public schools, William Henry Ruffner, after striving for so long to foster the public schools and secure a normal school, became the first principal of the new institution, appointed by the board of visitors.

In return for its $10,000 annuity, the Farmville school admitted "state students" tuition-free if they pledged to teach in the public schools upon graduation. Over the years, the school's annuity grew, and its curriculum expanded, but it enrolled no black women before the 1960s. Today the school is known as Longwood University, and men as well as women, black as well as white, attend it.

The College of William and Mary

Four years after the Old Dominion established a school at Farmville to train white women teachers, it provided similar training for white men. The College of William and Mary came on such hard times after the Civil War that it quietly suspended operations in 1881. The buildings were dilapidated, the student population had melted away, and the school had no funds. Among its small faculty was Lyon Gardiner Tyler, who held bachelor's and master's degrees from UVA. Even before the college closed, Tyler left to find a salary more adequate and more sure. Tyler, the son of former President John Tyler, would nonetheless turn up later to assist his father's alma mater.

Officers of the school had not wished to alter the classical nature of its curriculum, but they came to see that no alternative offered the school any chance of resurrection. Deciding to inaugurate a teacher-training program in return for a state subsidy, they framed a bill for consideration by the 1886 legislature. Nothing happened then, so they tried again in 1888. Elected to the House of Delegates in 1887, Tyler was on hand to push the William and Mary initiative at the 1888 session.

Given the earlier decisions, in 1882 and 1884, to establish normal schools at Petersburg and Farmville, spokesmen for William and Mary were able to argue to good effect that, while the state had undertaken to support schools at which white women, black women, and black men could obtain training to become teachers, nothing of the sort was available to white men. They argued, too, that the Tidewater region ought to obtain benefits from state spending on higher education, as did every other area of the state—Southside (the normal school at Farmville), Southwest (VAMC), Valley (VMI), and Piedmont (UVA).

Tyler and the College were successful in 1888. The legislature approved a measure that supplied William and Mary a stipend of $10,000 per year. In return, the College would resume operations and inaugurate a normal curriculum as well as a collegiate one. "State students," nominated from each county and city in Virginia, could enroll in the College without charge for tuition on pledging to teach for at least two years in the Virginia public schools. Of the 102 students who attended the school's first session after it reopened in 1888, half were state students. That year, the board of visitors appointed Tyler the school's new president, a position he held until he retired in 1919.

As the years went by, even as enrollment grew, state students remained about half the total. The legislature raised the College's stipend to $12,000 in 1890 and then to $15,000 in 1892. There it stayed into the early twentieth century.

The College was neither a state institution nor completely private. It was neither completely a college with a classical curriculum nor only a vocational school for training teachers. A hybrid, it limped along with chronic budgetary uncertainty. But the state annuity gave it more certainty than it had known for many years. William and Mary survived, and each year it supplied dozens of new teachers to staff Virginia's public schools.

Virginia Agricultural and Mechanical College

Virginia Agricultural and Mechanical College continued in the 1880s, as it had in the 1870s, to rely on the Morrill fund for its annual support. Thus it obtained scant financial benefit from the Readjusters' commitment to education, and turmoil—on campus and in the legislature alike—buffeted the college.

Should VAMC be organized on a more fully military basis? In the late 1870s, Professor James H. Lane, the chief proponent of the military alternative, opposed President Charles L. C. Minor, who continued, as he had from the beginning of the school and his presidency, to consider the military component as secondary and optional. The conflict erupted in a fistfight between Lane and Minor at a faculty meeting in March 1878. The school also found itself caught up in a fight in the legislature, itself bitterly divided over power and policy in state affairs.

The Board of Visitors resolved the campus dispute in favor of Lane in late 1879, when it fired President Minor and replaced him with the president of Emory and Henry. John Lee Buchanan entered his new office at VAMC in the spring of 1880. At the same time, the board directed a reorganization of campus life along military lines. All students must live in barracks, be subject to military discipline, and, if able-bodied, participate in regular drill. Enrollment had dropped to a new low, 50, so all students could for the first time be housed on campus, but the school's very survival seemed in doubt.

Controversy persisted through the early 1880s. Buchanan served as president from March 1880 until June that year, when the Readjuster legislature removed the Board of Visitors, named a new board, and directed the new board to replace all faculty and officers at the college. The new board declared VAMC not a military school after all, but an agricultural and mechanical one, and returned the military dimension to the subordinate position it had held during Minor's presidency. Professor Lane, so recently jubilant in victory, resigned in disgust, left the state, and soon found himself in charge of a cadet corps and an engineering program at what today is Auburn University.

Buchanan himself lasted only a short time as president, but the school lumbered along, in search of a president, a mission, and a means to achieve its objectives. The new board actually offered Buchanan his job back, but he declined, and the position went to Scott Ship (he later changed the spelling of his name to Shipp), previously on the faculty at VMI. Ship resigned, however, as soon as he discovered how little independence he and the school would have; he returned to VMI and subsequently served that school as its second superintendent. The board offered the presidency to William Henry Ruffner, but he declined, and a professor, John Hart, served as acting president during the academic year 1880–1881. Again the board offered the presidency to Ruffner, but he had no confidence that the circus would not resume. The board recycled an invitation to Buchanan, who, displaying greater confidence than Ruffner that he would be left alone to direct the school, resumed the post in August 1881.

The Democratic governor nominated a new Board of Visitors for the school in 1881, but the Readjuster-controlled Senate never saw its way to approving the appointments. Upon taking office in early 1882, the Readjuster governor, William E. Cameron, nominated another board. Confirmed by the Senate in January 1882, the new board met the same day, removed the president and professors, and named replacements.

The new president was Thomas Nelson Conrad, a Readjuster supporter, former president of the Preston and Olin Institute, and member of the VAMC faculty through the turnover since 1879. He kept his post for four years and was actually able to accomplish a great deal. He restored a military regimen of the sort that had been ordered in 1879 and rescinded in 1880. Yet his support of the Readjusters in the 1883 legislative elections left him vulnerable should the Democrats return to power.

Democrats took the legislature back in 1883, and their candidate, Fitzhugh Lee, won the governorship in 1885. Lee nominated a new board, made up entirely of Democrats. When approved by the Senate, the new board brought the big broom back out of the closet and swept out all the school's officers and faculty. The new president, a former Confederate general named Lunsford Lindsey Lomax, served from 1886 until 1891, even longer than Conrad had, though not as long as Minor did.

During the Lomax presidency, the legislature appropriated $20,000 in 1888 to erect Barracks Number One (later called Lane Hall in honor of the first commandant), the first major new building since the 1870s and the harbinger of a series of similar new buildings constructed in the Upper Quad over the next quarter-century. The new barracks could house all the cadets, and the old Preston and Olin building became a shop and classroom building.

The five presidents of VAMC

Barracks No. 1, later Lane Hall

After the directive of late 1879 (though the board went through changes and kept reversing course, so full reorganization took until 1882), all students had to live on campus—in barracks, subject to military discipline—and participate in regular drill. Those features of campus life, though subject to occasional reconsideration, remained largely intact for many years. In 1924, male juniors and seniors gained permission to choose a civilian option, and freshmen and sophomores did so in 1964.

Subject to Senate approval, governors nominated board members, and the board decided personnel questions. If state authorities grew dissatisfied, the faculty and president at VAMC were likely to find themselves seeking new employment.

Despite being caught up in an occasional violent storm, however, the new institution took root and grew in strength. It built up a following, and its leaders gained experience in operating the new kind of school. Beginning in 1886 and especially in 1891, they would generally be permitted to do so unhindered. They would get it right yet.

VAMC Amidst the Winds of Change

The Readjusters fostered a new fiscal environment in which expenditures for education flourished, at least relative to any previous time in Virginia's history. Students, black and white,

could attend public elementary schools and obtain the rudi-
ments of book learning. That meant that more students might
wish to continue their education, and those who wished to
might have a better chance at success.

The new environment also produced a much greater
demand for trained teachers, black and white, men and women.
The Readjuster legislature inaugurated a school at Petersburg
to train black teachers as well as offer collegiate courses.
Subsequent legislative sessions, with Democratic majorities,
inaugurated a school at Farmville to train white women as
teachers and funded a program at William and Mary to train
white male teachers.

Lost for a time with the emphasis on teacher training and
the turmoil in state politics in the 1880s, Virginia Agricultural
and Mechanical College muddled along, despite all the
uncertainty and disruption. In view of the support it received
from the Morrill Act fund, it never experienced the disastrous
finances that caused William and Mary to close down for a
few years. The 1890s would tell a happier story. The new
decade brought skilled and effective administrative leadership,
and it also brought the good fortune of political stability and
increased revenues.

References

Buck, *Development of Public Schools in Virginia*, 94–96.

Cato, "Higher Education for Women in Virginia," 292–325.

Cheek and Cheek, "John Mercer Langston."

Cochran, "Virginia Agricultural and Mechanical College," 106–59.

Dailey, *Before Jim Crow.*

Godson et al., *College of William and Mary*, 1: 401–11; 2: 439–55.

Kinnear, *The First 100 Years*, 91–141.

Kinnear, "History of Agricultural Education in Virginia," 239–66.

Langston, *From the Virginia Plantation to the National Capitol*, 409–37.

Temple, *Bugle's Echo*, 1: 147–78.

Toppin, *Loyal Sons and Daughters*, 13–21.

Wynes, *Race Relations in Virginia*, 16–38, 120–34.

The Preston and Olin building, c. 1900—after its conversion to a shop building and before it was destroyed by fire, as viewed from Main Street in the original sixteen squares

Chapter 5
1890s: VAMC
and Polytechnic Institute

The VAMC Board of Visitors, under the leadership of rector Charles E. Vawter Sr., recruited a new president to head the "Blacksburg college" as it neared completion of two decades of turmoil and experiment. John McLaren McBryde, who took the reins at Virginia Agricultural and Mechanical College in 1891, had previously led land-grant schools in Tennessee and South Carolina. He presided over his new institution as it made its way from the nineteenth century into the twentieth.

John McLaren McBryde, president, 1891–1907

During McBryde's first decade, the school grew larger and more complex and added the handle "and Polytechnic Institute" to its name. The first VAMC president with authority to hire and fire faculty, McBryde brought along such professors as Ellison A. Smyth Jr. and Robert James Davidson from South Carolina. Developments during his long tenure included the creation of a small graduate program. Beyond the realm of academics, intercollegiate sports became a part of the campus scene, and such symbols of twentieth-century Tech as the school colors, student yearbook, and school motto came along, as did the Highty-Tighties.

By the time McBryde retired in 1907, the institution had developed into a significant feature on the landscape of higher education in Virginia, and it had begun to look much more familiar to modern eyes. President McBryde's counterpart at Texas A&M in the 1890s, Lawrence Sullivan Ross, had a comparable impact on the institution over which he presided. Growth at both schools depended not only on political continuity and strong leadership but also on two acts of Congress that supplemented the Morrill Act of 1862—the Hatch Act of 1887 and a second Morrill Act in 1890. Both acts spurred changes in higher education in Virginia and throughout the nation.

The Hatch Act of 1887

The 1862 Morrill Act launched a new kind of education, supported in part by funds from the federal government and directed toward instruction in applied science. Twenty-five years later, Congress added a significant research function to the land-grant mission by funding agricultural experiment stations.

The Hatch Act's major sponsors were Senator James Z. George of Mississippi and Congressman William N. Hatch of Missouri. Its title promised to "establish agricultural experiment stations in connection with" the institutions supported under the terms of the 1862 Morrill Act. Beyond launching experiment stations in every state, the Hatch Act propelled the land-grant colleges into greater public favor by making the benefits of agricultural education more evident to citizens.

The Hatch Act offered to provide each state with an annual payment of $15,000. The 1862 act had provided a lump-sum amount to every state, which (as discussed in Chapter 1) had broad discretion as to its use. By contrast, the 1887 act authorized a fixed amount for every year, placed it directly under the control of land-grant colleges, and established compliance guidelines that the school had to meet in order to qualify for continuing payments.

Farm groups lobbied Congress for support of applied research, not pure research, which would come later. Farmers, regardless of whether they ever enrolled at a land-grant college, needed practical help with immediate problems. Congress specified the kinds of issues that the additional money might be employed to address—among them plant physiology and disease, soil analysis, crop rotation, and the production of butter and cheese.

Teaching *and* Research

Under the 1862 Morrill Act, members of the land-grant college faculty taught students mostly in classrooms and sometimes in laboratories. Teaching was their primary function, if not their only function. The Hatch Act redirected their activity beyond the classroom.

Senator George's own Mississippi exemplifies how the Hatch Act altered the activities at land-grant schools. Like many such schools, Mississippi A&M began in a small way to offer farmers' institutes and short courses for farmers—much like some schools offered teachers' institutes—in an effort to bring the school's benefits to state residents other than those who happened to be enrolled on campus. The Hatch Act, with its new funds from the federal government, made such work possible in a far grander way. Mississippi A&M managed to garner the entire fund for itself rather than divide it with its black counterpart, Alcorn. The school established its first experiment station at Starkville and soon planted branches in other parts of the state.

Teaching and research have ridden together through the past hundred years, but teaching typically rode alone during the first quarter-century after President Lincoln signed the land-grant college bill. After the Hatch Act, the experiment station became so thoroughly a part of the land-grant mission, people a few generations later would be hard pressed to comprehend that research had not been there all along. Moreover, the research done at experiment stations would so transform American agriculture that most people could have no idea how fully the tremendous variety of farm products, raised with great efficiency in enormous quantities, embodied huge twentieth-century improvements on nineteenth-century nature.

The 1890 Morrill Act

In 1890, Justin Morrill continued to serve in Congress. He retained his commitment to federal action in support of education, but he had moved from the House to the Senate, and he had modified his ideas of how Congress might foster a people's practical education. Never fully satisfied with the results of his first successful effort in Congress, he followed it up with proposals year after year, session after session, to supplement it. After a very long drought, he sponsored a second bill past all the obstacles that any successful proposal must overcome in Congress. The 1890 act provided "for the more complete endowment and support of colleges for the benefit of agriculture and mechanic arts."

Under the 1890 act, each state received an annual amount of cash from the federal treasury, beginning with $15,000 in 1890 and rising by $1,000 each year until it leveled off at $25,000 in 1900. Attractive as such an increase was, it came with strings attached.

Unlike the Morrill Act of 1862—enacted before emancipation and silent on race—the 1890 act offered annual payments only on condition that they benefit black students as well as white ones. The 1890 act—passed in the year of John Mercer Langston's brief tenure in the House of Representatives—stands as the last successful legislative measure of the Reconstruction era.

Republicans, in control of the White House and both houses of Congress, took advantage of their opportunity and enacted a considerable inducement to southern states to enhance black citizens' educational opportunities.

The 1890 Morrill Act did not require integrated facilities. It permitted segregation so long as a state "equitably divided" its land-grant funds between "a college for white students" and an "institution for colored students." The "separate-but-equal" doctrine is generally dated to the U.S. Supreme Court decision in the 1896 case *Plessy v. Ferguson*, but Congress had approved such an approach six years earlier. Both the 1890 act and the 1896 decision permitted segregation. Neither resulted in objectively equal opportunities, but the 1890 act spurred states to do more than they had been doing, and it supplied the funds to ease the way.

The South and the 1890 Morrill Act

Some southern states resembled Virginia in having already taken one action or another to supply black citizens with an institution at least partly funded with land-grant money. Chapter 3, on the 1870s, discussed Mississippi's actions. Also in the 1870s, Arkansas established a white school at Fayetteville and a black school at Pine Bluff, and Texas established a white school at College Station and a black one at Prairie View.

The Florida legislature acted only in the 1880s. In 1887 it authorized the State Normal College for Colored Students, which opened in Tallahassee that year. Responding to the 1890 Morrill Act, the State Board of Education renamed the institution to qualify under the act. The State Normal and Industrial College for Colored Students, available to a group making up 47 percent of the state's residents, received half of Florida's money from the 1890 act.

Most southern states had never divided the benefits. Georgia had shared the money for a time but then terminated the arrangement and put money only into a school for whites. Like Florida, rather than jeopardize access to land-grant funds for white schools, Georgia—together with other southern states that had not yet funded black land-grant schools—remedied the previous deficiency and founded what came to be known as the "colleges of 1890," as distinguished from the "colleges of 1862."

In Georgia's case, compliance with the new requirements meant establishing the Georgia State Industrial College in Savannah as a segregated coeducational branch of the University of Georgia. The new school opened in 1891 with free tuition to black residents of Georgia. It received both the $8,000 annuity that had gone for a time to Atlanta University and one-third of the new money. Richard R. Wright, president of the new land-grant school, was born a slave in 1853. He enrolled in the preparatory department at Atlanta University in 1869, the year of its founding, and graduated in 1876, when it served in effect as Georgia's land-grant institution for black citizens.

North Carolina offers a good example of a state that was slow to do much for whites and slower to do anything for blacks. Having lifted the initial land-grant designation and funds from the University of North Carolina, in 1887 the Tarheel State authorized a new land-grant school for whites; it went into operation in 1889. When Congress passed the 1890 Morrill Act, North Carolina's white authorities and citizenry wanted, of course, to obtain the additional funds dangled before it. To do so, however, seemed to require that comparable facilities be supplied black North Carolinians. The new white school's board of trustees made arrangements for black students to begin their studies at Shaw University, a private institution, pending legislative action to establish a new state-supported land-grant school for blacks. When the legislature next met in 1891, it authorized an "A. and M. College for the Colored Race," and the new school began operations at Greensboro in 1893.

Kentucky, to give another example, had been very slow to respond to demands for a school to train black teachers. It had finally acted only in 1886, when the legislature appropriated $7,000 for a building and an annual $3,000 for support, on condition that the new institution, State Normal School for Colored Persons, admit tuition-free all qualified students who pledged to teach at least two years in the black public schools for each year that they took classes. In the 1890s the school experienced a bonanza when the Kentucky legislature, seeking to qualify for federal funds under the Second Morrill Act, authorized new departments of agriculture and mechanics and supplied the school 14.5 percent of the combined 1862 and 1890 land-grant funds.

The West and the Morrill Acts

As new states in the West entered the Union, they benefited from both Morrill acts. Montana became a state in 1889, and in 1893 it chartered both the University of Montana in Missoula and a land-grant college in Bozeman that became Montana State University. Like some eastern states, some in the West combined their state university and land-grant school into a single institution. The University of Wyoming and the University of Idaho stand as examples.

Oklahoma became a state only in 1907. The year of its organization as a territory, in 1890, it established the University of Oklahoma in Norman and Oklahoma Agricultural and Mechanical College in Stillwater. The black town of Langston was born the same year, named for John Mercer Langston, the educator in Ohio, at Howard University, and at Virginia Normal and Collegiate Institute who took his seat in Congress that year. To satisfy the mandate of the 1890 Morrill Act and yet prevent racial integration at Oklahoma A&M, in 1897 the territorial legislature established a third school, this one in Langston.

The Colored Agricultural and Normal University of Oklahoma had as its mission "the instruction of both male

and female colored persons in the art of teaching" and in
the "agricultural, mechanical, and industrial arts." From
the beginning, black Oklahomans tended to call the school
Langston University, and in 1941 the legislature made it
official.

Virginia and the Hatch Act and 1890 Morrill Act

In 1886, in anticipation of the Hatch Act passed by Congress
the next year, the Virginia legislature created the Virginia
Agricultural Experiment Station and located it at Blacksburg.
Offering no state money, the legislature simply directed the
new federal funds, $15,000 per year, to the new unit.

The Board of Visitors transferred the VAMC farm to the
new station, and experimentation began on wheat, tomatoes,
and various other plants. VPI personnel also established an
orchard that included 119 varieties of apples and 56 varieties
of strawberries. The station had as its overriding objective the
production of practical knowledge and readable reports that
farmers in Virginia might immediately find useful. President
McBryde did much to spur the station's work, but the person
who proved most essential to its early success was William
B. Alwood. Professor Alwood had obtained his professional
training, especially in horticulture, in France and Germany,
where research in agriculture was far in advance of that in the
United States.

Congress's 1890 Morrill Act helped support VAMC's
new work under the 1887 Hatch Act. The Virginia legislature
divided its funds from the 1890 Morrill Act in the same manner
it had apportioned the money from the 1862 act, two-thirds
to Virginia Agricultural and Mechanical College, one-third
to Hampton Institute. Hampton Institute's share of the new
money, $5,000 in 1890, rose to $8,333 in 1900.

The share that went to VAMC, $10,000 in 1890, more than
doubled the college's revenue from Morrill Act funds. By 1900,
the Blacksburg school's share of the second infusion leveled off
at $16,667, and its combined annual revenue from the Morrill

funds of 1862 and 1890 had nearly tripled since the 1880s. The school's total income from state and federal funds reached VMI's level of funding, though it lagged well behind UVA's annuity from the state.

And Polytechnic Institute

The political stability of the period of McBryde's presidency, coupled with the rise in revenues, allowed VAMC to work toward fulfilling the broader

William B. Alwood, VPI agricultural researcher

vision of its mission articulated during the struggles of the late 1870s. The school should be organized, the board wrote then, "to teach all the classical and scientific subjects, as well as such as relate more immediately to agriculture and mechanics." It should "promote the liberal as well as the practical education of the industrial classes." And "degrees should not be confined to agricultural and mechanical instruction, but should likewise be awarded for distinction in those courses of study necessary to prepare the student for other professions and pursuits in life."

VAMC grew. It grew in student population from 150 at the beginning of McBryde's presidency in 1891 to more than 700 a dozen years later. It grew in physical plant through the construction of dozens of new buildings. It even grew a longer name. Agriculture and mechanics remained significant parts of the school's curriculum, but McBryde wanted the institution's

The professors of VPI, 1900–1901

name to reflect the broader instructional mission that had developed.

In 1896, the legislature granted McBryde's request and changed VAMC's name to Virginia Agricultural and Mechanical College and Polytechnic Institute. In popular usage, that long name was immediately shortened to Virginia Polytechnic Institute, Virginia Tech, or VPI. Later, the formal name would catch up with longtime usage and be officially shortened to Virginia Polytechnic Institute. That name, however, lasted only from 1944 to 1970, when the school became Virginia Polytechnic Institute and State University, a full name used with no more frequency than the 1896 version.

No longer VAMC, the school will appear throughout the remainder of this book as Virginia Tech or VPI.

Building Boom

During and after President McBryde's time at VPI, the school's physical environment changed in dramatic ways, even on the Upper Quad—the military quadrangle of brick buildings, the center of the campus during his tenure. Shortly before McBryde's arrival, Number One Barracks went up with money from an 1888 appropriation, and cadets moved into it from the old Preston and Olin Building. Permitting—and reflecting—a sharp rise in enrollment, other dormitories for cadets followed: Number Two Barracks in 1894, the first section of what would become Rasche Hall; Number Three Barracks, the first section of what became Brodie Hall, in 1900; Number Four Barracks, the old section of Shanks Hall, in 1902; and Number Five Barracks, the old section of Major Williams Hall, in 1904. These remained Tech's entire roster of dorms until the late 1920s.

Across campus, a second quadrangle of brick buildings began to go up as part of the Agricultural Experiment Station. The first new building, completed in 1907, was later named Sandy Hall. It reflected a measure enacted by the 1906 legislature, which provided $60,000 to complete and equip the

The Grove

"agricultural building." The same legislature established an annual appropriation of $5,000 to better support the Experiment Station that Tech directed under the 1887 Hatch Act.

The structure that has long been known as the Grove, built west of the main campus and on a hill south of Solitude, was designed as the home of the college president. President McBryde moved into it upon its completion in 1902. Not all subsequent presidents favored it as their official residence, but it continued to serve its original function into the 1960s. Then, for a time, it was remodeled for office use. Later presidents, however, toward the end of the twentieth century—James D. McComas and Paul E. Torgersen—made it their home, much as McBryde had at the start of the century.

McBryde's move to the Grove freed up his former home as a permanent infirmary. Tech had long had trouble finding space to look after cadets who fell ill, but no more. Occasionally renovated and enlarged, the building was named Henderson Hall in 1951 to commemorate Dr. William F. Henderson, who had served as college physician from 1890 to 1935.

From 1906 to 1945, or through most of Dr. Henderson's long tenure, Anna G. Hannas served as superintendent of the infirmary. Her gravestone in Blacksburg says of her that "to thousands of Tech students she was a minister of mercy and a devoted friend." Between them, Dr. Henderson and Superintendent Hannas cared for generations of cadets and helped to lessen the likelihood that families would face the horror of having a child go away to school and suddenly die.

Graduate Students

As Tech's student population soared to higher levels than ever before, the usual shortages developed—housing, classrooms, teachers. Graduate students offered a possible solution to one of those problems. President McBryde began a small graduate program in 1891, his first year at the helm. Throughout his presidency, the program remained small, but it did provide advanced training, and it also offered the possibility of immediate employment, as graduate students taught classes and received stipends. And some stayed on.

VPI thus supplied some of its own instructors. They did their undergraduate work at Blacksburg, stayed for graduate work, and then joined the teaching brigade, some of them for decades. One was Frank L. Robeson (class of 1904), longtime head of the physics department, who has a campus building named after him.

Another indication that Tech was maturing as an academic institution came when the school appointed its first professional librarian, Mary G. Lacy, in 1903. In the years that followed, Tech's library began to approach, even exceed, the most rudimentary level of offering students and faculty some reference and reading materials.

Beyond Academics

The Corps of Cadets dates its history to Virginia Tech's very beginnings, but in some important ways its history goes back only to the 1880s and 1890s. A renewed military organization of student life dates from 1882, and beginning in the fall of 1891, President McBryde's first year, a new organization called the Corps of Cadets undertook responsibility for supervising some aspects of campus life other than the military and the academic. McBryde's successor, President Barringer, went a bit farther in 1908, when he encouraged the Corps to draw up a constitution that began a tradition of student governance at Tech.

Organized athletic teams and games with other colleges also have their origins in the 1890s, not only at VPI but throughout America. In 1892 at Tech, a baseball program was initiated and a tennis association formed. Tech students had begun playing a bit of football in 1891—the same year the school formed the VAMC Athletic Association and adopted school colors and a school cheer—and the next year Professor E. A. Smyth offered some leadership in organizing a football team.

When the new Tech football team first ran onto the field that year, barely more players than a starting eleven suited up, with their leather helmets and all, but it was a beginning. One player later described how the 25-yard lines were marked by a plow, as were the sidelines. "The field was not as smooth as the bed of the Blacksburg railroad," he continued, and it "ran up and down hill, with interesting little hollows which hid the play from spectators on the other side of the field."

The first game, played in Radford, revealed football as a game that could stand skill and tactics, and not only strength and determination. For the 1893 season, Professor Smyth took himself to a rule book and applied his professional training to the applied science of developing a football team. The extraordinary Hunter Carpenter, who played for Tech from 1899 through 1905—with one year away playing for UNC, in a desperate effort to defeat UVA—was later named to the National Football Hall of Fame.

During McBryde's first year, Tech happened upon the following yell:

> Rip Rah Ree! Va., Va., Vee!
> Virginia, Virginia!
> A.M.C.

Clearly such a cry no longer satisfied the need when the school's name changed. VAMC did not rhyme with VPI, and thus, it is said, originated the term Hokie. Students held a contest, and O. M. Stull, class of 1896, kept a bit of tradition but entered a brave new world with phrasing that showed, already, the use of Tech and VPI as names connected with the school:

> Hoki, Hoki, Hoki Hy!
> Tech! Tech! V.P.I.!
> Sola-Rex, Sola Rah
> Polytech-Vir-gin-i-a!!
> Rae, Ri, V.P.I.

Hunter Carpenter,
VPI football great

Other accounts substitute "Techs" or "Polytechs" for "Tech," suggesting a name for the players rather than the school, and indeed VPI was long the preferred name for the school.

In 1896, Tech also acquired a new color combination, Chicago maroon and burnt orange. According to some comments at the time, sports uniforms in stripes in the previous choice of colors—black and gray—made athletes look like convicts.

In 1896, Tech also acquired a college seal, which the Board of Visitors made official years later (in 1963), and a motto, "Ut Prosim," "That I May Serve." Indicative of the development of extracurricular activities, a Glee Club was organized in 1894. Students began publishing a yearbook, *The Bugle*, in 1895; Claudius Lee (class of 1896) is credited with the name, though surely all cadets knew that the bugle regulated their daily lives from reveille to lights out.

And in 1903 publication began of a student newspaper, *The Virginia Tech*. As the original name of what would become the *Collegiate Times*, it also reveals a very early use of the preferred modern name of the institution.

In Loco Parentis

Athletics and academics grew together. From a late twentieth-century perspective, the school grew more recognizable. In the minds of the parents of Tech students from President McBryde's time, however, the land-grant school at Blacksburg remained as small as it had been when it was Virginia Agricultural and Mechanical College. In fact, parents seem often to have had their local school in mind when they thought of Tech, and assumed that President McBryde was as involved in their students' lives as the principal of the local school—as, in degree, he actually was.

McBryde fielded letters from concerned parents from across the state. Anxious that their sons would be all right, they conceived the school small enough that McBryde could know, and look after, all his charges. One letter said, "My boy is coming to your college today. Please give him a sunny room on the second floor and help him choose a good roommate." Another urged McBryde, "My two boys left this morning for your college. Charles is a husky boy and will get along. William is in poor health. Please see that he wears his hat and coat when the weather is bad."

Parents' concerns continued after their sons began school. One wrote, "My son joined the Y.M.C.A. and goes to the meetings but I do not know if it does any good. Where does he go after the meetings? Please let me know but don't tell him I asked." And another, "I sent my son some money. He writes that he got it but doesn't know what he did with it. Please check and let me know."

Other parents hoped that the school would manufacture good students even if out of unpromising materials. One man wrote McBryde, "No doubt you get a lot of letters from fathers telling you all about the fine qualities of their sons. Well I love my son very dearly but so far as books are concerned I have not discovered any fine qualities yet. Will you take him in your school and see if your professors can find any?"

Yet other parents saw the school's military dimension as suitable for instilling discipline. Thus McBryde was directed, "Your school is supposed to build character so I am sending you my son. I do not want him to smoke, chew, cuss, loaf or run around. He does all of these things now."

Supplemental Land-Grant Money

In the final years of McBryde's presidency, Congress offered further enhancements to the 1862 land-grant law. In 1906 it passed the Adams Act, which increased the amounts of money made available under the Hatch Act but specified that the new money was to be dedicated to pure research. The Adams Act provided each state's Agricultural Experiment Station with $3,000 per year, an amount slated to rise each year until it reached $15,000, a figure that matched the income from the Hatch Act.

The Nelson Amendment to the Agricultural Appropriations Act of 1907 brought still more money to land-grant colleges. By 1907, McBryde's last year at VPI and the school's 35th anniversary, the land-grant institution at Blacksburg could count on five pieces of federal money—the proceeds from the 1862 fund, the 1890 and 1907 supplements, and the proceeds from the Hatch Act of 1887 and the Adams Act of 1906.

With the Adams Act, pure research was added to practical research as an important function of the land-grant schools. Additional resources, attached to new responsibilities and new opportunities at those schools, came along still later. Beginning in the 1910s, extension—also termed "service" or "outreach"—entered what then became the land-grant college's triple mission of teaching, research, and service.

The acts of Congress in 1906 and 1907 contributed mightily to Virginia Tech's development, as they did to the nation's other land-grant schools. Both measures, like President McBryde's many accomplishments, did much to shape the institution. In addition, state actions in the new century's first decade reshaped higher education across Virginia, as the next chapter demonstrates.

References

Bettersworth, *People's University*, 66–77.

Bitter, *100 Things Virginia Tech Fans Should Know and Do before They Die*, 92–95, 164–66.

Cochran, "Virginia Agricultural and Mechanical College," 160–248.

Dethloff, *Texas A&M University*, 1: 154–225.

Kinnear, *The First 100 Years*, 143–82, 268–69.

Logan, "The Movement in North Carolina."

Martin, *Benching Jim Crow*, 1–26.

Neyland, *Historically Black Land-Grant Institutions*, 1–74.

Neyland and Riley, *Florida Agricultural and Mechanical University*, 1–20.

Patterson, *Langston University*, 1: 3–18.

Rainsford, *Congress and Higher Education*, 100–28.

Smyth, *RetroSpect*, 77–78, 96–97.

Wallenstein, *From Slave South to New South*, 167–69.

Young, *Virginia Agricultural Experiment Station*, 2–4, 11–14, 52, 67, 83.

Chapter 6
1900s: Hokie Stone and May Campaign

Claude A. Swanson, who was born in the very year that Congress passed the Morrill Land-Grant College Act, studied at Virginia Agricultural and Mechanical College for the academic year 1879–1880. He soon went into politics and— without a break, from 1893 until his death in 1939— served successively as U.S. congressman, Virginia governor, U.S. senator, and secretary of the navy.

Swanson's gubernatorial administration, 1900–1910, displayed more reform energy and commitment to education than any

Claude A. Swanson, Virginia governor, 1906–1910

governorship had since the Readjusters in the early 1880s. Great increases in state appropriations for public schools led to a surge in demand for public school teachers and the establishment of new institutions to train those teachers.

Joseph D. Eggleston Jr. served as state superintendent of public instruction during and after Swanson's governorship. He, too, energetically promoted educational improvements, from high schools to school libraries, and he went on to serve from 1913 to 1919 as president of Virginia Polytechnic Institute. He later served as president of Hampden-Sydney College (his alma mater) for twenty years, as a member of the State Board of Education, and

Joseph D. Eggleston Jr., state school superintendent and VPI president

as president of the Virginia Historical Society. The *Richmond Times-Dispatch* editorialized about him when he died that "no other Virginian of his generation touched the educational life of the Commonwealth at so many points or influenced it more importantly for the better."

During the first decade of the twentieth century, Virginia actively participated in the "Progressive Movement" and initiated commitments, unprecedented in the state's history, to improving education and transportation. During their four-year terms, Governors Andrew Jackson Montague and Claude A. Swanson alike demanded "good roads" and "good schools." Both kinds of improvements involved Virginia Polytechnic Institute and other public institutions of higher education. Both governors' elections came, however, after the Virginia Constitution of 1902 effectively eliminated black Virginians as a force in state politics, and black disfranchisement permitted a growing disparity at every level between public funds for white schools, among them VPI, and for black schools.

Across the state, the decade brought an enormous expansion in state support for elementary and secondary education. To satisfy the demand for more teachers, the decade also brought three new teachers' colleges for white women. Meantime, on the one hand, the state adopted the College of William and Mary as a state-funded institution and, on the other, it narrowed the curriculum and changed the name of Virginia Normal and Collegiate Institute to Virginia Normal and Industrial Institute.

The Virginia Constitution of 1902

The Virginia Constitution of 1902 provided the basis for all such efforts. The framers of the 1869 constitution, mindful that the postwar problems with the public debt originated in prewar investments in transportation schemes, barred the state from investing in "any work of internal improvement." Their counterparts three decades later qualified that flat prohibition with the phrase "except public roads." So the state had obtained a constitutional license, though requiring legislative authorization, to put state funds into improved transportation. The requisite legislation soon followed.

A 1906 act establishing a state highway commission, for example, called for the governor to appoint a state highway commissioner. The commission would also include a professor of civil engineering from each of the three leading state institutions of higher education—UVA, VMI, and VPI.

The new constitution also spoke of the public schools. Whatever features of the 1869 constitution white Virginians might wish to reject, the convention kept the requirement that the state "establish and maintain an efficient system of public free schools throughout the State." More specifically, the legislature had authority, though it was not obliged, to "establish agricultural, normal, manual training and technical schools"; the last category broadened the legislature's authority.

Voters would elect a state superintendent of public instruction for a four-year term, and he would head a reconstituted state Board of Education.

Lest there be any doubt about racial segregation, the constitution ordered: "White and colored children shall not be taught in the same school." This language was new to the 1902 constitution, for the 1869 charter had been silent on the question, though the legislative act establishing public schools in 1870 had used similar language. So segregation of Virginia schools was no innovation in 1902.

Hokie Stone Material, Neo-Gothic Design

Virginia Tech's early buildings were made of brick: the original Preston and Olin building; what would later be named Henderson Hall and Lane Hall; and additional structures on the Upper Quad. The years around 1900 brought a new architecture to the campus, in terms of both construction materials and building design.

Private funds paid for the YMCA building, completed in 1901 at the edge of the Upper Quad. Unlike all previous major buildings on campus, the YMCA building was constructed of stone, rough blocks of it, quarried nearby and later named "Hokie Stone."

New buildings that soon followed reflected appropriations from the state, which was providing VPI with significantly more financial support than ever before. In 1905, work was completed on what at the time was the Chapel, built where Newman Library is today. It served for a time also as a gym and an auditorium, and beginning in 1915 it housed the library. Agricultural Hall (completed in 1907 and later named Price Hall) and subsequent buildings on the Agricultural Quad across campus came dressed in Hokie Stone. New buildings also featured a "neo-Gothic" (or "Collegiate Gothic") exterior design.

The year 1908 brought unaccustomed amenities to the VPI campus: running water in all the barracks, outdoor lights,

YMCA Building, 1902

and concrete walks connecting campus buildings. Eventually paved walkways would cut across the Drillfield, too—but the Drillfield itself lay years away in the future.

While new buildings went up, some buildings came down. VPI had barely moved its administrative offices and records into one building when it burned down in 1900, and with it went much of the material that might have been used to write a detailed account of the school's early history. Fire also consumed a new science studies building in 1905. Moreover, Tech's very first building, home of the Olin and Preston Institute (and then Preston and Olin Institute), burned in 1913, so a major feature of the physical campus was obliterated, such that future Hokies would have little idea just where their school had begun.

With the YMCA building, the Chapel, and Price Hall, Tech began to adopt a distinctive architecture. In the 1910s, the first incarnation of McBryde Hall emulated these buildings' stone facing as well as the new style, a combination that constituted a major continuing feature of the physical environment. Yet some modern buildings have a very different face, or have only a

The map on the facing page shows the location of buildings on the Tech campus in February 1908. The shaded buildings, identified with circled numbers, still stand in some form on the campus. The solid black buildings, identified with capital letters, are gone. The area marked "Drill Field" was not called by that name until 1926.

BUILDINGS STILL STANDING

1—Barracks No. 1 (Completed 1888; now known as Lane Hall)
2—Barracks No. 2 (Completed 1894; now known as old section of Rasche Dormitory)
3—Barracks No. 3 (Completed 1900; now known as old section of Brodie Dormitory)
4—Barracks No. 4(Completed; 1902; now known as old section of Shanks Dormitory)
5—Barracks No. 5 (Completed 1904; now known as old section of Major Williams Dormitory)
6—YMCA (Completed 1899; later known as Military Building; Student Personnel Building; Performing Arts Building)
7—Laundry (Completed 1903; now known as Building 201, housing the University's Security Division)
8—Infirmary (One section completed 1876 for use as the President's Home; converted to infirmary with completion of a second wing in 1902; both early wings are now known as the old section of Henderson Hall)
9—Agricultural Hall (Completed 1907; now known as Price)

BUILDINGS NO LONGER STANDING

A—Preston and Olin Building (The first and only building on campus until 1896; burned down in 1913)
B—Foundry/Forge Shop (Built 1882; razed 1917)
C—Steam Laundry (Wooden building; used earlier as machine shop)
D—Pavilion (Used at various times as drill hall, assembly hall, mess hall, gymnasium, dance hall; torn down in 1940)

E—Mess Hall (Known at times as Commencement Hall, German Hall, and Commerce Hall; razed in 1957)
F—Commandant's House (Originally built for Prof. John E. Christian; torn down in 1962)
G—Powder Magazine (Used to store ammunition for cadet training)
H—Chapel (Used at various times as auditorium, dance hall, gymnasium, and finally as the College Library. After the building burned in 1953 the present library was built on the site)
I—Gibboney Field (Track, baseball, and football; originally called Sheib Field; name changed to Miles Field in 1909)
J—Bleachers (Torn when Miles Stadium opened in 1926)
K—Greenhouses
L—Creamery
M—Horticulture Hall (Built in 1890 for Agriculture Experiment Station; also used at various times by the Agricultural Extension Division, several academic departments, and by women students; was torn down in 1936 to make way for approaches to Burruss Hall)
N—Administration Building (Used earlier as a residence for Prof. William B. Alwood; destroyed by fire in 1900; rebuilt in 1904 as an administration building)
O—Second Academic Building (Razed in 1957 to make way for the new section of Brodie Dormitory; contained College Library from 1877-1914)
P—First Academic Building (First major building built by the new College; used at various times for administrative offices and the mess hall in addition to academic departments; razed in 1957 to make way for new section of Rasche)
Q—Science Hall (Mostly destroyed by fire in 1905; rebuilt that year; remodeled as Barracks No. 7 in 1927; razed in 1957 to make way for new section of Shanks Dormitory)
R—Power House (Completed during 1900 for use as heating and electric power plant; Thomas Dormitory now occupies the site)
S—Marks the site of the wooden Field House (Built in 1914; burned down in 1923)

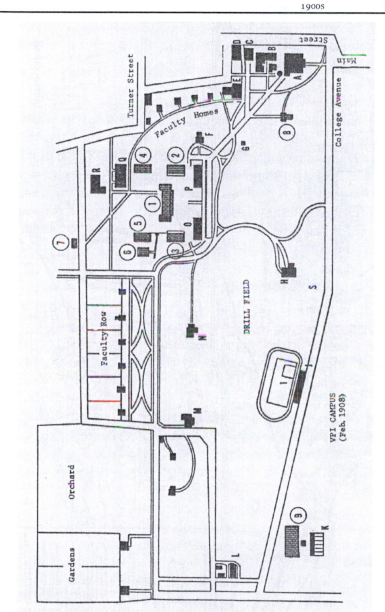

*Map of VPI campus, 1908. A Key to the map is on facing
p. 94. Note that the area marked "Drill Field" was not
called by that name until 1926.*

Hokie Stone lower story or two. The Board of Visitors adopted a resolution in 2010 directing that, in future, new structures have Hokie Stone exteriors.

The YMCA Building itself for many years not only housed the Y but also functioned as a student social center. In 1937, when the Student Activities Building (later named Squires) opened, the Y relocated there, and its former home became the Military Building until 1966. Then it served for a time as the Student Personnel Building. But beginning in 1972—after the Y relinquished its claim on the structure—it served for many years as the Performing Arts Building. Much more recently, a major overhaul expanded it for use as the home of the College of Liberal Arts and Human Sciences.

William and Mary

While Tech enjoyed its building boom, the people of the College of William and Mary suffered a series of financial scares, but the school ended up stronger than before. The state saved William and Mary in 1888, when the college lobbied for support of a normal school there to train white male teachers. Since then, the college had maintained its traditional classical curriculum and the teacher training program. Half the school's students were "state students," their tuition covered under a state stipend on the pledge that they would become teachers. Yet doubts arose from time to time that the college could count on the continuance of this arrangement.

First came a push in the legislature in 1898 to reduce funding for higher education. According to the proposal, UVA would suffer a cut of 20 percent, from $50,000 per year to $40,000, and VMI's reduction would be only slightly less, from $30,000 per year to $25,000. Even worse, William and Mary would take a cut of 50 percent, from $15,000 to $7,500. (With VPI dependent primarily on federal funds, the state could hardly do worse than continue to neglect additional funding.)

In the end, the legislature took no such action, but the Constitutional Convention of 1901–1902 occasioned an even worse threat. This time a proposal called for terminating all state support for any institution not owned by the state, and of course that would apply to William and Mary. If approved, this provision of the constitution, unlike the threatening legislation in 1898, would not be the kind that a more friendly legislature could later reverse. Again, college supporters turned back the threat, but William and Mary's president, Leon G. Tyler, and its board of visitors readily perceived the school's chronic fiscal vulnerability.

The William and Mary crowd understood that the resolution of 1888, vital as it had been at the time, no longer sufficed. President Tyler mused that the school was "neither fish . . . nor fowl," neither public nor private, neither free from the whims of any session's legislators nor independent of the annual stipend from the state. One member of his faculty, John Lesslie Hall, shared those concerns. Hall, a new breed of academician who, after studying at Randolph-Macon College and UVA, had gone to Johns Hopkins University to obtain a Ph.D., constituted the departments of English and history. He wrote to Tyler, "We *must* before long *give ourselves to the state.*"

And so it was. True, the legislature increased the annual stipend in 1904 to $25,000. But what the state gave, the state could take away. In 1906, the state accepted the school's offer to give up such independence as it had and become a state institution. The legislature approved the change, and Governor Claude A. Swanson signed the measure into law. The state of Virginia took possession of the College of William and Mary, and the governor appointed a new board of visitors.

The teacher training arrangement of 1888 persisted, but the institution faced the future with greater certainty. William and Mary continued half teachers' school and half college, but no longer would it be half private and half not. Like UVA, VMI, and VPI, as well as the newer institutions at Farmville and Petersburg, the College of William and Mary was now a public institution of higher education. The same legislature in 1906 increased the college's stipend from $25,000 to $35,000. At the next legislative session, in 1908, the stipend rose to $40,000, and in 1914 it grew again to $45,000, triple what it had been at the time of the threats back in 1898 and 1901.

At his retirement in 1919, President Tyler looked back and saw that the College's "struggle up to 1906 was for permission to live." In 1906 he had been able to tell the school's board of visitors that now, finally, "the Institution, like the Phoenix of old, risen from the ashes, was arrayed in plumage more attractive than it ever before possessed."

The May Campaign and the Public Schools

Education in Virginia in the first decade of the twentieth century was in a take-off mode. Not since the Readjuster years of the 1880s had so much been attempted and accomplished. The energies behind the educational crusade had various sources. When UVA gained a new president, Edwin A. Alderman, in 1904, he identified himself immediately with an agenda that reached far beyond his campus. He hoped to reach out and connect his school and "all its traditions and its powerful influence on southern thought," he said, "with the movement for the democratization of education," especially in Virginia.

Educational leaders called for a May Campaign for 1905. For a month they canvassed the state to broadcast their goal of a radically better system of education in the Old Dominion. It would require more money from the state. They wanted a standard nine-month school term, high schools even in rural counties, school libraries everywhere, consolidated schools and transportation to them, industrial education, and greater emphasis on teacher training.

The legislative session of 1906 brought a doubling of state appropriations for public schooling. Pushing far beyond a universal system of elementary schools, the Mann High School Act called for a state system of high schools. Schools at every level—albeit white schools generally far more than black— secured increased funding.

New Colleges to Produce More Teachers

The new high schools, in particular, soon generated an enormous additional demand for trained teachers. Many Virginians argued that, while the vast majority of teachers were women, the state supported four institutions of higher education for white men—UVA, VMI, VPI, and William and Mary—and only one for white women, the school at Farmville. Surely, they said, the state should foster increased opportunities for training women to teach. The legislature soon established three new teachers' colleges to supplement the work at Farmville.

Virginia displayed a happy combination of will, need, and resources. Yet divided minds could still thwart decisions. Many towns across the Commonwealth—particularly towns outside the Southside, where Farmville was—jockeyed to obtain a "normal school," among them Newport News and Manassas. Three towns—Fredericksburg, Harrisonburg, and Radford—appeared to lead the pack, but few people were optimistic that more than one school, let alone three, would be established anytime soon. Perhaps none at all would be, for some legislators opposed squandering the state's money on more schools for training teachers, and any combination of candidates might prevent any other town from reaching its goal. The battle over the normal schools had much the ring to it of the "War of the Colleges," when the land-grant money was so avidly sought by competing schools in the early 1870s.

A majority of legislators in 1908 favored establishment of a new school somewhere, but the House of Delegates approved a college in or near Fredericksburg, while the Senate settled on one in the Harrisonburg area. Resolution came, by the narrowest of margins, when both schools gained approval. The eastern and western portions of Virginia would each get a new school for white women to train for teaching.

The biennial budget contained start-up money for Harrisonburg the first year and for Fredericksburg the second year. Both schools initially carried the name Normal and

Industrial School for Women. One eventually became known as James Madison University, the other as the University of Mary Washington.

A decision in the legislature left much unfinished business elsewhere. At each town, rival sections and landowners jousted over the exact location of the new school. Each school's new board of visitors had to decide on a president. The Harrisonburg school selected a young man named Julian Ashby Burruss, a native of Richmond who sported a degree in civil engineering from Virginia Polytechnic Institute in 1898, a master's degree from Columbia University, and considerable progress toward a Ph.D. from the University of Chicago.

Various members of the faculty at Fredericksburg had obtained their schooling at VMI, UVA, or Farmville. The school began operations in September 1911 with 110 students. Tuition—$30 per year for paying students—was free for students who committed themselves to teach in the Virginia public schools for at least four years. Thus the school could recruit students with advertisements that promised an education "Free to Day Students Who Expect to Teach."

In addition to the older school at Farmville and the new schools at Fredericksburg and Harrisonburg, the 1910 legislature established a fourth school to train white women as teachers. Radford, in the southwestern part of the state, would have a school, too, one later known as Radford University. The 1910 law concerning Radford carried stipulations similar to those of the 1908 law regarding Fredericksburg and Harrisonburg. The community must provide an acceptable site or $20,000 in cash; and young women, nominated by their local school superintendents, might attend the school tuition-free provided they gave "satisfactory evidence of an intention to teach" in Virginia's public schools for at least four years after they finished.

The new schools offered training opportunities in every major section of the state. Yet so spotty was the availability of a thorough high school education that these schools could not assume that the students they admitted had the preparation to begin college work. Like the colleges and normal schools that preceded them, the schools at Harrisonburg, Fredericksburg, and Radford worked with students at whatever level of preparation they brought to the encounter. Later, especially given the 1906 high school law, the schools could impose higher entrance requirements.

Virginia Normal and Industrial Institute

During the new century's first decade, the University of Virginia obtained its first increase in annual support since the time of the Readjusters. The largesse that the legislature displayed toward white institutions of higher education was not matched at the black college near Petersburg.

Virginia Normal and Collegiate Institute, an artifact of the Readjuster revolution of the early 1880s, survived through the 1890s before getting its wings severely clipped. Since the late 1880s, VNCI had to get by with an annuity of only $15,000, rather than the $20,000 specified in the 1882 law that launched it. After first undercutting the school's autonomy and its black leadership in 1877, beginning in 1890 the state made the board of visitors entirely white, in stark contrast with the original bill's requirement that six of the seven members be African American.

The 1902 legislature terminated the collegiate program and changed the school's name to Virginia Normal and Industrial Institute. In 1901 and 1902, therefore, members of the last graduating classes in the collegiate department obtained their degrees. But in 1908, the legislature did at least restore the full $20,000 annuity.

Thus the Virginia Normal and Industrial Institute regained the level of state financial support it had enjoyed as the Virginia Normal and Collegiate Institute for a time in the 1880s, though the other schools were by that time receiving far greater funding than had been the case two decades earlier. During the same decade that the legislature hiked its support of higher education in general, and created three new schools to train white women teachers in particular, it narrowed the curriculum at the black school.

The 1901 constitutional convention was called in part to address the perceived need to take away the right to vote from as many as possible of the kinds of people, black and white, who had voted for the Readjusters. That same convention left the Petersburg school off a list of institutions from which the state Board of Education was to be drawn. The board of visitors from each of Virginia's major public schools would nominate a member of the faculty for consideration by the Senate, which would select among these "experienced educators" three people to fill four-year terms on the state board. Those schools were UVA, VMI, VPI, the College of William and Mary (so long as it continued to be appropriated annual state funds), the (white only) state School for the Deaf and Blind, and the Farmville school (the other three teachers' colleges did not yet exist). The Senate did not even have the discretion to consider appointing a black Virginian to the state Board of Education.

Race, Region, State Funds, and Educational Opportunity

Segregated access was one thing, utter exclusion another. Virginia authorities had long sustained a school for youth who were deaf or blind, as long as they were also white, but had never made such schooling available to black Virginians. In 1906 the legislature finally voted to end black exclusion; the School for Colored Deaf and Blind Children opened in 1909.

Yet segregated access itself supplied constant opportunities for white authorities to discriminate in levels of funding. The fate of Virginia Normal and Collegiate during these years symbolized the racial disparity in state funding of education. Black elementary schools lagged far behind white elementary schools in the state funds they obtained in 1900. At that time, per capita spending on white children was roughly double that on black children. By the 1910s, the gap had grown far greater, and black elementary and "training" schools lagged far behind white elementary and high schools.

Discrimination that denied black children an equal educational opportunity also worked against large numbers of white children. State money went to the counties on the basis of student population. County authorities, always white, allocated that money as they saw fit. Authorities in predominantly black counties put most of their money into schools for whites.

White schools in black counties therefore obtained far more money per student than did either black schools in black counties or white schools in white counties. The larger the black proportion—and in the early twentieth century, many eastern counties still had black majorities—the larger the subsidy to white schools from state funds. In black counties in 1915, the average white teacher's salary, measured in per-student terms, was eight times as great as the average black teacher's salary.

This discrimination—this double discrimination, one a function of the other—did not pass unnoticed by white Virginians in the western, whiter counties. At the constitutional convention in 1901, one of them challenged his eastern counterparts: "You will tax the people in Frederick County to educate the [black] children of the Black Belt, and then you will not apply it to the education of the [black] children in the Black Belt." And that is exactly what they did.

This behavior had implications for all three groups in terms of their access to higher education and their chances for success in college. Black students who enrolled at Virginia Normal and Industrial and at Hampton Institute, like white students from western Virginia who enrolled at VPI, generally brought with them to the encounter far less schooling—measured in tax dollars, at least—than did the students, typically from eastern Virginia, who went off to UVA or William and Mary.

Coeducation in the Future?

By 1900, many institutions of higher education in the Northeast were coeducational, and even more in the West were. Like most white southern colleges, by contrast, VPI admitted only male applicants. Students wishing to go courting looked around the village of Blacksburg. Alternatively, they might make their way to Christiansburg Female Institute, though getting from Blacksburg to Christiansburg could be daunting before train service connected the towns at the turn of the century.

None of Virginia's public institutions of higher education admitted white women as well as white men to any program. That was not necessarily true, however, of private schools. Among white men's schools, one, Roanoke College, admitted women during the Civil War and resumed the experiment in 1930 in the face of the Great Depression. Beginning in the 1890s the school admitted an occasional female student as a "special student," but only if she were related to a member of the faculty or the board of trustees. The first two to finish, Julia Louise Abbot of Strasburg and Julia E. Painter of Salem, both completed their studies in 1895, though they and other women who graduated before 1922 received only certificates, not diplomas.

Another men's school, Richmond College, graduated Lulie Gaines Winston with a B.S. in 1899. The daughter of a professor of physics at the school, she placed first in her class. In 1914, when the institution moved west from downtown to the present location of the University of Richmond, a separate women's counterpart, Westhampton College, was established there as well.

Several other institutions, though they may have straddled the line separating colleges from secondary schools, were coeducational from their beginnings. New Market Polytechnic Institute, organized in 1870 (and a candidate then for the land-grant funds), achieved collegiate ranking by the Federal Bureau of Education in 1889–1890, whereupon it became the first college in Virginia to be listed there as coeducational.

Bridgewater College began life in 1880 as a coeducational institution, Spring Creek Normal School and Collegiate Institute, though it was first recognized as a college only in 1893. Fredericksburg College, first recognized as a college in 1895, was coeducational from its origins in 1893 until it closed in 1914, soon after the state established a female teachers' college in Fredericksburg.

By 1900, women as well as men enrolled at land-grant schools everywhere outside the South. In the Midwest, some institutions admitted women from the 1860s or 1870s. Even in the South, all would admit women by the 1960s or 1970s. Among states in the former Confederacy, Tennessee proved a pioneer in the early 1890s when—as was often the case—it softened military requirements at about the same time as it lowered the bar to female admissions. The University of Tennessee terminated its military regimen for all students, even made military drill optional after the sophomore year, and then began to admit women.

Progress and Persistence

VPI admitted a few women as degree candidates as early as 1921, but their integration into many facets of school life proved slow, and the numbers of women long remained small. For the most part, Virginia maintained separate-sex programs in its public institutions of higher education through the land-grant system's centennial year in 1962. Separate-race schools began the process of integration in the 1950s or 1960s.

The years of Claude Swanson's governorship set the tone for much of the twentieth century. Nineteenth-century Virginians constructed an educational foundation on which their twentieth-century successors could build. Before the 1860s, the legislature established the Literary Fund, the University of Virginia, and the Virginia Military Institute, but it outlawed schools for black Virginians. In the 1870s or 1880s, it created a system of public schools for each race, from elementary schools to institutions of higher education. Virginia

Agricultural and Mechanical College came first, spurred by the Morrill Land-Grant College Act. Virginia Normal and Collegiate Institute near Petersburg followed in the 1880s, as did the State Female Normal School in Farmville.

The twentieth century's first decade brought substantial further growth, and the next half-century's political and educational leaders built on the legislation of the Swanson years. During that half-century they also responded to initiatives from the federal government, which, as the next several chapters detail, supplied increasing resources but also laid down new ground rules for their use. Virginia Polytechnic Institute's growth and development occurred in that context.

References

Alvey, *History of Mary Washington College*, 6–45.

Buck, *Development of Public Schools in Virginia*, 121–62.

Cato, "Higher Education for Women in Virginia," 249–68.

"Dr. Joseph Dupuy Eggleston," *Richmond Times-Dispatch*, March 15, 1953.

Ferrell, *Claude A. Swanson of Virginia*, 6, 70–85.

Godson et al., *College of William and Mary*, 2: 470–80, 500–1.

Harlan, *Separate and Unequal*, 135–69.

Jones, *History of James Madison University*, 3–20.

Kinnear, *The First 100 Years*, 158–80.

Kinnear, "History of Agricultural Education in Virginia," 281–323.

Larsen, *Montague of Virginia*, 89–181.

Lewis-Smith, *Radford College*, 8–15.

Miller, *"Dear Old Roanoke,"* 33, 92–93, 120, 156.

Montgomery et al., *History of the University of Tennessee*, 47–48.

Overton, "Joseph Dupuy Eggleston, Junior."

Pezzoni, "Our Native Stone."

Toppin, *Loyal Sons and Daughters*, 51–59, 77–84.

Chapter 7
1910s: Agricultural Extension and the Great War

Ella Graham Agnew, a native of Prince Edward County, has a building named for her at Virginia Tech, where she retired from her work in 1919, two years before the school permitted the first women students to enroll. She has been described as having become, in 1910 in the region around her home county, "the first home demonstration agent in America and the first woman to serve as a field worker" for the U.S. Department of Agriculture.

Ella G. Agnew, home demonstration agent

Agnew's career neither began nor ended in Blacksburg. It led her to a South African college in the 1890s, followed by work throughout rural America with the YWCA, and eventually the directorship of the women's department of the Works Projects Administration in Virginia during the Great Depression in the 1930s.

Tech retained Ella Agnew as a veteran home demonstration agent when it inaugurated Extension work in 1914 under the Smith-Lever Act passed by Congress that year. For the next

Lloyd W. Williams '07

two years, she continued to work in Southside Virginia, but then she moved to Blacksburg when the Extension service found permanent quarters at VPI.

Another Virginian also embodied Tech's contacts with a wider world in the 1910s. Lloyd W. Williams, a resident of Berryville, was captain of Company A and president of the Mechanical Engineering Club before graduating with the Virginia Tech class of 1907. Ten years later, when the United States entered World War One, he went to France with the Marines.

Especially as a school that promoted military training, Tech sent many of its students and graduates to Europe in 1917 and 1918 to fight in World War One. Shortly after Williams arrived, the story goes, a French officer with forces that were pulling back urged Williams and his men to retreat too. Williams is reported to have responded: "Retreat? Hell, no. We've just come." On June 11, 1917, days after his thirtieth birthday, he died in action, the first Virginian to die in the war.

As these two examples suggest, though Tech's influence never was confined to Blacksburg, never had it stretched as far as it did in the 1910s. The Smith-Lever Act of 1914 broadened VPI's responsibilities and impact in Virginia. Federal legislation continued to affect Tech's evolution, and Tech students, faculty, and alumni found themselves caught up in international events.

Presidents Barringer and Eggleston

After John McBryde announced his intent to step down
from the VPI presidency, the Board of Visitors selected Paul
Barringer, a professor and former faculty chairman at the
University of Virginia, where he had earned an M.D. Barringer
served at Tech from 1907 to 1913. Innovations of the Barringer
presidency included a professorship of forestry; programs in
agricultural, chemical, and mining engineering; a college honor
code; and a loud whistle that shrieked when it was time for
each class to end. Barringer upgraded the graduate program
that McBryde had inaugurated. And the athletic program added
another sport, basketball, in 1908–1909; Tech's first intercollegiate basketball game took place in the old library building.

Barringer's successor, Joseph Dupuy Eggleston Jr., served
from 1913 to 1919. Before accepting the presidency of VPI,
Eggleston served from 1906 to 1912 as state superintendent
of public instruction and then briefly with the U.S. Office of
Education. During
his time at Tech, a
student fee paid for
construction of a field
house, and the school
bought sixty acres on
which the Graduate
Life Center is currently
located. A new Alumni
Gateway entrance to
campus stood at the
intersection of Main
Street and College
Avenue from 1914,
shortly after fire
destroyed the Preston
and Olin Building,
until it was moved up

McBryde building

the hill on Main Street in 1936. Tech also adopted a major new mission in Extension and played significant roles in World War One.

Tech continued to offer a curriculum that focused on agriculture and engineering, though with far more students in engineering than in agriculture. Graduates worked in about equal numbers in agriculture, mechanical engineering, civil engineering, and electrical engineering. Smaller numbers went into business, chemistry, teaching, mining engineering, law, or the ministry.

Congress brought changes that affected Tech's teaching and service missions. The most significant of these was the Smith-Lever Act of 1914, but an allied measure, the Smith-Hughes Act of 1917, also proved important to education and agriculture across Virginia. The school began offering courses in vocational agriculture in the late 1910s and even home economics in the early 1920s.

The Smith-Lever Act

President Woodrow Wilson signed the Smith-Lever Act in 1914. Named for Senator Hoke Smith of Georgia and Congressman Ashbury Lever of South Carolina, the Smith-Lever Act added extension work to the official responsibilities of the land-grant schools. The federal government would supply each state $10,000 each year if its legislature accepted the act's offer and provisions. Congress sought to link the U.S. Department of Agriculture with the land-grant schools on a mission to reach people who, though not attending any of the colleges, could benefit from "useful and practical information on subjects relating to agriculture and home economics."

The Smith-Lever Act changed the relationship between the federal government and the land-grant colleges, much as it changed their mission. The state (or the college, the community, or private contributions) had to supply matching funds. The school must have a director of Extension, approved by the secretary of agriculture. And the school's Extension program must meet with the approval of the Federal Extension Division of the Department of Agriculture.

In 1914, Virginia already had the beginnings of an Extension system to build on. As state school superintendent, Joseph D. Eggleston learned from Hampton Institute's Dr. H. B. Frissell of demonstration work being done in Mississippi under the leadership of Seaman A. Knapp. Eggleston invited Knapp to explain his work to leading Virginians, among them Governor Claude Swanson and a farmer in Nottoway County named T. O. Sandy. Under Sandy's direction, and without Tech's involvement, farm demonstration work began in 1907. Sandy soon hired a man named Southall Farrar to promote corn clubs for boys, and he also hired Ella Agnew to promote poultry, garden, and canning clubs—especially tomato clubs—for girls.

President Barringer displayed little interest in what Sandy was doing, but school superintendent Eggleston saw great potential and pushed successfully for legislation in 1910 to establish a state United Agricultural Board to coordinate such efforts. When Eggleston doffed his hat as state superintendent and donned a new one as president of VPI, he entered a position that enabled him to see that Tech take the lead in Extension work across Virginia.

President Eggleston earnestly sought greater appropriations from the Virginia legislature, and he sought control of the Extension work. He gained half his objective. Demonstration work in Virginia began on a small scale in 1907, but only with the Smith-Lever Act's additional funds, together with Eggleston's presidency and the assignment of Extension responsibilities to Tech, did such work become a significant part of the school's mission.

Tech established an Agricultural Extension Division in 1914. In 1916, T. O. Sandy and Ella Agnew moved from Burkeville to Blacksburg. There, for another three years before

Agnew moved on, they continued to work together as closely as the two buildings that are named for them stand today in Virginia Tech's Agricultural Quad.

The Smith-Lever Act added greatly to the mission and the activities of land-grant colleges across America. The act paid early dividends during World War One, when the nation's farmers produced extra quantities of food to feed American troops and America's allies. Extension agents worked in virtually every county telling farm families that "corn, wheat, and meat" would win the war.

Once the nation's agricultural Extension program was launched, it grew rapidly. In subsequent legislation in the 1920s, 1930s, and 1940s, Congress greatly increased funding for Extension services. In fact, federal funding for Extension overtook that for research, just as federal funding for research overtook that for instruction. By mid-century, annual federal funding for Extension amounted to $32 million, while experiment stations received $12 million and instruction only $5 million.

Future Farmers

The Agricultural Appropriations Act of 1907 carried the Nelson Amendment, which granted states supplemental funds each year—beginning at $5,000 and rising to $25,000—to pay for training teachers of agriculture and mechanics. In view of the rules of race in the 1890 Morrill Act, two-thirds of the proceeds in Virginia went to VPI, while the other one-third went to the black land-grant school, Hampton Institute. In 1908, Virginia inaugurated an agricultural high school for each congressional district.

In 1917 Congress passed the Smith-Hughes Act, designed to enhance the teaching of vocational agriculture in the nation's secondary schools. The act directed funds to train high school teachers, and it allotted money to the high schools themselves to support teaching vocational agriculture and home economics. The agenda of the original Morrill Act was now broadened to reach high school students, who might or might not ever go to college.

As so often before and after, the 1917 act of Congress altered operations at Virginia Tech. The State Board of Education wanted to divide responsibility for training of secondary teachers among the University of Virginia, William and Mary, and Virginia Tech, with students emphasizing technical agriculture at Blacksburg during their first two years and then, for the next two years, attending either of the two white men's schools that offered teacher training. The Federal Board of Vocational Education promptly rejected the state plan and directed that the entire program be located at Virginia Tech.

Tech established a new Department of Agricultural Education, and Dabney S. Lancaster, a member of the Department of Animal Husbandry, took charge of it. Tech entered a new dimension of service to the state when it took on the task of preparing teachers who would go into the high schools to teach agriculture.

Directly connected with Tech's new combination of emphasis on agriculture, Extension, and education was the emergence of the Future Farmers of America. Walter S. Newman (class of 1919 and future president of Tech) left VPI's agricultural education department in 1925 to become state supervisor of agricultural education. At a meeting at Tech in 1925, he and three current members of his old department—Henry C. Groseclose (class of 1923), Edmund C. Magill, and Harry W. Sanders (class of 1916 and head of the vocational education department from 1940 to 1962)—developed the idea of an organization for farm boys studying agriculture. By 1928 their efforts had led not only to the organization of a statewide Future Farmers of Virginia but also to a nationwide organization, Future Farmers of America.

'Til the Angel Gabriel Blows His Horn

President Eggleston found it endlessly disappointing that he could not convince Virginia legislators to be less stingy in their

appropriations to Tech. At the beginning of his presidency, he
reviewed the figures from the previous decade. Aside from
occasional funds for new construction or equipment, and aside,
too, from student tuition and fees, Tech depended on federal
money from the Morrill Act and subsequent legislation and—
an innovation early in the century—annual allocations from the
legislature. The annual receipts from the Morrill funds came
to $33,333. The state annuity doubled from $30,000 in fiscal
1904 to $60,000 in fiscal 1909, but there it had stuck. Worse,
after four years at that level, it was reduced to $55,000 for
fiscal 1913. Eggleston obtained a return to the $60,000 figure,
yet he had occasion to exclaim, "VPI is the worst supported
agricultural and mechanical college in the United States, both
as to annuity and as to buildings and equipment."

Eggleston needed to see the annuity rise, not fall or stag-
nate, or he could not accomplish his goals and the mission
he saw for VPI. He spoke of how his faculty had no funds to
pay for travel to professional meetings—or even to respond to
requests from Virginians across the state for the expert advice
that the faculty would be delighted to supply. Tech had "the
men, the ability, and the willingness," he concluded, but "not
the money." Tech had a library, but could not afford to buy
books for it, had shops, but could not buy or repair equipment.
Faculty were paid far less, he said, at VPI than at VMI or UVA.
To nearly every request, no matter how urgent, his reply had to
be "no funds."

The money increased a little through the decade, first
back up to $60,000 and then to $71,000, though World War
One brought inflation that eroded those dollars' purchasing
power. In 1918, Eggleston tried again, once more describing
the impossibility of serving the state without more resources
and, once more, comparing Virginia with other states in the
financial support of land-grant colleges. He termed the Virginia
figure "the lowest of any land-grant annuity in the South." He
compared Tech's support with that of South Carolina's white

school ($230,000), Georgia's ($220,000), North Carolina's ($122,500), even Alabama's ($115,000). VPI's figure was identical to little Rhode Island's, he complained, and "Rhode Island can be put in Pittsylvania, Halifax, and Charlotte counties and not fill them." He managed to extract only slightly more funds.

President Eggleston told his faculty that, if a school's effectiveness depended on teaching, buildings, and equipment, they were going to have make up for inadequate infrastructure and equipment with superior teaching. Waiting for adequate classrooms and laboratories, he advised, was tantamount to waiting until "the angel Gabriel blows his horn." And yet Tech's classroom had become the entire state, he continued, and the new Extension work offered Tech faculty a wonderful opportunity "to make the state of Virginia the campus for Virginia Polytechnic Institute."

World War One

World War One had an impact on every state school in Virginia. At UVA, for example, enrollment dropped from 1,064 in 1916–1917 to 761 the next year and 536 in 1918–1919, despite the presence of the Students' Army Training Corps (SATC).

William and Mary saw its enrollment of regular students, which had peaked at 244 in 1905–1906, plummet to less than 150 in 1917–1918 and 1918–1919. Students left for war, and they left, too, for work in defense plants. The school lost so many students to a nearby DuPont powder plant, it rented out dormitory space for the plant's workers. Of the 131 students in 1918–1919, 24 were women, and only 26 were regular male students.

From President Lyon G. Tyler's perspective, the only thing that kept William and Mary going was his success in attracting a unit of the Students' Army Training Corps. The federal government paid all fees for the nearly 100 young men who enrolled at William and Mary under the military program. The

SATC at William and Mary—commanded by Major William P. Stone, a former professor of military science and tactics at VPI—prepared men for commissions as military officers.

Tech, like William and Mary and UVA, had special students come to campus for training for the war. An SATC unit of 550 men—roughly equal in size to Tech's normal enrollment—came to Tech in 1918. Faculty scrambled to supply instruction in mechanical engineering and other disciplines, while special instructors trained men for quartermaster service, the medical corps, chemical warfare service, and other specialties.

President Eggleston noted that the "distressing condition" of a terrible war put a premium on Tech's virtues and accomplishments. "In a time of stress and danger, the country calls for men prepared in one or more of three lines: military, agriculture, and engineering. When the government called for men trained militarily, VPI said at once, 'We are ready,' and the War Department is finding out . . . that VPI is ready." Eggleston went on: "When the government called for engineers, VPI said, 'We are ready,' and the government is finding out the truth of this statement also." The same went for agriculture, with the great need for increased food production. One newspaper concluded about Tech's contribution to the war effort that "the people of Virginia should be grateful to VPI for what it is doing for them as well as for America."

Virginia's Black Land-Grant Schools

In the 1910s, Virginia Normal and Industrial Institute participated in a rise in funding for all the state's institutions of higher education. The annuity rose in $5,000 increments to $25,000 in 1915 and $30,000 in 1918. At the end of the decade, moreover, it became a land-grant school.

Hampton Institute received one-third of Virginia's land-grant funds from 1872 to 1920. On the recommendation of Governor Westmoreland Davis, however, the Virginia legislature lifted the land-grant funds from Hampton Institute, the private school that had, in effect, been designated Virginia's black land-grant school for as long as the Blacksburg institution had been the state's white land-grant school. That money, amounting to $27,000 per year, now went to Virginia Normal and Industrial Institute.

Virginia continued to divide its land-grant funds between two schools, one white and one black, but no longer would it provide the black share to a private institution. Beginning in the 1920s, Virginia Normal and Industrial Institute—an all-black school, a state-supported institution that had not existed at the time the land-grant designations were originally made back in 1872—became Virginia's other land-grant school and began to receive federal money, as well as state funds, though much more money went to Virginia Polytechnic Institute than to Virginia Normal and Industrial.

Having succeeded in securing the land-grant designation, VNII President John M. Gandy proceeded to secure restoration of a four-year collegiate program in 1923, and the first bachelor's degrees were awarded under the new regime in 1925. The school acquired a new name in 1930, Virginia State College for Negroes. By 1930, too, the state transferred Cooperative Extension work under the Smith-Lever Act from Hampton Institute to Virginia State. The Virginia State College for Negroes did much the same kinds of agricultural Extension work and home demonstration work among black Virginians as Virginia Polytechnic Institute did among white Virginians.

Extension, War, and Coeducation

The combination of Extension and World War One altered the probability that women would be incorporated into VPI and the other remaining all-male land-grant institutions. Ella Agnew's work in Extension in Virginia stood as an example of women's emerging involvement in the land-grant mission across America.

Maryland demonstrated even sooner how much more might happen. At Maryland Agricultural College, a disastrous campus fire in 1912 destroyed many buildings, including the barracks, and the old military system never fully revived. At about the same time, the Smith-Lever Act of 1914 pressured land-grant colleges to inaugurate courses in home economics and train women as agricultural home demonstration agents. The school underwent rapid change.

Its name became Maryland State College. President Harry J. Patterson relinquished the president's house so that it could house women students, and the school admitted two women in 1916. The first, Charlotte Vaux, received a two-year certificate in 1918. By the time the second, Elizabeth Hook, earned a four-year degree in 1920, more than twenty women were studying at the school. Only later would the school be renamed the University of Maryland, but the future was already happening.

Major Williams

Virginia's institutions of higher education suffered disruption while contributing to the war, and many students, faculty, and alumni made great sacrifices. From UVA, 2,700 went off to war, and 80 died. After the war, a monument, "Soaring like an Eagle," went up on the grounds to honor one of them, an aviator named James Rogers McConnell.

VPI sent 2,297 alumni to the war—a figure given as 42 percent of all its alumni to that point. Twenty-six (their names are inscribed on the War Memorial above the Chapel) died in battle in France, or of disease, or while in training. In 1926, Tech dedicated the new War Memorial Gym to Tech men who had died in the war.

Some veterans of the Great War subsequently enrolled at VPI. Earle D. Gregory, who was awarded the Congressional Medal of Honor, enrolled at Tech in 1919 and graduated in 1923. Though a disabled veteran and Medal of Honor winner, he joined the Corps of Cadets. In 1963 the Corps honored him by renaming the elite drill team previously called the "Pershing Rifles" the "Gregory Guard."

Major Williams Hall is named in honor of one of the Tech alumni who died in uniform in Europe during World War One. For his gallant leadership in France, Lloyd W. Williams was posthumously awarded the Distinguished Service Cross and promoted to major. In 1957, 40 years after his death and 50 years after his graduation from VPI, the school named a newly-expanded barracks Major Williams Hall in his honor. It consisted of buildings constructed in 1904 (Barracks No. 5) and 1927 (Barracks No. 6), renovated in 1957

Earle Davis Gregory, from France to Blacksburg, 1919

when a third section was built to connect them. In the 1990s it was repurposed and expanded, and several departments in the liberal arts, including history, have their offices there.

Julian A. Burruss, President

President Eggleston stepped down from his post in 1919 to take a similar position at Hampden-Sydney College. Julian A. Burruss, the man who replaced him, served more than a quarter-century, much the longest of any Virginia Tech president. In many ways, the Burruss administration transformed Tech. As the next few chapters will detail, the school's curriculum, its enrollment policies, and its physical environment all showed dramatic change. So did the policy on mandatory participation in the Corps of Cadets. The undergraduate population came to include male and female civilians as well as male cadets.

None of Burruss's predecessors was a Virginia Tech alumnus, and none had a Ph.D., a degree routinely expected of his successors. In 1921, two years after he assumed the presidency at Tech, he completed the requirements for a Ph.D. from the University of Chicago. His dissertation, in finance, carried the title "A Study of Business Administration of Colleges Based on an Examination of the Practices of Land-Grant Colleges in the Making and Using of Budgets."

References

"Annual Report of the Principal," *The Southern Workman* 49 (June 1920), 276–79.

Calcott, *University of Maryland*, 244–50.

Dabney, *Mr. Jefferson's University*, 56–66.

Dabney, *Virginia Commonwealth University*, 61–65, 88.

Kinnear, *The First 100 Years*, 183–252, 285–87.

Kinnear, "History of Agricultural Education in Virginia," 324–543.

Godson et al., *College of William and Mary*, 2: 504–6, 542.

Overton, "Joseph Dupuy Eggleston, Junior."

Sue Quinn, "Miss Ella G. Agnew," *Richmond Times-Dispatch*, October 20, 1944.

Rainsford, *Congress and Higher Education*, 127–29.

Sutphin and Hillison, "History of Extension Work in Virginia Prior to Smith-Lever."

Toppin, *Loyal Sons and Daughters*, 77–89.

Wise, *Drawing out the Man*, 100–6.

Interlude
Golden Jubilee, 1922

Virginia Tech turned 50 in 1922. To celebrate, the school designated several days of "Golden Jubilee" in late May. At the close of spring term exams, the world traveled by train to Christiansburg and then by automobile to Blacksburg. On the parade grounds, a huge circus tent went up. Pup tents sprouted like mushrooms to house cadets who relinquished their rooms in the Upper Quad to visitors, some of whom may have borrowed the same room they had been assigned as cadets 10, 20, or 30 years earlier.

At least one graduate of every class in the school's history participated, and the entire class of 1875 came, as did John T. Cowan, the last surviving member of the very first Board of Visitors, appointed in 1872. Among the many speakers was Claude Swanson—former Tech student from the VAMC years, former Virginia governor, and U.S. senator. All alumni were white men, to be sure, though a few women had enrolled the previous year.

One day was "College Day." Governor E. Lee Trinkle spoke, followed by three representative spokesmen. President Edwin A. Alderman of the University of Virginia, speaking for the state public institutions of higher education, recalled the school's growth through hard times. "It stirs the spirit," he said, "to think how you have triumphed over your difficulties." After 50 sometimes troubled years, he told his audience, UVA's "younger brother" appeared "poised on the threshold of a new era, secure in the affection of the Commonwealth and the loyalty of your sons." The president of Washington and Lee

University, Henry Louis Smith, spoke for Virginia's private institutions, and Ohio State University's president, William O. Thompson, spoke on behalf of the nation's land-grant schools. At an evening program on "technical education in America," speakers represented agriculture, engineering, and applied science.

Another day was "Alumni Day." J. J. "Pop" Owens, spudmeister and steward, directed a fine luncheon at the college dining hall. One alumnus observed with grumpy satisfaction, "well, they never fed like this when I was here." Lyle Kinnear suggests that the jazz orchestra that played at the luncheon may have supplied many visitors with their first direct exposure to the jazz age.

Before long, the music played second fiddle to resounding college cheers. Members of classes from the VAMC years, thirty years before, rendered "Rip, Rah, Ree." Alumni from the second quarter-century challenged them with "Hokie, Hokie, Hi." Velocity as well as decibels picked up, and cadets from various generations shared lost cheers, forgotten songs, and old pranks.

Lawrence W. Priddy

A business meeting followed the lunch. Lawrence W. Priddy (class of 1897)—he had been the driving force behind financing the YMCA building and was currently president of the Alumni Association—urged alumni on that May 30th to contribute $50,000 to construct a "war memorial hall" that would include a gymnasium, space for student organizations, and

War Memorial Gym, newly completed, 1926

rooms where visiting alumni might stay when they visited their alma mater. Pledges surged past the proposed amount. The crowd reelected Priddy president of the Alumni Association and directed him to press ahead on the memorial.

Various speakers brought their political agendas to the jubilee—reminders today of the burning issues of that earlier time. Washington and Lee's president expressed his gratitude for Tech's fostering an education that would save democracy from the bolshevism of the new Soviet Union. Ohio State's president championed the League of Nations. The president of the Gulf Smokeless Coal Company, class of 1902, worried about United Mine Workers leader John L. Lewis. Historian William E. Dodd, class of 1895 and the 1922 commencement speaker, warned against too many immigrants from strange places in Europe.

Virginia Agricultural and Mechanical College and Polytechnic Institute attained the age of 50. Students, faculty, alumni, and citizens had much to celebrate. People in attendance could recall such things as the improbable victory in obtaining a share of Virginia's Morrill Act money; the uncertainty, turbulence, even desperation of the first two decades; and Tech's gradual growth under President John McLaren McBryde and his successors through Julian A. Burruss.

The assembled alumni at that "Golden Jubilee" had collectively participated in the school's development from an institution that struggled to carry out the teaching function to one that pushed research and extension as well. The people of Virginia Tech had collectively seen the school develop a broader curriculum and erect a collection of new buildings—as well as adopt a new name and new colors; begin a graduate program, a yearbook, and a school newspaper; and promote intercollegiate sports and various other campus activities. They had seen it become a major player in higher education in Virginia as well as a sturdy representative of the nation's land-grant system.

References

J. F. Donalson, "Sidelights on the V.P.I. Golden Jubilee Celebration," *Roanoke Times*, May 31, 1922.

Kinnear, *The First 100 Years*, 265–68.

"Lawrence Priddy, Insurance Man, 70," *New York Times*, September 4, 1944.

Chapter 8
1920s: The First Women Students

Julian A. Burruss served as president of Virginia Tech for more than a quarter-century, from soon after the end of World War One until the final year of World War Two. Before coming to Blacksburg in 1919, Burruss served for eleven years as the first president of the teachers' college for white women at Harrisonburg, where he played a central role in shaping the school. In many ways, Burruss reshaped his new school.

Julian A. Burruss,
president, 1919–1945

The Civil War transformed the status of African Americans, both men and women, and thus their educational opportunities. Beyond those changes, World War One altered the status of women, particularly white women. A half-century after the end of slavery, black women and white women alike were citizens, but then again they were not—either group—everywhere full citizens. When World War One broke out in 1914, women in many states—in every state in the South—were barred from voting. Educational opportunities in the South had greatly expanded in the previous half-century, for white women as well as white men, black women as well as black men. Yet all schools in the region had racial restrictions, and in Virginia most white colleges, including all those that were state-supported, enrolled only men or only women.

At the time, VPI was one of only a few remaining land-grant colleges to exclude all women from enrolling as degree candidates. The land-grant movement had fostered coeducation across the North and West, and the few holdouts, like VPI, were southern schools, particularly schools in states from the former Confederacy, and especially those that mandated a military regimen. Among southern white land-grant schools, the University of Tennessee—the exception that proved the rule—had admitted women since the 1890s, but only after it terminated its military regimen. UVA and VMI, like VPI, excluded women before the 1920s. VMI would long remain all-male, but a few women enrolled in the 1920s at Virginia Tech and the University of Virginia.

Early Exceptions to Female Exclusion

The declaration regarding female exclusion, as so many statements about the past, is not necessarily quite true. Tech had in recent years permitted some women to take an occasional course during the summer, but not to become degree candidates.

At the University of Virginia, Caroline Preston applied in 1892 for admission to study math. Actually she asked only that she be permitted to take the exam that male students were required to pass for a B.A. in the School of Mathematics. Her request was granted, so long as she agreed to take the exam separately from the men and, if successful, to accept a certificate, not a degree, attesting to her achievement. She obtained the certificate. Another female applicant, Addis M. Boyce also sought to study math, as a graduate student.

Enough was enough. By large majorities, the UVA faculty and board of visitors determined in 1894 to exclude women. Members of the faculty conjured up compelling reasons for their stand: "According to medical authority, the strain on young women in severe competitive work (in the higher schools of learning) does often physically unsex them, and they afterwards fail in the demands of motherhood." Whatever their thoughts along these lines, men associated with every school—faculty, students, alumni, visitors, administrators—worried about the implications of change for school traditions and the need to modify procedures or facilities.

During the 1910s, a group of Virginia women, chief among them Mary-Cooke Branch Munford, pushed for the admission of white women, if not to the University of Virginia campus itself, then to a coordinate college in Charlottesville. UVA alumni, politically powerful, scuttled such proposals, and the undergraduate school at the University would not admit women (without sharp restrictions) until the 1970s. Along the way, though, the effort to gain greater educational opportunities for Virginia's white women gained a measure of success, at UVA and other schools. Pearl Vivian Willoughby earned a Ph.D. at UVA in 1923 with a dissertation on "The Achievement of Modern Dramaturgy."

William and Mary

During and soon after World War One, substantial change occurred in Virginia's public policy. After the end of slavery, the state had displayed no reluctance to permit black women and black men to study together at institutions supported with public funds. As a private school and then also a land-grant school for black Virginians, Hampton Institute had always admitted women as well as men. So, from its inception, had the state-supported Virginia Normal and Collegiate Institute.

State-supported schools for white students were very different. The College of William and Mary was the first to adopt a policy of admitting both sexes. The school came on hard times during the nineteenth century. Already two hundred years old by the 1890s, it had faltered with the rise of UVA and then struggled to survive in the difficult years after the Civil War. It needed state funds, and in 1906 it became a public college.

The process started in 1888, when, responding to a request

from William and Mary, the state authorized a program to train white men as teachers there and gave an annual stipend to support the program. Responding to another initiative from the College, in 1918 the legislature authorized it to admit white women. Opponents were unable to prevent the change.

The College of William and Mary therefore became the first state school in Virginia to admit white women as well as white men. Since the black school at Petersburg had had its authority to grant baccalaureate degrees terminated back in 1902, in 1918 William and Mary became for a brief period the only coeducational state-supported college for either race.

The University of Virginia

In 1920 the Virginia legislature faced the question of whether to ratify the proposed Nineteenth Amendment, which declared it the nation's policy not to let any state deprive people of the right to vote, either in state or federal elections, on the basis of gender. Legislators showed no enthusiasm for the measure, but they recognized that enough states would likely ratify it that it would become the law of the land no matter what Virginia's policymakers wanted or did. Thus they amended the Virginia voter registration laws to accommodate the change. Nor was that the only change that year in women's access to new roles.

In some northern and western states, women became lawyers soon after the Civil War, but as late as the 1910s none could practice law in the courts of Virginia. It is not that none had ever tried to gain admission to the bar in Virginia or that none had the training required of men. Annie Smith studied law with her husband, who studied the subject at UVA, but a local judge rejected her effort in 1889 to become a lawyer. Twice she tried to get legislators to supply a solution, but they thought the whole idea a hoot and refused to change the law to let her become a practicing attorney.

That led Belva Lockwood, an accomplished lawyer in Washington, D.C., to visit Richmond in 1894 and 1895 in an effort to succeed where Annie Smith had failed. In the end, she fared no better. The judges on the state supreme court recognized her right in 1894, but the next year a whole new panel of judges reversed the decision and refused to permit her to represent a client in a case at that court. Rather than accommodate Annie Smith and Belva Lockwood, the legislature tightened the language of the law—changing "persons" to "male persons"—to make it even less likely that any woman could succeed in such an effort.

But the change in political status that the vote would bring led legislators to reconsider the question in 1920. Thus, though in no way mindful of the reformers at Seneca Falls, New York, or the demands they had voiced back in 1848, the Virginia General Assembly—in the same year that it conceded one of the leading demands from 1848, the right to vote—conceded another. It changed the statute to allow all persons, "male and female," to qualify for the practice of law. Moreover, the University of Virginia promptly began to admit women—white women—to its professional schools.

That fall, in 1920, three women—"these new and strange beings," according to the law school dean, William M. Lile, in his next report to the university president—began their legal studies at Virginia's only public law school. One, the law school librarian, Catherine Lipop, was convinced that she could better assist students and faculty if she better understood what they were trying to do.

The other two, Rose M. Davis and Elizabeth N. Tompkins, wanted to become practicing attorneys. Both passed the bar exam when they took it in 1922. Rose Davis went right to work, but Elizabeth Tompkins returned to school to complete the three-year degree in 1923. Thus, after nearly a century of training Virginia lawyers, Thomas Jefferson's university graduated its first female law student.

Medical College of Virginia

The story differed little in medicine, except that a few Virginia women succeeded in the field of medicine long before the 1920s. As early as the 1850s and 1860s, Virginia women attended medical school, but not in Virginia. Excluded from educational opportunities in their native state, they went to school elsewhere. In 1857, Orianna Russell Moon, a native of Albemarle County, graduated from the Female Medical College of Pennsylvania and thus became the first southern woman to earn a degree in medicine, only eight years after Elizabeth Blackwell became the first northern woman to do so. In 1864, Rebecca Lee, a native of Richmond, earned a medical degree, from the New England Woman's Medical College, and became the first African American woman to do so.

Virginia women continued to obtain medical degrees through the 1870s, 1880s, and 1890s from the Woman's Medical College of Pennsylvania; the Woman's Medical College of Baltimore; and Dr. Elizabeth Blackwell's institution, the Woman's Medical College of the New York Infirmary for Women and Children. Virginia graduates from the Pennsylvania school included Chertsey Hopkins from Warm Springs, Lynchburg's Rosalie B. Slaughter, Christiansburg's Phandora J. Simpson, and Norfolk's Elizabeth French Collins.

In medicine, unlike law, women with degrees earned in other states could practice their profession in Virginia. The first two such people that the Board of Medical Examiners approved were Dr. C. Lee Haynes, a white woman, in 1890, and Dr. Sarah G. Jones, a black woman, in 1893.

Toward the end of the century, Dr. Emily Chenault Runyon gained admission to the Richmond Academy of Medicine, though one member snorted in dissent at the decision. A few years earlier, he had written that to let women practice either law or medicine "aims at the complete destruction of society, subversion of religion, and reign of chaos."

The Medical College of Virginia rejected a woman who applied for admission to study dentistry in 1905, when the faculty voted "not to admit any females." At the dawn of the twentieth century, as had been the case fifty or a hundred years earlier, no woman could study medicine and obtain a degree at any school in Virginia.

That situation changed in 1918. A measure failed in the legislature that would have directed UVA and MCV to end their exclusion of women from professional programs, but MCV changed its policy anyway. Responding instead to wartime conditions, the Medical College of Virginia's schools of dentistry, medicine, and pharmacy decided to admit women beginning in 1918.

By 1922, at least two women had graduated from each of the three programs. They came from around the state. The pioneer graduates in dentistry included Petersburg's Esther Margaret Cummins, Wytheville's Constance O. Haller, and Roanoke's Tillie Lyons. Those in pharmacy included Norfolk's Margaret Ella Savage and Richmond's Ruth Vincent. The early female graduate who proved to have the most notable career of all was Mary Baughman, who practiced medicine in Richmond for many years.

In the 1920s, the University of Virginia also enrolled white women in medicine. Sarah Ruth Dean earned her M.D. there in 1922. It was not yet possible for Rebecca Lee—indeed for any African American, male or female—to attend medical school in Virginia. On the gender front, if not on race, much had changed just since the United States entered World War One in 1917.

Virginia Polytechnic Institute

Against this backdrop, the president of VPI, Julian Burruss, approached his Board of Visitors in January 1921 with a proposal. It was time, he urged, for his school to end its ban on admitting Virginians just because they were female. As the campus newspaper, *The Virginia Tech*, reported, he spoke of the need to supply training for industrial jobs of the sort that women had filled so well and so necessarily in the recent war effort. He believed that the right to vote embodied full citizenship for women, and that a land-grant school could therefore no longer legitimately exclude them. He argued, too, that, if the state were to accommodate women somewhere in technical courses, it could do so far more efficiently at a school that already had the facilities and offered the programs.

Burruss no doubt spoke from experience when he asserted that women could handle the intellectual rigors of challenging college work. Before coming to Tech, he had served for eleven years as the first president of the teachers college in Harrisonburg. He reminded his audience that women had demonstrated an ability to contribute in all kinds of ways to the industrial and military effort that permitted the United States to make the difference in the Allied victory in the Great War. And he pointed to the precedents, the very recent precedents, of women successfully enrolling in the College of William and Mary, the Medical College of Virginia, and the University of Virginia.

The Board of Visitors went along with President Burruss. That fall, five young women enrolled as full-time students, and another seven attended part-time. They surprised the writers of *The Virginia Tech* in one respect. The campus newspaper speculated that the women would wish to study "horticulture, landscape gardening, and other branches of agriculture." Instead, Ruth Louise Terrett enrolled in civil engineering, Billie Kent Kabrich in applied chemistry, and the other three—Mary E. Brumfield, Lucy Lee Lancaster, and Carrie T. Sibold—studied applied biology.

Tech's First Women Students

The five took right to their new academic environment. Mary Brumfield, a transfer student from Westhampton College (the women's unit of the University of Richmond), had followed her father, Dr. William A. Brumfield, after he took up his new post as health officer and professor of hygiene at VPI. She finished in 1923 and promptly became a Tech graduate student.

*VPI's first five women graduates: Mary Brumfield (B.S.
'23, M.S. '25) and Ruth Terrett, Lucy Lee Lancaster, Louise
Jacobs, Carrie Sibold (all B.S. '25)*

The four who had entered as freshmen remained together
for two years. Then they lost one of their number, Billie Kent
Kabrich, who married and left school, but a transfer chemistry
major, Louise Jacobs, took her place. As amended, the quartet
earned their degrees in 1925, at the same time as Brumfield
earned her master's. The ranks of Tech graduates no longer
included only men, and Brumfield was a double-alumna.

Though admitted to degree programs, female students were
by no means quickly integrated into all the college's activities.
Burruss had made it clear in his proposal to the Board of
Visitors that women would remain excluded from the military,
and the cadets, for their part, excluded women from many of
the school's extracurricular activities. Coeds were told to keep
away from the Upper Quad, though that was the location of
the bookstore. It was as if the five were enrolled in the same
institution but attended two different colleges in much the same
location.

Women might graduate from Virginia Tech, but their photos would not appear in the school yearbook, the *Bugle*. As an answer to the *Bugle*, the female graduates of 1925 produced the *Tin Horn*, and the classes of 1929, 1930, and 1931 did the same. The first edition—which consisted of typescript, hand lettering, and pasted photographs—carried a guarantee, inscribed on authentic paper, that it was bound in "real leather." The second edition, four years later, actually was bound in leather, although it, like its predecessor, sported photographs pasted onto the pages and was hand-produced. The 1930 *Tin Horn* carried a boast that it was "our first printed annual."

The women of VPI established many separate activities. During 1923–1924, the third year of coeducation, some organized a basketball team, and they all celebrated what one of them called "our victory in having won" a "co-ed room in the Library." By 1929, they had established a Women Students' Organization. Frances Vivian Vernon, one of the four seniors that year, served as its president and also as editor-in-chief of the *Tin Horn*.

Into the 1930s, a group of female thespians put on plays in which women played the male roles as well as the female roles (just as men maintained a group in which they played both male and female roles). One club member wrote after practice one evening, "Thought I would die laughing at Bernice McCoy and Martha Rice, dressed in men's clothing, trying to sing a lullaby in a deep voice to a leather coat which served as a baby."

For the female graduates of 1925, the experience of attending VPI gave considerable shape to their personal or professional lives. Two of them married classmates—demonstrating that not all cadets objected greatly at VPI's having enrolled women students. Mary Brumfield married William Roane Garnett (B.S. '23, electrical engineering), and Louise Jacobs married Charles Meade Stull (B.S. '25, mining engineering). Carrie Sibold and Lucy Lee Lancaster, both single, stayed in their hometown and worked for VPI, Sibold early on as a stenographer.

Lancaster began working in the college library as a student, then continued until her retirement in 1975, fifty years after her graduation. She took time away in the 1930s to earn a master's degree in library science in New York. And she traveled much of the world, whether to visit Mayan ruins or a place in Germany from which at least one of her ancestors had come to the New River Valley back in colonial times.

Coeducation at VPI after Ten Years

During the year 1930–1931, after nearly a decade of coeducation, the female cohorts remained small: ten sophomores, ten juniors. Excluded from male organizations, female students maintained their own clubs. Their Chemistry Club had six members, the Biology Club nine, and the Business Club ten, while Home Economics numbered sixteen. The basketball team had eleven members, the Glee Club fourteen, the Dramatic Club sixteen.

Twelve women graduated from VPI in 1931, nine of them from little Blacksburg. Six majored in business, two in home economics, and four in science or engineering. As one of them wrote, in 1930 they "went with the corps to Roanoke for the last time" for the traditional football game with VMI on Thanksgiving day. "We beat VMI at last," she chortled, though they nearly froze. The weather that day was "wonderful for Eskimos."

A sampling of the graduates that year conveys something of student life for the few women enrolled at Tech in the early years. Betty Conner, a Blacksburg resident and biology major, played basketball all four years, captained the team her senior year, and also served as senior class president. Catherine Slusser, another biology major from Blacksburg, joined the Biology Club all four years as well as the Glee Club and Dramatic Club her junior and senior years. She was president of her junior class and, active in the Women Students' Organization, served as secretary her sophomore year and president her senior year.

Other seniors reported similar experiences. Waneta McCoy, yet another student from Blacksburg, studied business administration, played basketball, joined the Dramatic Club, and served as president of the Business Club. Martha Rice, from Richmond, majored in civil engineering; in each of her final two years she participated in the Glee Club, the Dramatic Club, the basketball team, and the *Tin Horn*, which she edited her senior year. Clara Chrisman was president of the Dramatic Club and business manager of that club as well as of the *Tin Horn*, while Sybil Gilmore, the only female senior from out of state (West Virginia), was a student assistant in English.

Each of the female graduates had joined multiple female groups, and most had obtained leadership positions. Then they graduated and, armed with their VPI experience, headed out into the Great Depression. It is often remarked that single-sex women's schools offered greater opportunities for leadership development than coeducational schools did, but perhaps the kind of intra-institutional gender segregation that VPI displayed also performed in that manner.

Virginia State College

In 1921, when President Burruss justified the inclusion of women students, he stated that the school should "no longer discriminate against a large part of the people of the state supporting it." Looking back generations later, we can see what many black Virginians might have felt then. Black Virginians paid state taxes, too, and there were nearly as many black women and black men, combined, as there were white women. Yet only white women were permitted to leave the ranks of the categorically excluded. The state continued to exclude black Virginians absolutely in the 1920s, as it would through the 1930s and 1940s. Tech had begun to enroll women, but, as with men, only if they were not African American.

By the time women became degree candidates at Virginia Tech, nearly four decades had passed since the establishment of Virginia Normal and Collegiate Institute. That school had,

from the very beginning, educated black men and black women
in the same institution. By 1902, under the new disfranchising
constitution, the legislature had terminated the college part
of the curriculum and changed the name to Virginia Normal
and Industrial Institute. In the 1920s, while the white men's
schools were going about the difficult business of admitting
white women, the black school went through its own significant
changes. As the previous chapter showed, the Petersburg
school became a land-grant institution, its collegiate curriculum
returned, and it obtained a new name to reflect its identity,
Virginia State College for Negroes.

As Virginia entered a second half-century of land-grant
education, Virginia Polytechnic Institute enrolled white
students, men and women, and Virginia State College educated
black students, men and women.

Coeducation in the South

Women's admission to all-male white southern schools during
and soon after World War One was neither impossible nor inev-
itable. Among Virginia schools, MCV acted before legislation
mandated an end to female exclusion. No law, state or federal,
said Tech had to admit women either. The change came because
President Burruss took a forceful initiative.

The experience at other southern schools suggests the
range of possibilities. The previous chapter told how Maryland
changed its policy to admit women beginning in 1916.

At the other extreme, highlighting the range of discretion
and the importance of leadership on the question of female
inclusion, Texas Agricultural and Mechanical College displayed
a contrasting pattern, though the beginnings looked similar.
The daughters of one professor took classes in the 1890s,
even completed the curriculum in civil engineering, but were
awarded no degrees. Other women students followed. Women
enrolled when a summer session was held in 1901 and again
beginning in 1909. During World War One, the school hired a
woman to teach botany. In the early 1920s, dozens of women

studied at the school, as married veterans brought their wives to Bryan and some enrolled as "special unofficial students." In 1925, Mary Evelyn Crawford, the sister of a mechanical engineering professor, became the first woman to obtain a degree from the school.

Yet all these promising indications that Texas A&M was moving toward coeducation led nowhere. A court challenge in 1933 to the exclusion of local women ended with the judge deciding that the institution had full discretion in the matter. The school changed its policy so that even the wives and daughters of faculty could no longer take classes. Only in the 1960s, as it became a university, did Texas A&M go coeducational.

North Carolina State College of Agriculture and Engineering offered a mid-range example, more like Virginia Tech but with a longer start-up time. The board of trustees decided in 1899 to admit white women to all academic programs. Change nonetheless proved slow. Even before 1899, women had attended summer sessions, in fact had outnumbered men, and they continued to do so. Few enrolled during the regular year, however, and until 1927 even completion of requirements did not secure a degree. That year, Mary E. Yarborough received an M.S. diploma in chemistry, Charlotte R. Nelson a B.S. in education, and Jane S. McKimmon—who had completed all degree requirements two years earlier and then waited while trustees dithered—a B.S. in business administration.

Mississippi Agricultural and Mechanical College, which had admitted some women as early as 1882, ended coeducation in 1912 but restored it in 1930. Mississippi thus embarked on a gradual move to full coeducation at almost the same time Texas terminated its experiment.

Women Citizens, Female Scholars

The 1920s proved ambiguous for coeducation at southern white land-grant schools, yet something was happening. Maryland State College awarded its first degree to a woman in 1920, Virginia Tech in 1923, and North Carolina State College in

1927. Even Texas A&M awarded its first in 1925, the same year that Virginia Tech graduated its first coeducational class. A half-century after the South's land-grant era began, more and more white schools were making space for women as well as men.

At VPI, moreover, women were beginning not only to enroll as students but also to join the teaching faculty. As early as 1920, Anna Montgomery Campbell (daughter of Professor Theodoric Campbell) served as an instructor in English, and by the end of the decade Ella Gertrude Russell was instructor in chemistry, and Mabel Huey Cowgill in architectural drawing. By the late 1920s, Maude Emma Wallace was filling the place previously held by Mary Moore Davis as state agent for home demonstration work in the Extension Division. Also by then, regular faculty in the new home economics program included an associate professor, Martha Dabney Dinwiddie, and three assistant professors: Mary Bland McGowan, Margaret Minnis, and Emma Weld.

References

Cato, "Higher Education for Women in Virginia," 325–44.

Corks and Curls (University of Virginia yearbook; 1924), 149.

Cox, *Generations of Women Leaders*, 7–11.

Dabney, *Mr. Jefferson's University*, 50–52, 67–69, 144–46.

Dabney, *Virginia Commonwealth University*, 51, 65.

Dethloff, *Texas A&M University*, 2: 409–15.

Godson et al., *College of William and Mary*, 2: 506–11.

Goree, "Steps toward Redefinition."

Kinnear, *The First 100 Years*, 262–65.

Lucy Lee Lancaster, "Burruss Opened Doors of Tech to Coeds," *Roanoke Times*, March 19, 1972.

Lebsock, *Virginia Women*, 98–100.

Lockmiller, *North Carolina State College*, 82–83, 170–71.

Tin Horn (1925); (1929); (1930); (1931), 12–13.

Wallenstein, *Blue Laws and Black Codes*, 60–81.

Walsh, *Doctors Wanted, No Women Need Apply.*

"Aggie Hall," 1920

The Old Library, 1920

Chapter 9
1930s: Great Depression and New Construction

J. Ambler Johnston, class of 1904, served Tech and its Alumni Association through a long lifetime. Together with W. Leigh Carneal, he founded the firm of Carneal and Johnston, which designed many Tech buildings and gave the school its distinctive architecture. In the 1910s, Carneal and Johnston designed the McBryde Building of Mechanic Arts that—consistent with President Eggleston's directive that a new prototype for Tech buildings be adopted—used a local limestone that came to be

J. Ambler Johnston, alumnus and architect

known as Hokie Stone and, just as important, a "neo-Gothic" design.

The firm's impact on VPI's physical environment became more visible in the 1920s, but it became dominant only in the 1930s. During those two decades, the Drillfield took on its modern contours, as new buildings went up around it. In other

*Paul N. Derring,
YMCA secretary at VPI*

ways, too, Johnston's impact persisted a century and more after he enrolled at a school that had just recently adopted the name Virginia Agricultural and Mechanical College and Polytechnic Institute.

While J. Ambler Johnston's work transformed the visible campus, Paul N. Derring's work did much the same for the spirit of the place. Derring came to VPI in 1918. A 1917 graduate of William and Mary, he wished to contribute to the war effort but, totally blind, he could not volunteer for the military, so he worked for the Young Men's Christian Association. His service at Tech, at first with soldiers as well as civilians, continued with students, as secretary of the Tech YMCA, during the 1920s and 1930s and on—past a celebration during the Second World War of his twenty-five years at Tech—into the 1960s.

Countless students recalled Derring as "my daddy while I was at VPI" or "a Dad away from home." They knew him as the man who supplied wise and generous counsel when they were students—at first in his office in the YMCA building, just off the Upper Quad, and later in the Student Activities Building (later Squires Student Center)—and who instantly recognized them by their voices when they stopped by campus even years later. Derring started freshman orientation in 1927. He brought many speakers to campus, and the YMCA "Chariot" took students to meetings far from Tech. After one such meeting in Greensboro, North Carolina, in the late 1930s, a female student asked him, "Mr. Derring, just what is your job at VPI?"

When he replied—condensing his Christianity and his job description—"To save young men," she squealed. "Oh, please save me one!"

Three Legacies from the 1920s

Tech entered the 1930s with legacies from the recent past that transformed its physical environment, restricted its curricular development, and reconfigured its student population.

Drill Field

Julian Burruss, who spoke often during his presidency of his hopes for "a greater VPI," took office in 1919. Soon afterwards, Tech embarked on a major plan of physical development. The brick buildings of the Upper Quadrangle—the core of the early twentieth-century campus—would be maintained, and in fact new construction there in 1927 supplied Tech with Barracks Number Six, which later became part of Major Williams, as well as Barracks Number Seven, a renovated version of the Science Hall.

In the main, however, the campus would grow to the west, with a series of new buildings constructed with a limestone facing, and to the south with new athletic facilities. The late 1920s brought the construction of Patton Hall and Davidson Hall. Two new sports facilities opened in 1926, the War Memorial Gymnasium, dedicated to the memory of all Tech men who had died in the Great War, and Miles Stadium.

Aside from the Hokie Stone of such buildings as Patton Hall and the War Memorial Gym, Tech's most distinctive environmental feature is the Drillfield, which lies between those two buildings. It is easy to assume that it has always been there, easy to imagine that cadets marched on that very Drillfield in the 1910s, the 1890s, the 1870s—even that the founders happened upon the Drillfield and decided to center a military school there. Such is not the case.

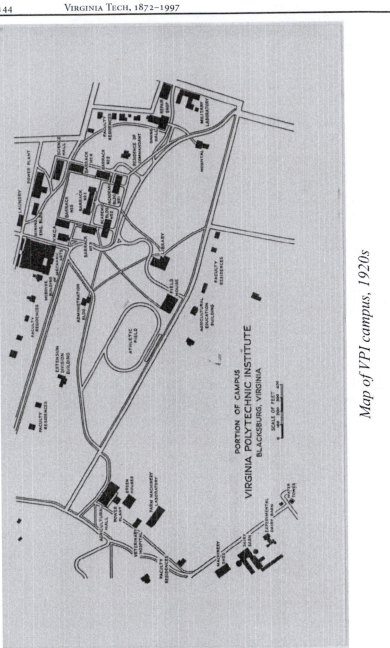

Map of VPI campus, 1920s

In fact, Burruss's early plan, as he described it, called for "a central recreation and drill field, approximately three times the area of the old athletic field, which forms the eastern end. This expanse is to be left open forever, and around it are to be grouped the buildings of the new plant. These structures are [to be] designed in the modified Tudor type of architecture, with walls of limestone quarried on the campus."

The "old athletic field" and "drill field," then, took up far less space than the current Drillfield, and it was in the area where the War Memorial is today. The Burruss plan was implemented during the 1920s and further developed in the 1930s.

Liberal Arts?

At about the same time that Tech teams were beginning play at Miles Stadium and classes were first being held at what would later be called Patton Hall, Tech's academic program came under heavy attack. The 1927 legislature ordered a survey of higher education in Virginia, and it directed a commission to review the report and make recommendations to be considered at the next session. One of those recommendations would have left all graduate study in the exclusive jurisdiction of UVA. Another would have eliminated "all work of the nature of liberal arts" at VPI. The commission would have had Tech narrow its curricular focus to the core areas of "agriculture and mechanic arts." Even courses in home economics and business administration would be permitted only as preparation for work in the two core areas.

In the end, Tech's leaders and supporters fended off these proposals, but success had its costs. With legislators as his primary audience, and despite his wishes for a "greater VPI," Burruss felt compelled to declare: "The Virginia Polytechnic Institute does not aspire to be a university, or a liberal arts college." For the present, at least, he voiced Tech's ambitions as focusing on the areas of "agriculture, industry, and business" and looking to the advancement of Virginia's "agricultural, industrial, and commercial interests." Accepting the notion of Tech's "restricted fields" of research and instruction in these areas, he concluded: "We simply want to develop our present field of service and to raise our work to the highest possible standard."

Burruss directed the same language to his faculty. Frightened by the threats from the legislature that he had to navigate, he made it clear to all department heads that they must "scrutinize mercilessly" all instructional work and all research, too, to be sure—and this is a clear summary of the college's mission, according to this narrow view—that it served to promote "the agricultural, commercial, and industrial development of the Commonwealth of Virginia."

Corps of Cadets: Optional after Two

VPI remained a school with a strong military component in the 1930s, but there, too, the previous decade had left its mark, and not only because of the enrollment of a small number of female students. Tech had long had a problem with student discipline. Rather than help, the Corps of Cadets seemed to college authorities to foster rowdy—albeit creative—behavior. The sophomore banquet fostered the greatest displays.

In June 1925 the sophomores decided, according to one, that they would "put on a celebration bigger and better than anything ever seen" on the Upper Quad. As another of them wrote, they set out "to collect quadrangle decorations." And they cannot be faulted for lack of effort. Steamrollers disappeared from a nearby construction site and reappeared on the cadets' domain. Cows mooed from fourth-story windows, a hive of bees patrolled another floor, and every type of farm critter and implement to be found in western Virginia perched somewhere inside or on a roof of the barracks.

A faculty report responded to one of these annual affairs of the 1920s by noting that, among all the land-grant schools across the continent, only three made four years of military training compulsory, and only two (VPI and Texas A&M) housed students in barracks all four years. Perhaps it was time for a change at Tech. The president and faculty proposed abolishing the Corps of Cadets entirely and reorganizing the school on a fully civilian basis. Moreover, Burruss wished to upgrade the academic performance as well as the quality of discipline that students had to display in order to stay in school.

The Board of Visitors would not go so far as to do away with the Corps, but it adopted a change that carried extraordinary implications for the school. Membership in the Corps would remain mandatory for most male students during their first two years, but during the second two years it became optional. The change went into effect for the 1924–1925 year.

For many years, most students opted to stay in the Corps of Cadets all four years, but some did not. Thus a group of civilian students gradually grew among Tech's undergraduate men. Moreover, once the military became optional, the school had leverage to encourage better behavior by students who wished to remain cadets. As President Burruss put it, "It is true that juniors and seniors will not be required to take military— yes, but neither will military be required to take juniors and seniors."

As the antics of the sophomore banquet of 1925 made clear, the change in policy announced the year before did not immediately transform life on campus in ways that had been hoped. But the 1925 display proved to be cathartic. It had no sequel. Students and faculty appear to have worked more smoothly together in the years that followed. One alumnus tried to explain the change. "We became less hostile," he said. "We seemed to be groping for ways to make our activities more constructive . . . for the greater VPI which just about everybody seemed to be talking about." Within a very few years, the struggle for a "greater VPI" would be hard enough anyway.

VPI and the Great Depression

Virginia could not escape the Great Depression, which began with the Crash of October 1929, deepened through 1932, and, along the way, savaged life—public and private—across Virginia, across the nation, indeed throughout much of the world.

During this time, VPI—especially the Extension service—had an impact on Virginia farmers in two ways. County Extension agents attempted to assist farmers through the agony of sharply dropping prices for agricultural commodities. Emphasizing subsistence as a primary strategy for getting through the hard times, they reversed the approach of the 1910s, when the nation needed increased production. Instead, they spoke in the 1930s of "depression proofing" and the "cow, sow, and hen program." In addition, they helped implement the New Deal's first Agricultural Adjustment Act, passed in 1933. They explained the AAA program and distributed its benefits checks. John Redd Hutcheson, Extension director at Tech, lauded the AAA as "the greatest educational experience that farmers have ever had."

Despite the hard times, and they were hard indeed, Tech came to the end of the decade more prosperous than ever before. In particular, the New Deal response to the Depression had an impact on the school both immediate and enduring.

From Hard Times to Graduate Studies

An economic downturn as sharp and protracted as the Great Depression had ominous implications for an institution dependent on state funds. As legislators in the early 1930s played Mother Hubbard and gazed at the depleted state coffers, they acted to reduce funding at VPI. In 1932 alone the legislature cut the general appropriation for Tech by 7.5 percent, and faculty salaries declined 10 percent. Over the duration of the Depression, faculty salaries declined by 20 percent and general state appropriations by even more. The cuts were substantial but not deadly.

Tech actually cut only one program—home economics. That program went away in 1933 but reappeared three years later, when the school made an effort to recruit students and give the restored department a strong launching. Among the students recruited were Kathleen Mansfield, a freshman, and Eva Foster, who transferred as a junior from the teachers' college at Harrisonburg. Two people on the faculty of home economics made a huge difference, right away and for many years afterwards. Maude E. Wallace, who had been very much involved in Extension ever since 1927, continued in that role and on the faculty as well. Dr. Mildred Thurow Tate arrived in 1937 as an assistant professor of the restored program of home economics, She soon began a campaign for a residence hall for female students; she also soon became the first dean of women.

By the end of the decade, indeed, Tech's curriculum had grown, and Tech had more undergraduates and more graduate students than ever before. New areas of study included rural sociology, ceramic engineering, poultry husbandry, and industrial physics. A new graduate program was begun in power and fuel engineering. Studies leading to the Ph.D. began in biology, chemistry, chemical engineering, and agricultural economics. Tech awarded its first doctorate in 1942, to Nathan Sugarman in chemistry.

Tech might not be yet offering the trappings of "a liberal arts college"—Burruss never entirely escaped his fright from a decade earlier—but it was surely true by the 1940s that UVA had no franchise on graduate study in Virginia.

Branch Campuses

In the years around 1930, all the state-supported institutions of higher education in Virginia—except, that is, VMI and the white women's normal schools—began to develop programs far away from their home campuses. Beginning in 1935, for example, black students enrolled in a program that, long associated with Virginia Union University and then Virginia State, eventually became Norfolk State University. William and Mary adopted a Richmond Division in 1925 (it became the Richmond Professional Institute of the College of William and Mary in 1939) and also a program in Norfolk in 1930.

Tech and UVA did much the same. For many years, a majority of VPI students had earned their degrees in engineering. In the 1930s, Tech began offering lower-division engineering courses at branch schools—"extension divisions"—in various cities. It established the first in Richmond in 1930, in association with William and Mary. It developed another in Norfolk in 1931 in conjunction with William and Mary's division there. In 1932, it also established branches at Lynchburg College and Bluefield College. These connections persisted into the 1960s, when most branch campuses became separate universities or components of a new system of community colleges.

Public Works and the New Deal

The Great Depression led to Franklin D. Roosevelt's New Deal, and the New Deal brought opportunities that transformed the Tech landscape. A major emphasis of the New Deal response to the Depression was to supply federal funds to create public works jobs. People could not buy if they had no money, and they had no money if they remained unemployed. Moreover, if they did not buy, then others could not sell, so still others could not produce. The way to break effectively through the downward cycle of employment in America, according to the New Deal approach, was to put people to work creating things from which Americans would benefit for many years afterwards. Outside of Virginia, such projects took shape as the Key West Highway in Florida and LaGuardia Airport in New York.

In Virginia, major monuments to New Deal public works spending include the Blue Ridge Parkway and the University of Virginia's Alderman Library.

Federal public works money also made it possible for new construction to go up at various

Teaching and Administration Building (Burruss Hall), 1939

other public institutions of higher education, among them the College of William and Mary and what were then known as Madison College, Mary Washington College, and Virginia State College for Negroes. Federal funds paid much of the cost, too, of constructing a new building in downtown Richmond that, for many years, housed the Virginia State Library and the Virginia Supreme Court.

New Buildings and a Transformed Campus

Federal money did not just show up in the mail because someone in the nation's capital wanted to promote the nation's general welfare. It had to be sought. President Burruss strove mightily to obtain federal funding for new construction at Tech.

To list the buildings at Tech that went up with federal aid during the 1930s is to take a tour around the Drillfield. On one side of the Drillfield, a giant new building went up, called at the time the Teaching and Administration Building but later named Burruss Hall after the college president who made it happen. Work began in 1934, and the building opened in 1936 in time for that year's commencement exercises to fit comfortably in the new 3,000-seat auditorium.

Diagonally across the Drillfield from Burruss is Hutcheson Hall, completed in 1940 as Agricultural Hall. Behind it is Smyth Hall, the Natural Science Building or "Aggie Annex," completed in 1939. On one side of Smyth are Seitz Hall, completed in 1937 and originally called the Agricultural Engineering Hall; the Home Economics Building, later named Agnew Hall; and the Dairy Building, completed in 1931, even before the New Deal, and later named Saunders Hall.

At another corner of the Drillfield is the Eggleston complex. East Stone Dormitory Number 1, as it was called at first, was completed in 1935, and the east and west wings were added by 1940. In back of Eggleston is a companion site, Owens Dining Hall, also a product of the 1930s.

The list of New Deal structures goes on. The Student Activities Building (Squires) opened in 1937, and Paul Derring and the YMCA office moved there. Some faculty members obtained new housing on campus—and thus benefited from more than new buildings to teach in—when the Faculty Apartments, or Faculty Center, opened in 1935. Subsequently enlarged and renovated, as Squires has been as well, the Faculty Center later became known as the Donaldson Brown Continuing Education Center and then the Donaldson Brown Hotel and Conference Center—and still later the Graduate Life Center.

What has long been named Seitz Hall offers a glimpse at the ways in which construction of the new buildings of the 1930s drew on the energy of the community as well as the expertise of the college—and how both could benefit. Professor Charles E. Seitz and his colleagues in agricultural engineering designed their own building. Then they trained workers, as necessary, in such skills as carpentry, electricity, masonry, plumbing, and stonecutting, and they supervised the construction.

Virginia Tech's twenty-first century campus displays further monuments to the New Deal, while at the same time embodying significant other change. Completed in 1940 was Hillcrest, a residence hall for women (and immediately dubbed by cadets the "Skirt Barn"). Together with Agnew Hall, the home economics building down the hill, Hillcrest appeared to promise a permanent and prominent presence of women as faculty and students on the Virginia Tech campus.

A tour of the Tech campus would not be complete if it did not include the Duck Pond. In addition to all the major construction itemized here, the 1930s brought significant landscaping and tree planting and the construction of new walks, roads, and what, in recognition of the feathered life forms that flock there, came to be known as the Duck Pond. On the other side of Solitude, on the way up the hill toward Hillcrest and the Grove, is a large outdoor theatre (the Garden Theatre, or Amphitheatre), dedicated in 1935 but much later largely reclaimed by the woods.

Honor Roll

A tour around the Drillfield provides an honor roll of great names in Tech's past. Agnew Hall was named in 1949 for Ella Graham Agnew, the pioneering Extension agent of the 1910s. Seitz Hall honors Charles Edward Seitz, the founder and head of agricultural engineering from 1919 to 1954 whose tremendous influence extended around the state and across the country.

Eggleston Hall commemorates Tech's seventh president. Other buildings are named for Roy J. Holden, who taught geology for forty years and served as department head; William D. Saunders, who taught dairy husbandry for fifty years and directed the Agricultural Experiment Station; and Ellison A. Smyth Jr., who taught biology from 1891 to 1925 and also coached football for a time.

Hutcheson Hall honors two men, the Hutcheson brothers, who between them served the university for more than ninety years and studied or worked at Tech for a century. Thomas

Barksdale Hutcheson, class of 1906, was dean of agriculture at his death in 1950. John Redd Hutcheson, class of 1907, was director of Extension, president of VPI from 1945 to 1947, and then president of Tech's Educational Foundation. "Dr. Jack" and his older brother, as a plaque at the building says, each gave a lifetime of his best "to agriculture, Virginia, and alma mater."

Women of VPI

The inclusion of women students and faculty at VPI became greater at about the time Agnew and Hillcrest both opened in 1940. The numbers of graduating women—four seniors in 1925, twelve in 1931—grew slowly, and the road to their full inclusion in the life of the school proved uneven.

Male students and alumni did not put much stock in coeducation. On an overwhelmingly male campus, seniors selected the valedictorian and salutatorian each year. They did not necessarily pick the students with the highest and second-highest grades. In 1932, the year of Franklin D. Roosevelt's election as president, they snubbed the young woman with the highest academic average, Frances Rosamond Aldrich, a chemistry major from Pennsylvania, by naming her to neither position. Expressions of discontent ensued, and in the end her accomplishment was acknowledged at commencement.

At about the same time, Burruss had to fend off an antediluvian alumnus who vented his wish that coeducation at Tech be abandoned. Burruss let it be known that, in his opinion, to abandon coeducation would jeopardize Tech's federal funding as a land-grant school. The story goes that his antagonist gave up the fight with the glum statement, "Women's rights I'll never understand, but money I do understand."

Once again, as he had in 1921, President Burruss relied on an interpretation of the law and Tech's obligations as a land-grant college that, though he chose to believe it and deploy it, came from no known federal mandate, no court decision, no consensus among land-grant college presidents. To the contrary, Texas A&M College won a decision in local court in 1933 that left the matter of coeducation entirely up to the institution's authorities, and the school rolled back such changes as had permitted some women to enroll.

In 1936, the year President Roosevelt gained election to a second term, Tech women in the senior class upset some of their classmates by asking to be included in the *Bugle*. Fifteen years had passed since the first female students had enrolled as degree candidates at Tech, and eleven years had passed since the first group had graduated and appeared in the first *Tin Horn*. To be included in their college yearbook was still too much for Tech women to ask in 1936. Within five years, that and much else would change.

The 1941 *Bugle* contained the pictures of 439 graduates—316 of them (72 percent) cadets, 100 (23 percent) civilian men, and 23 (5 percent) women. Most of the women majored in the revived home economics program, and most reported having joined the new YWCA during their junior year. Many had transferred in from Madison College, Farmville, Radford, or elsewhere—Madeline Kruger, a chemistry major, had completed two years of study at VPI's Norfolk extension. Four were engaged in graduate work. Women students, like men, were being drawn from more distant places, though many were still local; six of the 23 lived in Blacksburg, and two more in Christiansburg, but one each—all graduate students—came from Pennsylvania, Texas, and California.

In the late 1920s, the female students organized a Women's Student Organization. After civilian male students—now that there were some—organized the Civilian Student Union as a student government but excluded women from it, women organized a counterpart Women's Student Union. As the three factions jockeyed—cadets, male civilians, and females—they might align themselves according to male and female or according to cadet and civilian, but they could not do both at once. In 1939, to counter the cadets' power in student governance, the male civilians invited the women to join them in a combined Civilian Student Union.

After the United States entered World War Two in 1941, the pressure to include women grew stronger as male students grew scarce. The Agriculture Club, for example, decided in April 1943 to admit home economics majors as members.

Women as well as men marched into Burruss Auditorium, where, together with their families and the faculty, they celebrated the completion of their studies at VPI. Coeducation—to some substantial degree—had come to Tech to stay. For a time, women had their own separate yearbook, their own separate basketball, thespian, and glee clubs, their own many things. Regardless, they had a place alongside men in the classrooms and laboratories, in commencement ceremonies, and on the roster of graduates, even eventually in student governance. Women as students were transitioning from exclusion to separation to inclusion.

Ella G. Agnew, Mary Moore Davis, and Maude E. Wallace, in 1947. Each in turn played leading roles in home economics on the VPI campus and, through Extension, across the state.

From Great Depression to World War

During the Burruss years, Tech began the integration of women into the faculty as well as into student life on campus. Beginning in 1924, moreover, male upperclassmen gained the option of whether to be in the Corps of

Cadets, and the numbers of civilian men edged up. By the late 1930s both changes were very much in evidence.

In the early 1930s, for the first time, bachelor's degrees awarded in a given year exceeded 200, and master's degrees 20; by 1940, both figures had more than doubled. Enrollment, never as high as 1,000 before 1923, or 2,000 before 1936, topped 3,000 by 1940. (See Appendices C and D.)

Despite the trauma of the Great Depression, VPI came through the 1930s stronger than ever before. Its physical plant was more fully developed, and its curriculum had never been so robust. As VPI built on the enlargement of its mission to include research and extension as well as instruction, it continued to increase its contributions to the social and economic well-being of the people of the Old Dominion.

Already by 1940, VPI was a very different place than it had been in 1920. The challenges to come in the next three decades would impose obligations and create opportunities that far exceeded anything yet seen there.

References

Alvey, *History of Mary Washington College*, 193–94, 233–36.

Cox, *Generations of Women Leaders*, 9–11, 33.

Dabney, *Mr. Jefferson's University*, 181–86.

Godson et al., *College of William and Mary*, 2: 667.

Heinemann, *Depression and New Deal in Virginia*, 25–26, 62–63, 109.

Kinnear, *The First 100 Years*, 268–85, 305–11.

Webster, *I Remember Paul*, 23, 29, 54.

*Dr. Hung-Yu Loh
(M.S. 1943),
professor of physics,
1940s–1970s*

*Major General Cecil R.
"Scribe" Moore
(B.S. 1916, M.S. 1917),
Eisenhower's chief
engineering officer in World
War Two Europe*

Chapter 10
1940s: World War Two

Great numbers of VPI students represented the World War Two generation across the 1940s—in wartime interruption to their schooling, in their wartime service in Europe or Asia, in their return to school under the G.I. Bill, in marriage and family formation, and in their subsequent professional careers.

Henry J. Dekker '44, rector in 1997

One was Henry Dekker. A native of Norfolk, he began his studies at the Norfolk branch in 1937 in chemical engineering, then (after working to save money) began classes at Blacksburg in 1940, class of 1944, where he studied business administration. By 1943 he had served as president of his class and president of the Corps of Cadets.

But then he fought in the Pacific during the war and served in Japan during the occupation; returned to Tech after three years away; and graduated as a civilian in 1947, the school's 75th anniversary year. He stayed on at Tech for four more years, first as instructor and graduate student, subsequently as school treasurer. During his time in Blacksburg, in 1949, he married Louisa Otey Gillet, a niece of VPI president Walter S. Newman's wife.

He left Blacksburg to work in the fabric and apparel industry and rose to the presidency of Louis Feraud. He, his wife, and their children lived far from Blacksburg, but then he retired and the couple returned. Long active in school affairs, Henry Dekker served on the Virginia Tech Board of Visitors, and in 1997, on the institution's 125th birthday, he presided as rector at Founders Day ceremonies.

Clifton C. Garvin Jr. followed a similar path from the 1940s to the 1990s. He graduated with honors in chemical engineering in 1943, married that year, and then spent three years in the Pacific Theater with the Army Corps of Engineers. After the war, he, like Dekker, returned to Tech, where he earned a master's degree. Then he went into the oil industry. From 1975 until his retirement in 1986 he served as CEO of Exxon Corporation. In the 1990s, he served as a member and then rector of the Virginia Tech Board of Visitors. At the 1997 Founders Day ceremonies, Henry Dekker presented Clifton Garvin with the William H. Ruffner Medal, the university's highest honor.

World War Two had tremendous consequences for institutions of higher education across America, and certainly for Virginia Tech. Many students and alumni went off to war. With the decline in male students, women suddenly made up a larger fraction of the student population, and they entered into student activities from which they had previously been excluded. Establishment of a Radford connection in 1944 turned back some of that advance. The G.I. Bill brought a different set of changes.

World War Two at Virginia Tech

The U.S. Congress enacted a peacetime draft in 1940— peacetime in the sense that the nation was not yet *at* war, not in the sense that there was *no* war. More than any other war in the history of the planet, this was a world war. On October 16, five hundred Tech students lined up in Squires Hall to register for the draft, and that number did not include the juniors and seniors who were enrolled in ROTC. Barely a year later, following Japan's attack in December 1941 at Pearl Harbor in Hawai'i, the U.S. entered the war. American troops, among them more than 7,000 former Tech students, soon fought in Europe, the Pacific, and elsewhere.

By the summer of 1941, the Hercules Powder/Radford Ordnance Works, located only a few miles away, was depleting the Tech workforce. Unable to compete with the plant's pay scale, the school lost platoons of secretaries, dining hall workers, and other employees. Many faculty members left Blacksburg to enter the military or take defense jobs.

The war also transformed the Blacksburg student population. Many students left school to enter active service. Tech facilitated early graduation through accelerated academic programs and mid-year commencement ceremonies. The number of regular students dropped from 3,382 in spring 1942, then 557 in spring 1944, to only 411 in spring 1945. The football program suspended operations for 1943 and 1944, and the student newspaper, *The Virginia Tech*, never appeared during 1944.

Yet campus depletion through mass exodus proved only part of the story. Beginning in March 1943, an Army Specialized Training Program (ASTP) at Tech trained army engineers. Enrollment rose from 186 the first quarter to more than 2,000. Other programs followed, among them a Specialized Training and Reassignment (STAR) unit. Enrolled like any other students in various classes, they earned college credit for their studies, and 46 completed the requirements for engineering degrees. VPI also ran three-month "engineering war training" programs for women to prepare "Rosie the Riveter" for jobs in industry.

War Memorial—the view from Alumni Mall

The Soldiers of VPI in World War Two

Tech graduates and faculty who remained on the home front
contributed to the war effort in agriculture, industry, and
government. Soldiers from VPI made huge accomplishments
on the war front. In South Asia, Brigadier General Lewis
Andrew "Abbie" Pick, class of 1914, oversaw construction
of a military road in Burma that came to be known as "Pick's
Pike." In Europe, Major General Cecil R. "Scribe" Moore (B.S.
1916, M.S. 1917) served as chief engineering officer for all of
Europe. In the spring of 1945, a group of former Tech students
and professors in uniform—coming together and celebrating
imminent victory in Europe—established in Naples, Italy, what
was called the school's first overseas alumni club.

Tech soldiers also made huge sacrifices. Three hundred
died in service. Three who died were awarded Congressional
Medals of Honor. First Lieutenant James W. Monteith Jr., class
of 1941, died leading his men at Normandy. Sergeant Herbert
J. Thomas, also class of 1941, sacrificed his life to save his
men when he threw himself on a grenade at Bougainville in the
Pacific. Second Lieutenant Robert E. Femoyer, class of 1944,
piloted a "Flying Fortress" over Europe. On his last flight, he
brought his crew safely back even though the plane had been

War Memorial—the view from the Drillfield

crippled by anti-aircraft fire and he himself had been mortally wounded. From 1949 on into the twenty-first century, each of the three men had a building at Tech named to commemorate him.

Postwar changes in Tech's physical environment included construction of the Alumni Mall, leading toward the Drillfield from Main Street, and a War Memorial Chapel, built between the Mall and the Drillfield. When completed in 1960, the Memorial Chapel commemorated all Tech's fallen soldiers of World War Two. Since then, it has also come to commemorate the dead from other wars, from World War One to the present. Above the Chapel itself are eight pylons that represent brotherhood, honor, leadership, sacrifice, service, loyalty, duty, and the university motto, "Ut Prosim," plus a cenotaph titled "Medal of Honor Alumni" that now lists eight names.

Coordinate Colleges

UVA and VPI each began an affiliation with a coordinate female college in 1944. In UVA's case the push for such an arrangement dated back to the 1910s, though its proponents had in mind a coordinate college in Charlottesville, not a drive of a couple of hours to Fredericksburg. In the case of VPI, the new arrangement, with a school only half an hour's drive away, retarded the process of gender integration that had begun in 1921.

Over the years, the white women's normal schools evolved from their origins and modified their curricula to offer more liberal arts courses. The State Normal and Industrial School for Women at Radford, for example, became Radford State Teachers College in 1924—a name that continued to reveal its origins and its main mission—and began to grant baccalaureate degrees in 1936. In 1928, the State Normal School for Women at Fredericksburg adopted the name State Teachers College at Fredericksburg. As both schools developed collegiate instruction, they evolved into schools that might be merged in some fashion with historically male colleges.

Mary Washington and UVA

In 1928, the campaign to provide UVA a coordinate women's college resurfaced, and the legislature established a commission to explore the question. Various schools and cities emerged as possible places for such a college, including the public teachers' schools at Harrisonburg and Fredericksburg, the private women's colleges at Hollins and Sweet Briar, and the cities of Lynchburg and Roanoke.

In 1932 the legislature passed a bill to designate the Fredericksburg school the liberal arts women's college of UVA. Spokesmen for UVA heartily approved, at the same time that they refused to hear of such a school in or anywhere near Charlottesville. Women's groups, for their part, rejected the idea since the Fredericksburg school did not approximate UVA as a liberal arts college. Citing the state's dismal financial condition and therefore the unavailability of funds to accomplish the proposed change, Governor John Garland Pollard vetoed the measure. Nothing had been settled.

The legislature approved a change of name for the school in 1938 to Mary Washington College, and in 1943 Governor Colgate W. Darden revived the 1932 proposal for partial consolidation. Such an arrangement gained approval in 1944. After a four-year transition period, Mary Washington College would be reinvented, converted into a school "with the same standards of admission and graduation as obtain for male students in the College of Arts and Sciences . . . at Charlottesville." The Fredericksburg school became "Mary Washington College of the University of Virginia," alternatively "The Woman's College of the University of Virginia"—much like its North Carolina counterpart at Greensboro.

VPI's Radford Connection

Governor Darden matched his call for coordination between UVA and Mary Washington with a call for a similar arrangement between VPI and Radford. Enacted at almost the same time as the UVA merger, in some key ways the VPI measure resembled its companion.

The 1944 connection led to a change of name for each school. Virginia Agricultural and Mechanical College and Polytechnic Institute assumed the shorter name by which it long been known anyway, Virginia Polytechnic Institute. At the same time, Radford State Teachers College became Radford College, Woman's Division of Virginia Polytechnic Institute.

In the years that followed, then, VPI had two main campuses, not just the one. The statute consistently termed Radford the "Woman's Division"; it referred to Blacksburg as either the "Men's Division" or the "Men's Campus." The very term "VPI" became ambiguous, officially comprising both campuses but more often used to refer just to Blacksburg. Reflecting the new arrangement, four women were added to the VPI Board of Visitors.

An early version of the consolidation of the two schools would have barred undergraduate women from living at the Blacksburg campus. Male students, in a gesture that contrasted with the earlier resistance to female enrollment, expressed strong opposition to the prospect of a reversion to all-male. As enacted, the bill permitted four categories of women to enroll as VPI students at Blacksburg: graduate students; undergraduates who had reached the age of 21; undergraduates who could be day students because their residence was in or near Blacksburg—thus permitting the daughters of faculty to enroll, as well as other nearby young women; and a residual category of students whom the Board of Visitors had discretion to approve.

Some female students had to make their way from Radford to Blacksburg to take a class, and some faculty from Blacksburg had to go to Radford to teach one. As a rule, undergraduate women students at Blacksburg could enroll only in the school's core curricula: engineering, agriculture, or business. Teacher training for female students was to be had at Radford. Both schools retained something of their programs in home economics, but with students taking their first two years at Radford and their final two years at Blacksburg.

Women, never plentiful at Blacksburg, continued nonetheless to play various campus roles during the years of the Radford connection. During the school year 1946–1947, for example, Freda Polansky (B.S. '47, industrial engineering) became the first female student editor-in-chief of *The Virginia Tech*. During 1949–1950, Doris Tomczak edited *The Virginia Tech Engineer*. Thora Elrath served as business manager of the 1950 *Bugle*, and managing editor of the 1951 edition, and she was also on the editorial staff of *The Virginia Tech* and president of the YWCA.

Most of the women students at Blacksburg—about a hundred—continued to live in Hillcrest. When Mary Virginia Jones, class of 1962, entered Tech in 1958, she was the only first-year woman studying mechanical engineering and one of only six first-year women studying engineering at all. She could enroll at Blacksburg because she was pursuing a program of study that Radford did not offer, also because as the daughter of a professor she lived nearby.

John R. Hutcheson, president,
1945–1947

Walter S. Newman, president,
1947–1962

The new dispensation did not affect graduate students. The first woman to earn a Ph.D. at Tech was Betty Delores Stough, in 1953; the second, Irene Monahan, in 1961.

End of the Burruss Era

Julian Burruss presided over VPI from 1919 to 1945. He accomplished the political engineering that brought the first women students to Tech in 1921 and also the vast construction of the New Deal years. At a dinner in June 1944 honoring him for his twenty-five years as president, it was announced that the Board of Visitors had given the Teaching and Administration Building a new name, Julian A. Burruss Hall.

Yet the president's job had become overwhelming for one man. The Board of Visitors had acted to relieve Burruss of some of the overwork by creating a new office, executive assistant to the president, and asking John Redd Hutcheson to take it on. Dr. Hutcheson earned his B.S. at Tech in 1907 and his M.S. in 1909. He served as a livestock specialist for the Virginia Agricultural Extension Service in the 1910s and then, for a time, as assistant director of Extension. Since 1919, in fact since the day Burruss was appointed president at VPI, Hutcheson had directed the Agricultural Extension Division.

The aging Burruss presided over the school until an automobile accident in early 1945 made it impossible for him to continue. Hutcheson agreed to serve as acting president and then, for a time, as president. He attempted to be less remote than Burruss had often seemed, in part by communicating more frequently—and by telephone rather than typed memo—and even by actually meeting with students and faculty.

When Burruss died two years after his accident, the *Roanoke World-News* observed that, in a state that "appreciates monuments to its heroes and great men, there could be no finer or more fitting memorial" for Burruss than the school that he had turned into "a magnificently expanded college of nation-wide reputation."

In the late 1940s, Tech adopted an administrative system that unburdened the president of many of the responsibilities that had overwhelmed Burruss in his later years. Hutcheson convinced the Board of Visitors that the school needed a financial and business manager, and he appointed Stuart K. Cassell (B.S. 1932, M.S. 1933) to the post. Beginning in 1945, English professor Dr. Paul H. Farrier filled the new post of director of admissions. When the Board created the position of vice-president, Dr. Walter S. Newman agreed to fill it.

In 1947, when President Hutcheson succumbed to a sustained bout of ill health, Vice-President Newman succeeded him, Tech's third consecutive president to be an alumnus. Hutcheson recovered and, when the Board of Visitors established the VPI Educational Foundation in 1948—today's Virginia Tech Foundation—it named Hutcheson as its president. He served ably in that capacity until his death in 1962.

Virginia State Retirement System

Until 1942, Virginia Tech offered no pension benefits, and professors often labored far longer than their declining health and energy made advisable. The Virginia legislature began that year to address the problem of pensions for state employees.

Under the Virginia State Retirement Act of 1942, teachers and other state employees could obtain pensions after reaching the age of 65 if they had at least 20 years of service. For people who were already state employees on July 1, 1942, joining the retirement system was optional but carried with it a mandatory retirement at age 70. For later employees, participation in the system was mandatory. In a manner similar to the way the new federal system of Social Security worked, both the employee and the state contributed into the retirement fund. In the early years, the pensions were so small that many faculty chose to continue teaching, and thus they bypassed the mandatory retirement feature and continued to draw salaries larger than the available pensions. Over the years, the pensions grew in size, so, even before participation in the retirement system became mandatory, pensions offered sufficient inducement for some old-timers to retire.

A host of venerable VPI professors retired from their posts in the years around 1950. Professor Charles W. Holdaway, for example, served on the faculty for forty-eight years, from the time of President John McBryde until the time of President Walter Newman, before he retired as head of dairy husbandry in 1952. Dr. Frank L. Robeson, class of 1904, retired as head of the physics department in 1954. Recruited from the University of Kentucky to replace him was future Virginia Tech president T. Marshall Hahn Jr.

The G.I. Bill and America

One of the great pieces of Congressional legislation of the twentieth century—comparable to the nineteenth-century

Morrill Acts of 1862 and 1890—was the Servicemen's
Readjustment Act of 1944, or G.I. Bill. Designed in part to
reward returning soldiers after the war, in part to boost their
opportunities in the postwar world, and in part to keep them
out of job market while the economy converted from wartime
to peacetime production, the G.I. Bill offered substantial
assistance toward obtaining a higher education.

The G.I. Bill applied to anyone who served honorably in
the war and whose military service had "impeded, delayed,
interrupted, or interfered with" his education, defined as
including all people who had been under the age of twenty-
five when they entered the military. Within specified limits,
the government would cover tuition costs as well as supply
a monthly subsistence allowance for living expenses.
Beneficiaries must begin their studies within two years of their
discharge from the military, and benefits would not extend
more than seven years past the end of the war.

In the late 1940s, the G.I. Bill had a tremendous impact on
returning veterans and on the schools across America in which
they enrolled. A great bulge of additional students—at Tech,
UVA, William and Mary, Virginia State, and a great many
other colleges around the country—made their way through the
curriculum. Having seen far too much death and destruction
and determined to make the most of the peace, they went out
to become the nation's next generation of teachers, engineers,
farmers, and businessmen. A second bulge of veterans passed
through Tech and those other schools after the Korean War.

The G.I. Bill and Virginia Tech

Thousands of older students, including Henry Dekker, enrolled
at Virginia Tech under the G.I. Bill. Total enrollment at the
Blacksburg campus reached 5,458 during the 1947–1948
academic year, the highest number yet. Where to put all these
students? Like many other schools, including UVA, Tech
adopted the idea of trailer parks—one that the vets dubbed

"Vetsville" near Solitude and another, "Cassell Heights," on the hill. Classrooms and housing alike were scrounged at the Radford Arsenal, which housed about 900 students and came soon to be known as "Rad-Tech." Women who had served during the war as WACs and WAVEs enrolled under the G.I. Bill mostly at the Radford campus.

The enrollment of veterans at Blacksburg peaked during 1948–1949, when total enrollment reached 5,689. The fall quarter of 1949 marked the completion of three new dormitories—Femoyer, Monteith, and Thomas, named for Tech's three recipients of the Congressional Medal of Honor for service during the war. The use of Rad-Tech ended, and with it the fleet of buses that students called "Yellow Perils." The federal government revved up use of the Radford facility as part of its Cold War activities.

Life in Blacksburg and at VPI changed as veterans of the war enrolled at Tech. Never since 1872 had first-time Tech students outnumbered returning students. The newcomers collectively brought little knowledge of Tech traditions and were disinclined to defer to them. Having just served during the war, most were finished with the military. They enrolled as civilians, who soon outnumbered cadets. Relations between cadets and civilians were sometimes tense, and veterans energized a movement demanding that "The Corps Must Go." The Corps did not go, but in 1964 participation became optional for all male undergraduates.

The Cosmopolitan Club

The Cosmopolitan Club reflected some North American students' interest in foreign cultures as well as the presence at VPI of some students from other countries. Its membership in 1949–1950, for example, included women from Germany, Bulgaria, and China, plus Puerto Rico, and men from Poland, Russia, Iran, Syria, India, Guatemala, Argentina, and Rhodesia.

Neither the Cosmopolitan Club nor the presence of students from Asia was entirely new to Virginia colleges in the late

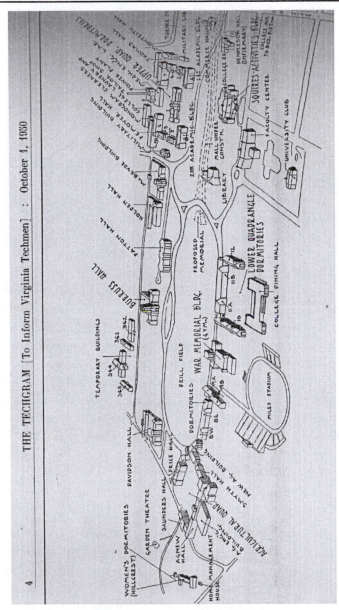

Map of VPI campus, 1950
How does it compare with your own observations?

1940s, though the number from Asia was—and by the 1940s some of the students of Asian ancestry were American born.

At Virginia Military Institute, cadets from China had enrolled as early as 1904; the first graduated in 1908; and others followed. Three generations of one Chinese family, the Wens, established their own VMI tradition by attending the school. The most famous VMI student from China, Sun Li-Jen, graduated in 1927 and returned to his homeland as an officer in the Chinese Nationalist Army, to which General Sun brought distinguished service through World War Two and after.

Cato Lee '27

VPI and UVA also enrolled an occasional Asian student as early as the 1920s. Tien-Lian Jeu, for example, after spending his freshman year at VMI, graduated from VPI in 1924 in electrical engineering. He overlapped at Tech for one year with his friend Cato Lee (Lee Kee-Tow), who had accompanied him across the Pacific from Hong King in 1920 but, younger than Jeu, attended Fork Union Military Academy before starting college.

Cato Lee graduated from VPI in mechanical engineering in 1927. The *Bugle* that year listed him as a member of the Cosmopolitan Club, though it offered no photograph of the group. It also said that, a "speedy hurdler," he had been a member of the varsity track and tennis teams. After quoting a line from Rudyard Kipling, the *Bugle* said with reference to Lee that "the gentleman of the East is not different from the gentleman of the West."

Among the members of the Cosmopolitan Club at mid-century was Yvonne Rohran Tung, class of 1950. Also from East Asia, she majored in horticulture, lived at Hillcrest, and belonged to the Baptist Student Union. Here was a student—not male, not white, not military; not Virginian or even American—who embodied everything that the early student population at Virginia Tech was not. So did her sister, Shiran Tung, who had graduated a year earlier.

Philip See Jung Lee, another ethnic Chinese student, represented a variation on key themes that Henry Dekker also embodied during the 1940s. See-Jung Lee entered the U.S. from China, a world at war, in 1940 at age 17 with his 16-year-old sister, Jee-Jung (Margaret), both of them welcomed by their father, Rev. Shau Yan Lee, who had come to America a decade earlier as a Baptist minister to Chinese Americans. They all escaped the Chinese Exclusion Act by virtue of his status and their young age. Soon they were both living in Norfolk, where Philip worked at a Chinese restaurant and Margaret attended Maury High School, the city's leading "white" high school. Then, from early 1943 until May 1945, he served in the U.S. Army, after which he promptly put the G.I. Bill to work by completing his lower-division studies at VPI's Norfolk division. During that time he married Helen Toylan Din, an ethnic Chinese former high school classmate of his sister's. Then he enrolled at the Blacksburg campus, where he graduated in 1949 in civil engineering, a profession he followed for the rest of his life.

In the 1940s, China also supplied a commencement speaker and a professor. The commencement speaker in September 1944—as World War Two continued in Asia with China an American ally—was Dr. W. C. Yang, the president of Soochow University. In 1948, Hung-Yu Loh joined the Virginia Tech faculty. Dr. Loh had earned a B.S. from Soochow University in 1931, an M.S. at Virginia Tech in 1943, and a Ph.D. from Johns Hopkins in 1946. He taught physics until he retired in the 1970s, and he won the Wine Award as the outstanding teacher in the School of Applied Science and Business Administration in 1959.

Membership in the Cosmopolitan Club signaled a student population that drew from places great distances from Virginia, and it signaled, too, the presence of nonwhite students on an "all-white" campus. Professor Hung-Yu Loh's three older children graduated in 1955, 1957, and 1961. Enrollment at Tech, although clearly not all-white, long remained completely non-African American. The first black applicant gained admission in 1953, the same year as another freshman, Dr. Loh's daughter Evanne. Both were strong students, but his taking classes was remarkable, hers remarkably unremarkable.

Yvonne Rohran Tung '50

References

Alvey, *Mary Washington College*, 175–79, 225–28, 256–314.

The Bugle (1927), 183; (1941); (1947), 122, 201; (1948), 80, 238; (1949), 153, 245; (1950), 104, 114, 337.

Corks and Curls (1923), 119, 123; (1924), 149.

Couper, *One Hundred Years at V.M.I.*, 4: 95.

Cox, *Generations of Women Leaders*, 13–15, 34–36.

Dabney, *Mr. Jefferson's University*, 230–70, 366–69.

Dethloff, *Texas A&M University*, 2: 450–500.

Godson et al., *College of William and Mary*, 2: 647, 697–712.

Humes, *How the G.I. Bill Transformed the American Dream*, 107–34.

Kinnear, *The First 100 Years*, 316–76.

Lee-aphon, *Cato Lee*.

Lewis-Smith, *Radford College*, 82–90.

Littlejohn and Ford, *Norfolk's Public Schools*, 8–47.

Robertson, *Historical Data Book*, 84, 91.

Wise, *Drawing out the Man*, 85.

Irving Linwood Peddrew III, 1953

Chapter 11
1950s: The First Black Students

Everywhere in the South, state-supported higher education was
born segregated, and it stayed that way for generations—even
though a huge shift took place after 1865, when African
Americans moved beyond absolute exclusion and gained some
sort of access. In the singular exception to the absolute rule of
segregation, the University of South Carolina accepted African
Americans into undergraduate programs and also the medical
school and the law school for four years in the 1870s, during
Reconstruction.

Virginia exemplified the regional pattern with its 1872
law dividing the Morrill Act's land-grant funds, two-thirds to
Virginia Agricultural and Mechanical College and one-third
to Hampton Institute. So the language in 1896 in *Plessy v.
Ferguson* regarding "equal, but separate" scarcely inaugurated
segregation—in higher education any more than in elementary
or secondary schooling.

At VPI, as early as the 1920s, an occasional Asian-
American or Asian applicant gained admittance, completed the
curriculum, and graduated. But just as the daughters of white
parents could not attend VPI until the 1920s, the sons and
daughters alike of black Virginians were categorically excluded
before the 1950s. The same was true at UVA and VMI.

At the Virginia Military Institute, a highly qualified black
Virginian applied for admission as early as 1953, yet not one
black cadet enrolled there before 1968. Similarly, of the four
Virginia schools that had started out as teachers' colleges
for white women, none admitted a black student until some

Charlie L. Yates '58

point in the 1960s. That leaves four historically white, state-supported institutions—the University of Virginia, the College of William and Mary, the Medical College of Virginia, and Virginia Polytechnic Institute—at each of which, under special circumstances, a very limited number of black students enrolled during the 1950s. They participated in what can be termed proto-desegregation, an early form of desegregation, scarcely the real thing.

This chapter briefly recounts the stories of the black pioneers at those four schools, especially VPI, where one lone soldier, Irving L. Peddrew III, stepped onto campus and began the process of desegregation in 1953. The next year, three more joined him. At VPI, the 1950s brought the enrollment of eight African Americans, never more than four at a time. All eight subsequently put their educations to good professional use. Five graduated from VPI—one among the first four, all of the next four—and three went on to earn either a doctorate or a law degree.

Charlie Lee Yates enrolled in 1954 and graduated in 1958, one of six honors graduates in mechanical engineering that year. Among historically-white, land-grant schools in the former Confederacy, only the University of Arkansas (which admitted black undergraduates beginning in 1955) and North Carolina State (1956) came close to matching the pioneer developments at VPI. At the other eight such institutions, black undergraduates did not even get to enroll before the 1960s. The flagship universities in those states, if separate institutions, displayed similar timelines.

Yates went on to earn a master's degree from Cal Tech and, after working for many years at Johns Hopkins University's Applied Physics Laboratory, earned a Ph.D. at Hopkins.

Returning to his alma mater, Dr. Yates taught mechanical engineering at Virginia Tech from 1979 to 1983. Then he left to set up an engineering program at Hampton Institute, and while away he served a term on Tech's Board of Visitors. Beginning in 1987, back again in Blacksburg, he taught aerospace engineering until his retirement in 2000. His license plates proclaimed—one can guess with some mixture of pride, affection, and defiance—"CLY58."

Up against Massive Resistance

Oliver W. Hill, born in 1907, grew up in Virginia before such opportunities as Charlie Yates experienced, and he helped bring about the changes that made them possible. Hill attended Howard University, first as an undergraduate and then, with no law school available to African Americans in Virginia, for a law degree. He graduated in 1933 with Thurgood Marshall. Later, from his law firm in Richmond, for decades he litigated civil rights cases in Virginia.

At mid-century, Hill occasionally traveled west across the Blue Ridge while looking after a case in federal court in Roanoke in which black parents from Pulaski County challenged the requirement that their children travel daily by bus to and from Christiansburg Institute to attend school. On one such trip, in April 1951, Hill stopped each way in Farmville, in Prince Edward County, in response to an urgent request by Barbara Johns and other black students there who had gone on strike against the crowded and dilapidated Moton High School. They wanted a school more equal to the white one. Hill offered to take their case but only on the condition that the suit attack segregation directly.

From Prince Edward, Hill and his colleagues ended up taking to the U.S. Supreme Court one of the cluster of cases called *Brown v. Board of Education*, decided in May 1954. That ruling declared that the traditional formula of "separate but equal" could no longer be applied to public schools: segregation itself violated the Fourteenth Amendment's Equal

Protection Clause. State-mandated racial segregation of public schools, both elementary and secondary, was unconstitutional and would have to go.

In the 1940s, education cases brought by black Virginians in the federal courts, all of them regarding elementary and secondary schooling, focused on extracting more of the "equal" from the old formula "separate but equal"; and then after 1950 the emphasis turned to attacking the "separate." The Prince Edward case exemplified the shift. One of the great questions in Virginia in the 1950s, especially after 1954, related to black access to white schools (white students were not seeking admittance to black schools).

Elementary and segregated education gained most of the headlines, yet higher education faced similar issues. The story at Virginia Tech can only be understood in the larger contexts of the state, the South, and the nation. And it illustrates how "desegregation," when it came, was a gradual process more than a specific event—not at all simply the enrollment of the first black student.

The Supreme Court decisions in *Brown v. Board of Education* in 1954 and 1955 overrode Virginia's constitutional requirement that "white and colored children shall not be taught in the same school." Yet, in response to *Brown*, Virginia threw what U.S. Senator Harry F. Byrd termed "Massive Resistance" in the way of the desegregation of public K–12 schools.

Rather than permit a black child to attend school with whites, the state shuttered some schools—and contemplated closing down the entire system of public schools throughout Virginia. So nowhere in Virginia did any of those schools integrate at all before 1959, and little if any change occurred in most places before well into the 1960s. Therefore the black students admitted to Tech in the 1950s all entered an overwhelmingly white institution from all-black high schools.

The process of racial desegregation at Tech, though slow and grudging, was far quicker and smoother than in Virginia's

K–12 schools—and quicker than at most institutions of higher
education in Virginia, whether private or public, or schools
at any level in the Deep South. Yet the top administrators at
Virginia's white institutions looked backwards on race, not
forwards.

As their top priority, they sought to safeguard their
institution, not foster social change. As Tech alumnus and
Blacksburg pastor Ellison A. Smyth later put it concerning
the Byrd Organization's power and VPI president Walter S.
Newman's anti-integration attitudes and behavior, it was "an
educational system where Richmond called all the signals. And
if you weren't in cahoots with the Richmond gang, you didn't
get the appropriations."

Maintaining Segregation in Higher Education, 1935–1950

The black applicants from the 1950s were by no means the
first to seek admission to a white institution in Virginia. Most
notably, Alice Jackson, a graduate of all-black Virginia Union
University in Richmond and a graduate student in French at
Smith College in Massachusetts, applied for admission to UVA
in 1935 to continue her studies in foreign languages. Before
1920, she would have been rejected for her gender as well
as her racial identity, but now it was on racial grounds alone.
Virginia legislators responded to Alice Jackson's effort with
two actions designed to deflect black applicants from white
schools.

Virginia State College for Negroes (its formal name then)
undertook to establish master's programs. The first, launched in
1937, were in elementary and secondary education, designed to
fit the needs of black teachers. Graduate programs in English,
history, home economics, mathematics, and sociology soon
followed. None of these would have addressed Alice Jackson's
aspirations, but a companion program did.

Under the Stephen-Donell Act of 1936, the state offered to cover qualifying black Virginians' costs at out-of-state schools—in tuition, living expenses, and transportation—to the extent, that is, that they exceeded the costs of obtaining a comparable education in Virginia. Hundreds of black Virginians took advantage of the grants program to attend schools like Columbia University, New York University, Howard University, and Meharry Medical College. The two New York schools offered strong graduate programs in education and thus attracted teachers. The two black schools most attracted people who wished to study law or medicine.

Almost as soon as these two programs went into effect, one of them fell short of a 1938 ruling by the U.S. Supreme Court. In a case that arose in Missouri, the Court ruled that a state, if offering a program like law to white citizens, must offer such a program, in-state, to black citizens too—though that might be at a segregated black school, the path forward that Missouri authorities chose. The law school at the University of Missouri could not reject black applicants, in this case Lloyd Gaines, just because the state offered to contribute toward his costs to study in another state. The Court was not ordering the white program to desegregate, but it was narrowing the constitutional grounds for outright rejection of black applicants to a graduate or professional program.

Though Virginia's program of modest grants regarding out-of-state schools could not have passed constitutional muster in federal court, black Virginians did not challenge it in court through the 1940s. Beneficiaries typically no doubt wanted to get on with their lives; considered the likelihood of legal victory dim; and calculated that they were going to have to front much of the money for their education anyway. The state treasury was offering to cover the additional costs of going outside the state, so they might as well go to a quality institution like Columbia University.

The Supreme Court, 1948–1950

During the twenty years before *Brown* v. *Board of Education*, however, various African Americans, like Lloyd Gaines, went to court to challenge their exclusion from "public" institutions of higher education. Those cases came out of the Deep South (the seven states that originally formed the Confederacy); the Upper South (states that seceded some months later, like Virginia); and the Border South (six other segregated states). In time as well as space, Virginia fell between the Border South and the Deep South. Black applicants who became plaintiffs in court cases challenging their exclusion on racial grounds were often able to force change.

Many cases were resolved in lower courts—sometimes state courts, usually federal—especially in the years around 1950. Resolution could take more than one form. In Florida, for example, a federal court ruling led the state to authorize some graduate and professional programs at the black land-grant school. In North Carolina, a federal court directed the UNC law school to accept qualified black applicants. In 1950, a state court directed the University of Missouri to enroll two black freshmen seeking technical programs as well as a black graduate student, and that same year a state court directed the University of Delaware to admit black undergraduates on the grounds that the flagship university was vastly superior to the black land-grant school, which had just lost its accreditation.

People whose cases reached the U.S. Supreme Court in the late 1940s came from Oklahoma and Texas. Ada Lois Sipuel Fisher, for one, did not mean so much to change anything in Virginia as to change something in Oklahoma, but she spurred change in both. An excellent student at Langston University (Oklahoma's black land-grant institution), she applied to the University of Oklahoma Law School in 1946, but the board of regents turned her down on racial grounds. With Thurgood Marshall as her chief lawyer, she took a case to the Supreme Court, which ruled that the state had to find her a place in law school. The sham substitute quickly erected did not satisfy her, so she took another case to the Supreme Court, and she won again. This time, she was permitted to enroll. Even the 1948 case led authorities at the University of Arkansas and the University of Delaware to change their rules and permit the enrollment of qualified black applicants in professional and graduate programs.

Two Supreme Court cases in June 1950—building on the rulings on Fisher's struggles—tightened the requirements imposed upon state authorities. *Sweatt v. Painter* and *McLaurin v. Oklahoma* made it clear that, not only must a segregated state supply black access to an appropriate in-state program, but that, if separate, that program must meet a definition of "equal" that included not only such quantifiable measures as numbers of courses or library books but also qualitative criteria like the school's reputation. The University of Texas Law School had to admit Heman Sweatt. And if a black student gained admittance to a previously white program, no school could—as Oklahoma had with Ada Lois Sipuel Fisher and George W. McLaurin— segregate that student (assign specially marked "colored" sections) in the classroom, the library, or the cafeteria.

Graduate Programs in Virginia, 1950–1953

The June 1950 Supreme Court rulings had immediate results at the University of Virginia. Gregory Swanson, a 1949 graduate of Howard University Law School, had passed the Virginia bar—and was working for the lawyer Oliver Hill—when he applied for admission to the law school at UVA to do graduate work. Despite the recent court decisions and the continuing lack of a law school for black Virginians, UVA turned down a qualified candidate and awaited a challenge in the courts. Unwilling to alienate alumni and legislators by appearing to give up too easily, university officials left it to judicial authorities to mandate Swanson's admission.

Hill and Swanson went to federal district court in Richmond; the court so ordered; and Swanson enrolled in

September 1950 for the fall semester. From that moment, although black students at historically-white institutions of higher education remained scant for many years, those in Virginia could no longer be clearly divided between all-black and no-black.

Black Virginians continued to seek admission to just the kinds of graduate and professional programs—law, medicine, education, the arts and sciences—that UVA offered. Racial barriers, however, had not vanished. Days after Swanson's admission, Robert A. Smithey applied to do graduate work in English and education. Virginia State offered such opportunities, though, and UVA was able to deflect Smithey there.

By contrast, another black applicant to UVA proved successful. Walter N. Ridley, a faculty member at Virginia State College, hoped to complete a doctoral program in education at UVA. Before Swanson's court victory, Ridley had experienced rejection there. Immediately afterwards, though, in September 1950 he gained admission. A new dean of education, Lindley J. Stiles, helped him quickly take advantage of the new possibility. Ridley became the first black doctoral student to enroll at any white public university in the South (and no black school had such a program) and, in 1953, the first to earn a doctoral degree there.

Faced with the new legal and constitutional environment, officials at the College of William and Mary, too, might accept a black applicant, though they gave it consideration for some time before determining that they had no choice. In 1951, they admitted Edward A. Travis to the Marshall-Wythe Law School, and in 1954 Travis became William and Mary's first black alumnus. Also in 1951, the school accepted Hulon Willis for a master's degree unavailable at Virginia State. Willis, a 1949 graduate of Virginia State, taught school in Norfolk and took classes in Williamsburg only in the summers before his graduation in 1956. Meantime, whenever feasible, William and Mary rejected other black applicants on racial grounds, for example Dorothy Smith in 1954 on the basis that Virginia State offered a graduate program in elementary education.

At the Richmond Professional Institute, a branch of William and Mary, some black applicants—among them James Gilliam—applied for fall 1950 but were turned back. For fall 1951, though, Hilda Yates Warden and a few others began classes as graduate students in the School of Social Work. She completed her master's degree in 1954.

Growing up as a black child in Richmond, not far from either (all-black) Virginia Union University or (no-black) Medical College of Virginia, Jean Louise Harris expected to attend the one but could scarcely dream of enrolling at the other. But her graduation from Virginia Union in 1951 came at a propitious time. She had figured on attending an out-of-state medical school—probably Howard University or Meharry Medical College—with assistance from a Virginia state scholarship. Instead, she found herself admitted into MCV. Not only did she complete her M.D. there in 1955, she (much later) taught there as a professor.

Virginia Tech, 1951–1953

VPI was exempt from many of the pressures to desegregate. Tech offered no graduate work in foreign languages, so Alice Jackson would never have considered applying there in 1935. Gregory Swanson sought only an institution with a law school, Walter Ridley a doctorate in education. Tech nevertheless offered graduate study in many fields unavailable at Virginia State.

And then there was engineering. The cases that reached the U.S. Supreme Court, from the Missouri case in the late 1930s through the Texas and Oklahoma cases decided in 1950, had all concerned schooling beyond the bachelor's degree, whether in law or some other field. Yet Virginia State College offered no engineering curriculum, even at the undergraduate level, while UVA and VPI both did.

Then again, an applicant to VPI might not wish to
study engineering. Everett Pierce Raney had taken classes
at Hampton Institute and then at Virginia State's Norfolk
Division (today's Norfolk State University). Having
completed the junior-college curriculum at Norfolk in business
administration, he sought in 1951 to continue his study in that
field at Tech. As college presidents customarily did in the early
1950s on questions such as Raney was raising, VPI president
Newman consulted J. Lindsay Almond Jr., the state attorney
general. Almond assured Newman that Virginia State offered
a bachelor's degree program in business administration, so
Raney had no need to go to Blacksburg. Tech rejected him.

In August 1951, President Newman received a letter from
the Virginia Teachers Association, representing the black
teachers of Virginia's black public schools, asking Newman
how VPI would treat applications from any among them
to study there. After consulting with the Board of Visitors,
Newman wrote back that Tech would admit qualified applicants
to programs that Virginia State College did not offer. Given the
range of master's programs that Virginia State had inaugurated
over the past dozen years or so (in the aftermath of Alice
Jackson's application to UVA), along with the absence at VPI
of doctoral study in education, Newman's letter conceded little
likelihood that Tech would receive an application from a black
teacher it could not reject.

Two years later, in 1953, Tech had yet to admit a black
student, graduate or undergraduate. But a related question
had arisen: How should the institution treat groups meeting
on campus with black as well as white participants? UVA
permitted black visitors to eat in the cafeteria; VPI did not.
One such occasion had arisen when the Virginia Social Science
Association, having in one or another recent year held its
annual conferences on both campuses, demanded that Newman
explain its shabby treatment of black guests at Tech. At a July
1953 meeting of the Board of Visitors, Newman explained that
Tech would "continue to have embarrassing situations" until

Floyd Wilson

it admitted its first black graduate student and opened all facilities to him.

Irving Peddrew and VPI, 1953–1956: Desegregation and Undergraduate Engineering

Already by then, Irving L. Peddrew III had applied for admission to study electrical engineering, not as a graduate student but as an undergraduate. He applied to UVA, but never heard back; to VMI, and was advised to consider Howard University; and to VPI.

President Newman made the rounds. He consulted Attorney General Almond and Governor John S. Battle. He told the BOV that admissions interviews had reported Peddrew a readily acceptable student and a "very decent sort of individual." The attorney general had made it clear to Newman that Tech had no legal leg to stand on if it rejected Peddrew and if he responded by taking a case to federal court. Peddrew has declared that he never meant to do any such thing, but VPI authorities had no such assurance. He would have been just as happy—much happier—to follow through on his plans to take a state scholarship to do out-of-state work in engineering at the University of Southern California.

Alas, Tech admitted Peddrew. Not any random freshman, Peddrew climbed through the narrow window of "graduate and professional programs"—among them undergraduate engineering. In September 1953, he became the first black student admitted to Tech. In fact, he became the very first black *undergraduate* admitted to an historically-white, state-supported, four-year institution of higher education in

Virginia or indeed—aside from South Carolina back in the 1870s—anywhere in the former Confederacy.

VPI officials therefore chose not to address all the conditions that Newman had pointed toward in his discussion of the Virginia Social Science Association. Peddrew was not a graduate student, nor was he admitted to all the school's facilities. Rather, he was defined as a "day military student"—typically, cadets who had obtained permission to marry and live off campus, not unmarried cadets who were required to live and eat off campus.

Lindsay Cherry, in the Hoge house

Peddrew—like each of the seven later black students at VPI during the 1950s—lived with an elderly black couple in town, Janie and William Hoge, at 306 East Clay Street, roughly a mile hike from the campus buildings where engineering classes were held. He had to walk home and back in the winter cold and slush if he wanted to eat a hot lunch. And, while he sought out the electrical engineering program, he understood that he did not have the option, as his white classmates did, to switch out of engineering—to change majors yet remain at VPI.

In 1954, three seniors at Norfolk's Booker T. Washington High School applied to VPI. Dr. Paul H. Farrier, the admissions director, traveled to Tidewater to interview the candidates and their families, and Newman went along to form his own judgment. Afterwards, he directed Farrier to admit Lindsay Cherry, Floyd Wilson, and Charlie Yates to the School of Engineering and the Corps of Cadets. The three comprised their own support group, and they reinforced Peddrew's ability to persist.

The three entering freshmen, all of whom lived with Mr. and Mrs. Hoge, followed different trajectories over the next four years. Charlie Yates stayed and graduated. Floyd Wilson, whom Lindsay Cherry has described as the brightest of them all, left after one year for a career in the U.S. Air Force. Lindsay Cherry, who had always suffered from eye problems, worked through the pain to accomplish his assignments, but, after the first of multiple eye surgeries, got a summer job in New York City with the U.S. Postal Service to help pay for his treatments and never returned. Later, after time in Asia courtesy of Uncle Sam, he returned to the USPS, but this time by no means still a mail sorter; and, over a distinguished career, deployed his gifts and his training to create or upgrade the data processing computer programs—shipping, inventory, payroll—that the USPS would rely upon across the nation.

Two vignettes suggest the impact Peddrew had on VPI, even as a stepson of the school. He recalls the graduating senior, for example, blue-eyed and blonde, who told him, "You possibly could imagine what I thought and what I've been led to think. But I want to tell you . . . you've changed my mind." And he recounts how, called to Burruss Hall in 1954, he was told that his performance had permitted officials to see the experiment as a success such that they should take a chance on the trio from Norfolk.

That said, the reason that Charlie Yates could be the first to graduate among the earliest black students was that Irving Peddrew chose to leave after his third year. His considerations were many. Most of all, after the close of that academic year he went to Southern California for six weeks to participate in a program, Students in Vocation, with the YMCA/YWCA. And with people getting to know each other pretty well, some asked him why, in view of his disappointment with his college life at VPI, did he feel he had to return—something along the lines, as he put it many years later, of "we think you deserve better than what you've been exposed to."

Some weeks earlier, Peddrew and his girlfriend had looked forward to attending the Ring Dance, but he had been advised by President Newman—and even by allies, supportive people he had met through Paul Derring's YMCA—not to attend, an experience that may well have shaped his predisposition, as it must have been a brutal reminder that, outside of classes, VPI was not his college.

Finding himself actually at the University of Southern California, the very place he had planned on attending college in the first place, certainly played into his thoughts and feelings. Finally, he knew that the experiment he had lived had worked out. Floyd Wilson had already left VPI, but Lindsay Cherry and Charlie Yates had settled in, and an additional black student had just finished his freshman year. Peddrew's work had been a success. He could move on.

Matthew M. Winston and Essex E. Finney Jr., 1955–1959

Tech admitted a fifth black freshman in 1955, Booker T. Washington High School valedictorian Matthew M. Winston, and then a transfer sophomore from Virginia State College—switching from one land-grant school to another—Essex E. Finney Jr., in 1956. Winston took Floyd Wilson's place at the Clay Street house; Finney took the place of Irving Peddrew.

Both knew to take literally the kind of language that Essex Finney saw in his acceptance letter: "We have decided that we can accept you at VPI . . . to take our course in agricultural engineering." In addition, President Newman called Winston into his office to urge him not to attend the Ring Dance his junior year. Newman referred to the wishes of "higher ups"—by whom Winston gathered he meant officials in Richmond—and also declared that "the townspeople would not stand for it."

Matthew M. Winston '59

Yet Winston has reported no recollection of hostile treatment from his classmates. To the contrary, he recalls their consternation when, if invited to go out for food or coffee, he explained that Virginia law did not permit him to accompany them off-campus, and school policy prevented such on campus. The sit-ins of February 1960 occurred the year after he graduated. So did the admission of the first black undergraduates at a host of southern land-grant schools: Tennessee, Clemson, Georgia, Florida, Auburn, Mississippi State, Texas A&M.

"I was not here on a crusade or mission," Winston would later recall. "I just wanted to go to school." Beyond that, the early black students fretted that, if they rocked the boat, they might be expelled. They kept their heads down and did the work.

Winston and Finney both graduated in 1959. Winston moved back to Tidewater, where he put his training in mechanical engineering to good effect in a career at Langley Research Center with NASA. Finney went on to earn a master's degree at Penn State and a Ph.D. at a second northern land-grant school, Michigan State, and he spent a distinguished career with the U.S. Department of Agriculture.

James Leslie Whitehurst Jr., 1959–1963

James Leslie Whitehurst Jr. and Robert Garfield Wells both entered Tech in 1959. Intent, like Matthew Winston, on obtaining the best possible education, Whitehurst later explained that he had picked Virginia Tech over Virginia State because Tech had "better laboratories, better professors, and better equipment." He chose Tech even though, since the black school offered physics, he understood that he had to major in electrical engineering instead.

Like their predecessors, the two had been admitted to classes, not to all student activities and facilities. Required to live and eat off campus, for their first year they stayed with the Hoges. Whitehurst later recounted how, when he went to the snack bar at Squires Hall, he was asked to leave. He had been a football star at Norcom, the black high school in Portsmouth, but, though given a uniform, he watched practices from the sidelines for some weeks in fall 1960 before giving up the idea of playing in college.

Whitehurst had found something he did not seem able to change, so he left the goal of integrating athletics to later students. Determined to push the remaining boundaries back wherever he could, for his junior year Cadet Whitehurst demanded a room in the barracks, and he called on the law for support. President Newman and the Board of Visitors directed the dean of students, James W. Dean, to devise a plan whereby Blacksburg residents would—family by family, business by business—be advised of and encouraged to approve VPI's plans to integrate the campus and the town. So he lived his junior year in Lane Hall and ate in Owens Dining Hall. Moreover, he rebuffed President Newman's request that he not attend the Ring Dance.

The school that James Whitehurst and Robert Wells graduated from in 1963 had changed in the decade since Irving Peddrew applied for admission. Whitehurst went on to serve as an Air Force pilot, then in 1975 earned a law degree at UVA. During that time, Governor Linwood Holton appointed him as the first African American on the VPI Board of Visitors (1970–1974).

In 1979 Whitehurst returned to Tech, where he spoke to students and recalled his time there. "Both the school and I grew a lot as a result of those years," he observed. Of the university administrators, he remarked, "They were under pressure. They were cautious in advancing toward integration. I think they were afraid of endangering their state appropriation. I always understood their perspective and tried to work with them." Perhaps so, but he had pressed hard, both about living on campus and about attending Ring Dance. It had often been an ordeal for him, but he had pushed VPI farther, as he put it, "toward integration."

A Survey of the Segregated States

Virginia serves well as an example of the timing, process, and degree of racial desegregation in the 1950s. At the undergraduate level, VPI had its echo in Charlottesville, where three black students were admitted in engineering, as at VPI, though not until 1955, two years after Peddrew.

Two did not stay. George W. Harris Jr., for one, transferred to a black school, Virginia Union University, where he was arrested for joining a February 1960 sit-in; then attended another black institution for law school; and later served for two decades as a judge in Roanoke.

Robert A. Bland, by contrast, persisted. He graduated in electrical engineering in 1959 and—like Charlie Yates and Essex Finney—later earned a doctorate. Not until after Bland had graduated at UVA did it become possible for a black undergraduate there to major in something other than engineering—or to live on campus.

The Supreme Court decisions of 1938 and 1948–1950—and, later on, *Brown v. Board of Education*—applied in principle to all segregated states. In 1953, at about the same time as Irving Peddrew enrolled at VPI, Oklahoma Agricultural and Mechanical College admitted three black undergraduates—two in electrical engineering and one in veterinary medicine. Oklahoma had recently enacted a measure approving the admission of black undergraduates, on condition that the courses they sought were unavailable at Langston University.

Other Border South states acted in much the same way, some of them a bit earlier. Holloway Fields earned a B.S. at the University of Kentucky in 1951, for example, and Elbert C. Whisner at the University of Delaware in 1952, both in electrical engineering. Each had been admitted under the special "graduate and professional" category, since the program of study he sought was not offered at his state's black land-grant. In the wake of *Brown v. Board of Education*, the University of Maryland, the University of Missouri, and West Virginia University all adopted a policy in 1954 to

permit *in-state* residents to enroll as
undergraduates regardless of their
racial identities or curricular wishes.

Change typically took longer in
the rest of the South. In early 1955,
during Irving Peddrew's sophomore
year at VPI, LeRoy Benjamin
Frasier Jr. and two other seniors at
all-black Hillside High School in
Durham applied for admission to
the University of North Carolina
in nearby Chapel Hill. Promptly
rejected on racial grounds, the three
took the matter to federal court. A
three-judge panel ruled that *Brown
v. Board of Education* was "as
applicable to schools for higher

*Essex Finney '59 on his
graduation day with Mr.
and Mrs. Hoge outside
their Clay Street home*

education as to schools on the lower level" and directed UNC
to process the trio's applications without regard to their race.
All three began classes at Chapel Hill that fall.

The university administration and the state of North
Carolina, disinclined to accept the outcome, appealed the
ruling to the U.S. Supreme Court. Meanwhile, UNC refused
to consider applicants who had not been party to the case. In
March 1956, in *Board of Trustees of the University of North
Carolina v. Frasier*, the Supreme Court upheld the lower
court's ruling.

The trio could remain at UNC, and other black
undergraduates could gain admission there as well. Moreover,
that summer or fall, black undergraduates began studying at (to
use the later names) both North Carolina State University and
the University of North Carolina at Greensboro.

Beginning in March 1956, therefore, *Brown v. Board
of Education* applied to all state-supported undergraduate
programs across America. No more should students have had
to act as though the rules from 1950–1954 still held. Nobody

should have been compelled to make the choice—as James Whitehurst thought he still did in 1959—between entering Virginia Polytechnic Institute as an engineering student and studying physics at Virginia State College.

The NC State Model in Sports

North Carolina State—starting three years after Peddrew's enrollment, but three years before Whitehurst's—moved quickly past VPI. The first cohort of black undergraduates, four in all, broke through barrier after barrier. Irwin Holmes and Walter Holmes (no relation) both moved into a campus dormitory in early 1957, the spring of their freshman year. Irwin Holmes and Manuel Crockett both joined the freshman indoor track team and that February set a precedent by competing against Chapel Hill.

Walter Holmes joined the football marching band. In the fall of his sophomore year, when NC State had an away game at Clemson, he marched out onto the field just like any other member of the band. The temerity that he—and the rest of the band, in fact NC State in general—showed their hosts stunned the crowd. The president of Clemson and the state attorney general issued a policy statement that, whatever might be permitted in another state, South Carolina's policies would have to be complied with at events held there.

Meanwhile, Irwin Holmes had switched from freshman track to freshman tennis, where he was the best player on the team. During his sophomore season—following Walter Holmes's trip to Clemson—both Clemson and the University of South Carolina balked at permitting him to play on their home courts. After his coach refused one alternative, going on the road without him, both South Carolina schools, in a compromise, agreed to play the matches at Raleigh instead. Holmes competed at NC State for three years on varsity, and in 1960, his senior year, he served as co-captain. During that time, white supremacy and black exclusion persisted on the two Deep South campuses.

All that said, like VPI and the two South Carolina schools, North Carolina State held off permitting black students to play on the football team—or basketball—until well into the 1960s.

VPI's Initial Steps toward Desegregation

With regard to black enrollment, VPI in the 1950s appears in a split image: on the one hand, the grudging and partial acceptance of the black pioneers; on the other hand, the fact that they were admitted at all—and before *Brown v. Board of Education*, and without a specific court order. After Peddrew began classes at VPI, two years elapsed before either UNC or UVA enrolled a black undergraduate. More than that, Whitehurst and Wells both completed their degrees before any black student, graduate or undergraduate, ever enrolled at Deep South land-grant schools Auburn or Mississippi State.

Gaining admission into a program, as at VPI, was scarcely the same as desegregating a school. None of the eight pioneer black students at VPI was free to select a major outside of engineering. Required as underclassmen to participate in the Corp of Cadets, they were nonetheless barred from living in the barracks. As for representing their school in intercollegiate athletics, that, too, was out of the question. Yet gaining admission at all was an absolute prerequisite to breaking down other barriers.

One by one, those additional barriers, too, eventually fell. Matthew Winston, graduating in 1959, never lived on campus and was urged to skip his Ring Dance. James Whitehurst set new precedents on both fronts. But he had to fight, and fight again, and he never played a down for his college's football team.

References

Interviews with Matthew M. Winston Sr. (in VT Stories) and with Irving L. Peddrew III, Charlie L. Yates, and Essex E. Finney Jr. (all on the website of Special Collections and University Archives).

Cherry, *The Life of Lindsay Cherry*.

Dean, James W. "The Early History of Affirmative Action at Virginia Tech: An Historical Account," *Diversity News* 1 (Spring 1995): 5–6.

Deel, "Virginia's Minimal Resistance."

Fisher, *The Autobiography of Ada Lois Sipuel Fisher*.

Hollis, *University of South Carolina*, 2: 61–79.

Kinnear, *The First 100 Years*, 396. Compare with Robertson, *Historical Data Book*, 24.

Kluger, *Simple Justice*, 256–84, 451–79.

Martin, "Black Education in Montgomery County," 68–72, 145–47.

Ollove, Michael. "Fighter Broke Racial Barriers at Virginia Tech," *Roanoke Times and World News*, May 13, 1979.

Smyth, Ellison A., interview with Michael A. Cooke, in the Black Appalachian Oral History Project, March 5, 1991, Special Collections and University Archives, Virginia Tech.

Trillin, *An Education in Georgia*.

Tushnet, *NAACP's Legal Strategy*, 49–143.

Wallenstein, "Desegregating the University of North Carolina."

Wallenstein, ed., *Higher Education and the Civil Rights Movement*.

Chapter 12
1960s: State University

Mississippi-born Laura Jane Harper arrived at VPI in 1949 as associate professor of foods and nutrition. In 1960, Dr. Harper became dean of the new School (later, College) of Home Economics, where she remained until she retired in 1980. For a time while the Radford and Blacksburg campuses were administratively connected, she directed the home economics programs at both places. Active in research in nutrition, she exemplified Virginia Tech's tripartite mission of research, teaching, and service as the school emerged

Laura Jane Harper, dean, Home Economics

as a major university. Moreover, she played crucial roles in fostering the personal and professional development of women, white and black alike, at a historically white-male institution. Dean Harper gave the Founders Day address in 1980, "Against the Odds: Women at VPI."

President T. Marshall Hahn Jr., who drove the extraordinary changes of the 1960s, came to know the nation's land-grant schools as a student, a professor, and an administrator. He earned his B.S. in physics in 1945 from the University of Kentucky at the age of eighteen and earned his Ph.D. at MIT in 1950. He returned to Kentucky, where he taught as associate professor and then professor, before moving to VPI in 1954 as department head in physics. He went to Kansas State

T. Marshall Hahn Jr.

University in 1959 as dean of the new College of Arts and Sciences, and he returned to Tech as president in 1962. Hahn entered upon the presidency at Virginia Tech with a vision of the school as a world-class university. His attempts to raise Tech to satisfy that vision came at a propitious time. Moreover, he understood that, to make that vision real, he would have to cultivate relationships with the Board of Visitors and other campus stakeholders, as well as with the state governor and legislature. Beyond all that, partly reflecting his tremendous input in state educational policy making, he had far greater financial support from the state budget than previous leaders of the school ever had.

President Hahn consistently termed VPI a "university." By 1970 it had become one in name, Virginia Polytechnic Institute and State University. Doctoral programs could be found in a wide range of areas, and master's degree programs in far more, including areas of inquiry far beyond the original scope of Virginia Agricultural and Mechanical College.

Among the decade's big changes, VPI's "woman's division" and "men's division" ended the institutional connection that had begun in 1944. At the same time, membership in the Corps of Cadets became an option, not a requirement—a pivotal event in Tech's history and one that occurred despite the opposition of many alumni. Tech's student population doubled in size, became mostly civilian, and grew considerably more diverse.

Public Policy and Higher Education

The public policy context of higher education underwent
extraordinary changes between the late 1950s and the early
1970s. The story is partly one of federal legislation, as this
chapter recounts, and partly one of state legislation, as the
following chapter will detail.

The Cold War framed much of federal policy in the generation after World War Two. The USSR's launching in 1957 of
Sputnik, the first man-made satellite in orbit, spurred the U.S.
government to direct unprecedented amounts of money toward
the training of scientists and engineers. The National Defense
Education Act of 1958 proved to be one of many measures
promoting higher education across America.

During the mid-1960s, Democrats controlled Congress,
Lyndon Johnson sat in the White House, and the Great Society
brought change in many spheres of life. Congress broadened
the scope of the National Defense Education Act in 1964 to
include disciplines like history and political science. It also
passed the Higher Education Facilities Act of 1963, which
supplied funds for construction; the Higher Education Act of
1965, which provided funds to colleges and universities; and
the Economic Opportunity Act of 1964 provided for work-
study, on-campus employment.

Other federal legislation addressed institutional discrimination on the basis of race or sex. The Civil Rights Act of
1964 specifically outlawed racial discrimination at facilities
that received federal funds. The Educational Amendments of
1972 similarly curtailed discrimination against women by any
program receiving federal funds. All these varied acts began
to change the ways that Tech and other institutions of higher
education conducted their business.

Arts and Sciences at a Land-Grant School

Midwestern land-grant schools had, early in their histories,
typically broadened their curricular offerings and become

full universities. Tech, by contrast, though it too had grown in degree, held back and remained close to its origins. One important consideration had long been state officials who spoke publicly of their concerns that the various schools were duplicating their efforts. A movement in the late 1920s had pushed to exclude all liberal arts courses from Tech's curriculum and close down the engineering school at UVA. President Burruss therefore always fretted about duplication, even while Tech offered ever more courses in the 1930s.

Long after Burruss stepped down, courses like history and English continued to be viewed as "service" courses, necessary evils perhaps, but not to be warmly embraced at a technical school and certainly not to offer degree programs. Their job description called for them to retain a subservient posture with respect to such core areas as agriculture and engineering.

By the 1960s, such concerns had diminished to the vanishing point. President Newman envisioned Tech as much more of a university, and President Hahn, from the time he arrived back on campus in 1962, spoke of Tech as "a land-grant university." As dean of the new College of Arts and Sciences, English professor G. Burke Johnston continued during the early Hahn years, as he had since his recruitment to VPI in 1950, to foster the emergence of the liberal arts.

The concept of a university is a potentially cosmic one. Such a school might offer a universe of courses to a universe of students. Or, as Cornell University founder Ezra Cornell put it, he wanted a school—and defined it as a "University"—"where any person can find instruction in any study." In stark contrast to the Virginia Agricultural and Mechanical College of the 1880s, the course offerings of the 1960s ranged far beyond the "agricultural and mechanical," and the student population began to include many women as well as men, more civilians than cadets, and people of all racial identities.

Changes in Tech's curriculum and organization, together with physical growth to match the academic expansion, came early in Hahn's administration. In August 1962, the State

Council of Higher Education approved a proposal that Tech begin granting degrees in English, history, and political science. In 1963, for the first time, Tech awarded B.S. diplomas to students with majors in these fields, among them history grads John M. Katon and Joseph H. Umbarger.

Word came in December 1963 that Tech had its first Rhodes Scholar, William Walker Lewis Jr. Excelling alike at athletics and academics, the younger Lewis majored in physics with a perfect grade point average and also captained the tennis team.

New programs continued to gain approval. In 1966, master's programs in two disciplines only recently approved for bachelor's degrees, English and history, were added. Tech recognized a new technical area by adding a B.S. major in computer science in 1970, the same year it marked the emergence of the arts and humanities at Tech with a B.A. in theatre arts—and the same year Tech officially became a university.

The Separation of VPI and Radford

The legislature combined the Blacksburg campus with Radford College in 1944. Twenty years later, it separated them, and each went on to develop into a university.

Leadership at the Blacksburg campus initiated the uncoupling. Both schools had grown prodigiously since 1944—the "Men's Campus" to the largest school in Virginia, the "Woman's Division" to the largest among the women's colleges. Coordinating the two institutions had never been easy or smooth, and their growing size made such ever more difficult. From Hahn's perspective, moreover, the Blacksburg campus could never become a research powerhouse if the salary schedules of the two campuses remained linked. At Radford, one might gain promotion and tenure by completing the dissertation; Blacksburg's expectations were moving toward substantial published scholarship.

After the division between the Radford and Blacksburg campuses, women students could enroll as freshmen in any academic program Tech offered, and they quickly began

attending the Blacksburg campus in ever larger numbers. Total
enrollment there reached 10,000 for the first time in fall semester 1968 and 11,000 a year later. While undergraduate men
contributed to this growth—after all, they comprised half of the
baby boom—the number of women students topped 1,000 for
the first time in fall 1968.

Graduate enrollment also continued to surge. The last year
with fewer than 200 graduate degrees awarded was 1961. By
1975 the total exceeded 1,000 (see Appendix D).

Reorganizing a University

Sometimes it seemed everything was changing at Tech. A combined student government replaced the old division between
civilian and cadet governments in 1966, and M. Garland
Rigney, a political science major, became the new group's
first president. In January 1970, the undergraduate newspaper
traded in the name *The Virginia Tech*, which dated from 1903,
for a new one, *The Collegiate Times*.

Tech gave up its long-distance undergraduate divisions to
a new statewide system of community colleges (as discussed
in the next chapter). Far-flung graduate centers began to take
their place as offshoots from the Blacksburg campus. In a
major reorganization, various activities were brought together
in 1966 as the Research Division and the Extension Division.
No longer would agriculture and home economics dominate
the Extension functions, as Tech's outreach programs reflected
Virginia's increasing urbanization.

In the 1950s, Tech maintained three "schools": the School
of Agriculture, the School of Engineering (in 1955 it became
the School of Engineering and Architecture), and the School of
Applied Science and Business Administration. The latter school
grew and divided. A School of Home Economics emerged
from it in 1960. A separate School of Business Administration
gained approval that year and emerged in 1961 as the School
of Business. The remainder became the School of Science

and General Studies and then, in 1963, the School of Arts and Sciences.

In 1964, each of these components became a "College" instead of a "School," and architecture broke away from engineering. By the early 1970s, Tech had colleges of Agriculture, Engineering, Architecture, Business, Arts and Sciences, and Home Economics, as well as a Graduate School and a new College of Education.

Faculty Tenure, Student Evaluations

Student evaluations and faculty tenure alike originated in the 1950s and shaped academic life in the 1960s. Neither played any role in Virginia Tech's early years. In the 1880s, the Board of Visitors could, if it wished, make an abrupt and clean sweep of president and faculty. Beginning with President McBryde in the 1890s, the board generally let the president decide who to hire and who to fire. The new dispensation persisted into the 1950s.

In 1953, President Newman discovered to his consternation that things might have to change with respect to faculty personnel. After the Southern Association of Colleges and Secondary Schools criticized Tech for having failed to adopt a tenure policy, Newman appointed a faculty committee to report back. It drafted a policy statement based on a declaration by the American Association of University Professors dating from 1940. The Board of Visitors quickly adopted the new way of doing the business of hiring and firing faculty.

In the 1950s, therefore, Tech put into place a system that evolved a bit but endured. After a probationary period, faculty would be retained or let go, and if retained it would be with considerable employment security. Thus originated the world of the 1980s and 1990s and beyond in which assistant professors, if they satisfied what typically were fairly stringent criteria for retention, became tenured, usually with promotion to associate professor. Associate professors—though not all ever made the attempt—might satisfy a further set of requirements and gain promotion to full professor. Such promotions had to make their way past review by the department, the college, central administration, and the Board of Visitors.

A related development, also originating in the 1950s, led to students evaluating at least some of their courses. Student course evaluations became widespread only in the 1970s, after the organization of the Faculty Senate in 1969. Not all courses were evaluated at first. Regardless, student assessments of their faculty offered only one basis for annual performance evaluation and only one basis for decisions regarding faculty retention, promotion, and merit pay raises. Yet instruction remained a central part of Tech's mission, and evaluations by students offered one systematic means of informing personnel decisions—even if course evaluations had as one ostensible purpose simply helping teachers improve their teaching.

Black Athletes and Black Women at Tech

Black students came to Blacksburg in 1966, no longer just one or two or three at a time—or under prohibitive restrictions as to housing and curricula—but suddenly in double-digits, and some had been actively recruited with a scholarship funded by the Rockefeller Foundation. Six were young women: Linda Adams, "Jackie" Butler, Linda Edmonds, "Freddi" Hairston, Marguerite Harper, and Chiquita Hudson. From Tech's origins in 1872, forty-nine years elapsed before the first white women enrolled; thirteen years went by between the first black male student in 1953 and the first black women.

Chiquita Hudson—a graduate of Phenix High, also the school in Hampton that had produced Irving Peddrew thirteen years earlier, and the only engineering major among the six—was ill and died after her first year. Freddi Hairston married and left school after two years—and later earned a Ph.D. and became a professor, as Dr. LaVerne Higgins. Linda Adams—who had become VPI's first black female student when she enrolled in 1964 at a branch campus in Clifton Forge—came to the Blacksburg campus as a junior, studying statistics, and finished in 1968, Tech's first black female graduate.

Chiquita Hudson, Marguerite Harper, and Linda Adams

The other three graduated within four years, Marguerite Harper with a major in history and Jackie Butler in sociology. Everything about Harper and Butler embodied the new Virginia Tech—not only were they female students, but they were African American, and they majored in history and sociology, not in home economics or engineering. Whether because of restrictions on gender or on race or on curricular offerings, nothing of the sort could have happened before the 1960s. Harper went on to become an award-winning high school teacher. Linda Edmonds, who had planned to attend Hampton Institute, not a white school, graduated in clothing and textiles and subsequently earned a master's at Michigan State and a doctorate in business from Virginia Tech.

The first black men and black women of VPI found a campus where they could thrive academically but often did not feel at home socially. In spring 1968, several of those who came to Blacksburg in 1966 or 1967—including Stan Harris, Larry Beale, and Jim Watkins—formed a new group primarily for black students, a VPI chapter of Groove Phi Groove.

For the very first black students, in the 1950s, admission to Tech carried with it little more than the privilege of taking classes toward a degree. By the time James Whitehurst graduated in 1963, thanks to his efforts black students could eat and room on campus. Whitehurst failed, however, in his effort to break through the racial barrier and join the football team.

Virginia's public institutions of higher education began to field integrated sports teams in the late 1960s and early 1970s. The first black athlete recruited to an historically white public institution in Virginia enrolled at Old Dominion College on a basketball scholarship in 1965, Arthur "Buttons" Speakes. At Virginia Tech, the first African American intercollegiate athletes enrolled in 1967. Larry Beale joined the freshman basketball team that year, and Jerry Gaines—Tech's first black student to receive an athletic scholarship—starred on the track team. Intercollegiate athletics for female students—regardless of racial identity—developed in the years afterwards.

So sports integration for men had begun. A biracial basketball team from Virginia Tech won the NIT in 1973. In the 1990s such Tech athletes as Eugene Chung, Antonio Freeman, and Jim Druckenmiller entered the National Football League after embodying the multiracial make-up of Tech's sports teams.

Male Cadets—Black and White—at VMI and VPI

Should military training be required of all male students? At a land-grant school, the question had to be addressed, and tradition went further than the 1862 Morrill Act in shaping each school's answer. At Tech, membership in the Corps of Cadets, long mandatory, became optional for juniors and seniors beginning in 1924–1925, but it remained required for the first two years. Forty years later, effective with the 1964–1965 academic year, the Board of Visitors made it voluntary even for first-year men.

The Corps of Cadets at Virginia Tech and Virginia Military Institute alike remained all male and all white or, rather, all non-African American, into the 1950s. The first black students at Tech in the 1950s, all men, had to participate in the Corps for at least their first two years, just as white male students then did. Virginia Military Institute finally admitted its first black cadets in 1968: Larry H. Foster, Harry W. Gore Jr., Adam L.

Randolph III, Richard E. Valentine Jr., and Philip L. Wilkerson Jr. During the next few years, the black cadets of VMI entered into the life of the school much as white cadets there did. Gore served as managing editor of the school newspaper, *The V.M.I. Cadet*, and Valentine as assistant editor of the 1972 yearbook, *The Bomb*. Wilkerson became a company commander.

Collectively, black VMI cadets influenced school traditions by bringing a perspective that clashed with the past. When they declined to give the customary salute to Robert E. Lee as they passed Lee Chapel, some white cadets emulated them. And the tradition of playing "Dixie" at athletic events soon faded.

At Virginia Tech, the dual changes of the 1960s on gender and the military led to a transformed student population. During the academic year 1963–1964—the year before the split with Radford and the conversion of the Corps to an option for men—the student population on the Blacksburg campus, roughly 6,500, included about 2,000 members of the Corps and fewer than 300 women. By 1971–1972, the aggregate student population had doubled to 13,000; membership in the Corps had dropped below 600; and the number of women students neared 4,000, none of them yet permitted to become cadets.

America's Land-Grant Schools in the 1960s

At the beginning of the 1960s, many of the nation's land-grant schools retained ample evidence of their beginnings as agricultural and mechanical colleges. Many land-grant institutions outside the South, however, had begun as coeducational schools, moved early on to a wider curriculum, and had become full-fledged universities. Other schools were well advanced in the transition. Most land-grant schools were public, though M.I.T. and Cornell University were both private.

Into the 1950s and beyond, seventeen states, from Delaware to Oklahoma as well as from Florida to Texas, retained a dual system with one land-grant school for whites and another for blacks. At some point in the 1950s or 1960s, the historically white schools—the land-grant schools and state universities alike where, as in Virginia, these were separate institutions—all admitted their first African American students. Some, like VPI and West Virginia University, did so with relative ease by the mid-1950s, though in very small numbers and without enthusiasm, as the previous chapter showed. At others—the universities of Georgia, Alabama, and Mississippi—the first gesture toward racial desegregation came with public pain, anger, and at least the threat of violence. By the end of the 1960s, however, this great transition, too, was well under way.

By the 1960s, most land-grant schools admitted men and women more or less alike. Rutgers, though, long maintained separate undergraduate schools for men and women, and VPI's coordinate arrangement with Radford did much to curtail full gender integration.

On the gender front, a late battle over enrollment took place at Texas A&M, a school that replicated Tech's history though with its own twists. There, as so often, the question of coeducation was tangled with the question of compulsory military education. Texas A&M confirmed its stand in the 1950s and stood alone not only in maintaining a mandatory participation in the military for virtually all students but also in remaining all-male. Both changes came in the 1960s. A lawsuit filed by women seeking coeducation ended up at the U.S. Supreme Court, but the Court looked the other way. The board of directors, acting on its own, decided in 1963 that women could be admitted to the school provided they were the wives or daughters of students or faculty, pursued a program of study unavailable elsewhere in Texas, or did graduate work. In 1965, Texas A&M abolished compulsory participation in its Corps of Cadets. By 1971 women were admitted with none of the previous restrictions, and in 1972 a women's dormitory opened on campus.

As land-grant schools took on new identities, they adopted new names. Some shed their earlier identities when they did so—Kansas State University, North Carolina State University, Oklahoma State University. Texas Agricultural and Mechanical College became Texas A&M University in 1963. In 1971, Texas A&M advertised itself as "a coeducational university admitting all qualified men and women to all academic studies on the same basis without regard to race, creed, color or national origin." During the 1960s, in short, Texas A&M displayed the kinds of adjustments under President James Earl Rudder that Virginia Tech did under President T. Marshall Hahn.

Students Contesting Students over Flags

Many issues divided the nation during the 1960s, none more than race or the Vietnam War. The war was long and costly, far longer for Americans than World War One or Two, and 46 former students at VPI have their names inscribed on the campus War Memorial. Opposition to the war mounted as the decade unfolded, and demonstrations came to Tech, as they did to a great many of the nation's campuses.

Southern schools with white traditions also faced challenges from students—among them Marguerite Harper—who objected when the band played "Dixie" at football games or the Confederate battle flag snapped in the wind. Black students at white schools encountered traditions they found objectionable, and whites were often bewildered when objections were registered.

Early one April morning in 1968, the Corps of Cadets' flag detail, as usual, raised the flags of Virginia and the United States at Burruss Hall. Soon after 6 o'clock that morning, hours after the murder in Memphis of Martin Luther King Jr., a small interracial group of Tech students went to Burruss and lowered the flags to half-mast.

The Virginia Tech ran a story, "Students Stage Vigil at Burruss to Honor King," that told how the group—described as "displaying black arm bands" and conducting "a sit-in"—stayed at their post at the flagpole to talk among themselves and to discuss issues with other students. One group member noted with approval afterwards that they had occasioned considerable "thinking and talking." Around noon, however, a larger group of students forcibly raised the flags again. A short while later, President Lyndon Johnson directed that all U.S. flags be lowered to half-mast.

Two years later, Tech students punctuated the end of the 1960s with the school's largest demonstration of the decade. President Richard M. Nixon's widening of the Vietnam War— the incursion into Cambodia in May 1970—led to confrontations across the country that left four young people dead at Kent State University in Ohio and two at Jackson State in Mississippi. At Tech, more than one hundred students occupied Williams Hall overnight and were arrested.

A New McBryde, a New Squires

An array of new buildings went up during the 1960s and into the 1970s. A new home for work in biochemistry and nutrition (later named Engel Hall), for example, was completed during fall 1961. In January 1962, the men's basketball team first played a game in what would soon become known as Cassell Coliseum, rather than the much smaller War Memorial Gym, dating from 1926.

Many more followed. Lane Stadium—named for Edward H. Lane, class of 1910—was dedicated in 1965; it replaced the much smaller Miles Stadium, which also dated from 1926. Other new structures included a new McBryde Hall, built on the site of the earlier one from the 1910s. The new McBryde functioned as a metaphor for the great changes at Tech since its early days. The original McBryde Building of Mechanic Arts was a shop building, complete with lathes, saws, forges, and planes. The McBryde of the 1970s and 1980s housed the departments of history, political science, and sociology, as well as math and an even newer major, computer science.

Derring Hall, which opened in 1969, was named for Paul

Derring, who worked with students as YMCA secretary and in other capacities from 1918 to 1964. Squires Hall, the old Student Activities Building, had a facelift and more between 1966 and 1970, as renovation tripled it in size, and it emerged with a new name, Squires Student Center. If one could start over, it would seem more appropriate to have named the Student Activities Building after Paul Derring.

In a race to keep up with demands for space, Tech embarked on still other construction in the late 1960s and early 1970s. Cowgill Hall—named for Clinton H. Cowgill, who headed the architectural engineering department from 1928 to 1956—provided a new home for the newly separate College of Architecture. The College of Home Economics moved in 1969 into Wallace Hall, named for Maude E. Wallace, who served as state home demonstration agent and then assistant director of Extension between 1929 and 1959. Burruss gained more space at the back, and Lane Stadium gained thousands of additional seats. The Carol M. Newman Library, named for a professor of English, 1903–1941 (he was also widely considered the patron saint of extracurricular activities at VPI), opened in 1955 and doubled in volume two decades later.

The construction of I-81, the interstate highway that runs past Christiansburg on its way from Pennsylvania to Tennessee, brought Blacksburg and Virginia Tech far closer in time than ever before to northern and even eastern Virginia. Earth movers were working on Christiansburg Mountain in 1969, at the same time that renovation continued at Squires.

Housing a Growing Town and School

New student housing went up off campus and on. By early 1962, buildings soon to be named Barringer Hall (named for Tech's sixth president) and Vawter Hall (named for Charles Erastus Vawter Sr., member of the BOV, 1886–1900, and its extremely influential rector, 1891–1900) were in use. Additional residence halls, built between 1964 and 1970, included Lee Hall, named for Claudius Lee, who served on the faculty from his graduation in 1896 until 1946; O'Shaughnessy Hall, named for Louis O'Shaughnessy, professor of mathematics and civil engineering from 1918 to 1954; Newman Hall, named for Tech's tenth president; Miles Hall, named for C. P. "Sally" Miles, class of 1901, athlete, coach, and athletic director; and Ambler Johnston Hall, named for J. Ambler Johnston, class of 1904 and campus architect.

Those new residence halls were all meant for male students. Where to put the additional women? Beginning in 1966, Tech converted two men's dormitories, Eggleston and Campbell, to residence halls for women, and then, to replace Hillcrest (which, expanded, became a dorm for male athletes), constructed a new high-rise home for women, Slusher Hall—named for Clarice Slusher, class of 1927 (VPI's third entering cohort of female freshmen) and the school's registrar from 1937 to 1963. It opened in 1972.

As Tech grew, so did Blacksburg. The school ran out of space to house students, and the community became home to the surplus. Not that students tended to mind, for after a year or two on campus, many of them welcomed the freedom as well as the responsibility of fending more for themselves and finding their own places. For that to happen, there had to be places. In the 1960s and in succeeding decades, supply did not always keep up with demand.

The history of Tech has always been also a history of the surrounding community. Harry H. Hunt III and Peter Snyder helped transform the community. Hunt was an mortgage underwriter operating out of Virginia Beach, and Snyder had been a student at Virginia Tech, when they met in 1965 and formed a partnership. That winter, they began putting up a constellation of apartment buildings, Terrace View. By 1973, in eight phases, they had built a total of 808 apartments.

A rapidly growing college community needs homes for faculty and graduate students as well as for undergraduates. West on Price's Fork Road, beginning in 1968 the Snyder Hunt partnership built Oak Manor, a community of 120 townhouses.

On what had been a farm a little farther out toward Price's Fork, between 1973 and 1984 Snyder Hunt built Hethwood, a planned urban development of 300 single-family houses, 300 townhouses, and the Foxridge complex of more than 1,600 apartments, together with amenities like a shopping center and basketball and tennis courts. Tech continued to grow, and Foxridge added still more apartments.

The Politics of Inclusion

In the 1960s, the land-grant system turned one hundred years old. In Virginia, a politics of inclusion renovated the entire system of higher education. A broadening of political participation pointed toward increased funding of public schools, enhanced access to higher education, and a more diverse student population. Federal work-study aid facilitated access by the sons and daughters of lower-income families, as did the new community college system discussed in the next chapter.

Virginia Tech exemplified the tremendous changes at public institutions of higher education across America, especially at land-grant schools in the South. A white men's military school, emphasizing engineering and agriculture, underwent swift if partial transformation. The dual decisions of 1964—one regarding Radford College and women, the other concerning the Corps of Cadets and men—did much to open the school to people who could not or would not have attended under the old rules. The changing policy environment represented by the Civil Rights Act of 1964, together with the new curricular offerings, did so as well. The Virginia Tech of 1970 was hardly the same school as the VPI of the early 1960s.

Working effectively with campus stakeholders and state authorities alike, President Hahn—together with his various allies—had created a university. In curriculum, student population, and so much more, Tech became a university. White women enrolled in far larger numbers than ever before. So did black students, both men and, beginning in 1966, women. Policy developments of the 1960s followed a path charted by the Morrill Acts of 1862 and 1890 and the G.I. Bill. Public education became more public.

And major institutions of higher education changed to align more closely with the "ideal type" (as the sociologist Max Weber might have termed it) of university. During the 1960s and early 1970s, the stand-alone land-grant institutions (like Virginia Tech) and the stand-alone flagship state universities (like the University of Virginia) converged in becoming similar, universities in the sense both of no social groups excluded from enrollment and no areas of human inquiry excluded from the curriculum.

It is easy to assume that the land-grants comprised the cluster doing the moving, as if trending toward a model already in place at the flagship schools. But flagship universities, including UVA, were changing substantially as well. And, in social terms, Virginia Tech preceded UVA, by several years, when it recruited white women, black women, and black men beginning by 1966.

References

Black Women at Virginia Tech Oral History Project, Special Collections and University Archives, Newman Library.

Cox, *Generations of Women Leaders*, 15–19, 39–50.

Dethloff, *Texas A&M University*, 2: 555–74.

Graham, *Federal Education Policy in the Kennedy and Johnson Years*.

Kinnear, *The First 100 Years*, 383–466.

Mattingly, "'We Were No Different': Virginia Military Institute Integrated 50 Years Ago," *Richmond Times-Dispatch*, December 20, 2018.

Miles, "Laura Jane Harper."

Minogue, "Students Stage Vigil at Burruss to Honor King," *The Virginia Tech*, April 10, 1968.

Strother and Wallenstein, *From VPI to State University*.

Thelin, *Going to College in the 1960s*.

Wallenstein, "The Morrill Land-Grant College Act of 1862," 107–17.

Centenial Celebration, 1972

The year 1972 occasioned a huge celebration at Virginia Tech, another in a series of major markers in its history. During four days in May 1922, looking back to its origins as a land-grant college in 1872, Virginia Polytechnic Institute had celebrated its Golden Jubilee. In 1962, it had celebrated its ninetieth birthday as a land-grant school in conjunction with the centenary of the Morrill Land-Grant College Act. And in 1972, Virginia Polytechnic Institute and State University celebrated the official completion of its first hundred years.

A campus publication, *The Techgram*, observed in September 1971 that the school was beginning its hundredth academic year and also kicking off a year-long centennial celebration. Enrollment reached roughly 13,000—appropriately enough, writers might have noted, one hundred times the figure from Virginia Agricultural and Mechanical College's first year.

Three major new buildings approached completion. One was Whittemore Hall, named for John W. Whittemore, faculty member for 35 years and dean of engineering from 1952 to 1963. Another was Cheatham Hall, designed to house programs in forestry and wildlife and named after Julian N. Cheatham, class of 1933 and executive vice-president of the Georgia-Pacific Corporation. The third was McBryde Hall, built on the site of the former McBryde Building, named for Tech's fifth president, and home of several departments in the new College of Arts and Sciences: foreign languages, mathematics, history, sociology, political science, and computer science.

Other kinds of monuments to Tech's growth also emerged in the centennial year. Scheduled for publication at the beginning of March 1972 was a 500-page book, a heroic undertaking, *The First 100 Years: A History of Virginia Polytechnic Institute and State University*. Its author was Duncan Lyle Kinnear, better known as Lyle or "Deacon."

Dr. Kinnear brought impressive credentials to his task. Having earned his bachelor's and master's degrees at Tech, he had taught psychology and education at his alma mater since 1936, so he had an intimate acquaintance with the school's more recent history. His dissertation, completed at Ohio State University in 1952, explored "A History of Agricultural Education in Virginia," so he also brought training in history and knowledge of his topic's early years. With the inducement of "one year of reduced teaching responsibilities and one year of no teaching" (as he reported) so he could focus on the assignment at hand, he agreed to take it on.

Kinnear rued that he had to proceed with very little previous written work on which to draw. Regarding Tech's faculty and staff of the first hundred years, he observed as he finished his book, "Everyone was so busy getting the job done that nobody worried about putting it down on paper."

"Beyond a shadow of a doubt," Kinnear wrote, "VPI in its first century was more concerned with making history by rendering service on all fronts than it was with recording this history." Yet he was committed to recounting "the contributions of its programs, faculty, and alumni to the state and the nation," and he had reason to be gratified with the response. One reviewer, Guy Friddell, spoke in glowing terms about how well Kinnear had gone about "light[ing] the candles" for Tech's "100th birthday."

Tech planned what was called a "Centennial Founders Day Program." March 19 marked the precise day the school turned a hundred, but the Board of Visitors, recognizing that March 19 of that year fell on a Sunday and during spring break, opted to schedule the observance five days later.

The Founders Day festivities harked back to the Golden
Jubilee in lining up participants. These included direct
descendants of the first student, of the first Board of Visitors,
and of every president of the institution beginning with
the first, Charles L. C. Minor, from 1872. Some speakers
represented the U.S. Department of Health, Education, and
Welfare; the State Council of Higher Education for Virginia;
or the State Board of Community Colleges. Another speaker
was John W. Hancock Jr., class of 1925 and president of the
VPI Educational Foundation, which had sponsored Kinnear's
book. President T. Marshall Hahn noted that Tech had begun
as a "people's university" and vowed that it would remain
one. Wilson B. Bell, the director of university development,
expressed the wish that Founders Day "become an annual event
on campus," a wish that came true for many years.

Various events followed during the year of celebration.
The evening after Founders Day, three women from Tech's
first coeducational class—Mary Brumfield Garnett, Lucy Lee
Lancaster, and Carrie T. Sibold—were feted at a dinner at the
Donaldson Brown Center for Continuing Education.

At a "rededication ceremony" for McBryde Hall in April,
faculty gathered and took their places in students' seats. Told
they should prepare for class by reading about President
McBryde, they took notes instead while Kinnear recited
McBryde's accomplishments. William C. Havard Jr., dean of
the College of Arts and Sciences, also spoke. During the same
ceremony, President Hahn, alumnus and architect J. Ambler
Johnston, and history department head and Civil War historian
James I. Robertson Jr. celebrated a bequest from Frank L.
Curtis to the history department in support of research in
Virginia history and the history of the Civil War.

Centennial Montgomery County Day took place on May
23 to recall the county's support of the school at that crucial
moment a hundred years before when the offer of $20,000 to
help launch a land-grant institution swung legislative votes to
the support of a little Methodist school located just up a small

hill from Blacksburg's sixteen squares. The 1972 Tech Board of Visitors, together with descendants of the 1872 county board of supervisors, attended a luncheon that ended with a huge cake that had 100 candles. Tech and the county's public schools alike dismissed afternoon classes, and thousands of people turned out to watch or march in a parade around campus and through downtown Blacksburg.

The Board of Visitors took various actions during the centennial year that set the stage for developments across the next quarter-century. The board approved a system of fraternities and sororities. It also established an Academy of Teaching Excellence; created the position of Alumni Distinguished Professor and named geology professor F. Donald Bloss the first ADP; and inaugurated Alumni Scholarships, the first five of which went to entering freshmen in 1972. The Alumni professorships and scholarships reflected initiatives of the Alumni Association, which wished to offer men and women who had once studied at Tech opportunities to observe the centennial celebration in tangible, continuing ways. And the Alumni Association was acting in accordance with President Hahn's observation that no better uses could be made of private contributions to the university.

Commencement took place as a centennial activity, and television newsman David Brinkley spoke at the graduation ceremony at Lane Stadium. Graduates—President Hahn designated them the "centennial graduation class"—numbered 2,118 who received bachelor's degrees, 385 who completed master's programs, and 114 who earned doctorates. Nearly as many people completed doctoral programs in the centennial year as had attended Tech in its first year. For its part, Virginia Tech commenced its second hundred years.

References

Bloss, *WWII, Mineralogy, and Me: A Memoir.*

Kinnear, *The First 100 Years,* vii–xiv.

Strother, Warren, "The View from Here," *Context* 6 (Summer 1972): 1–3.

Techgram, September 1971 through December 1972.

Chapter 13
1970s: A New World of Politics and Education

In the 1960s, Mills E. Godwin Jr. symbolized how much both he and the state had changed in a decade. He had been a leader in the Massive Resistance movement in the 1950s, when Virginia authorities responded to *Brown v. Board of Education* by preparing to close down any K–12 school, even the entire state system of public schools, rather than permit black children to enroll in "all-white" schools.

But after Godwin gained election to the governorship of Virginia in 1965, from his first day in office he expressed a commitment to public education. More state funds must be obtained, he urged, so that more could be invested in education—not only in elementary and secondary schools but also the existing four-year colleges and universities, plus a tier of two-year institutions to be created. Governor Godwin approached a legislature, moreover, that proved receptive to his agenda. As with President Hahn at Virginia Tech, Governor Godwin pushed ambitious plans at a propitious time. He and Hahn worked together to achieve much.

At Tech in the 1970s, the tremendous changes between 1962 and 1966 continued to unfold. Enrollment continued its sharp rise, chased by building construction. Emphasis on research continued to grow. Women, black as well as white, entered the Corps of Cadets. Between the early 1960s and the late 1970s, moreover, big changes reshaped higher education across the Commonwealth, and President Hahn had a mighty hand in some of those as well.

The year 1966 marked a transformation in the policy environment of higher education in Virginia. As is usual with historical change, one could see precursors that pointed toward it, and not everything changed all at once, but the events of 1966 led to the emergence of an educational universe in the 1970s vastly different from that even a decade earlier and radically different from a century before. Two state-initiated changes emerging in the decade beginning in 1966 had to do with better funding and new institutions. Both changes depended on a revamping of the political universe in Virginia that followed an urbanizing population, an enlarged electorate, and a reapportioned legislature.

The 1950s: Slow Growth, SCHEV, and a "Coordinated System"

During the 1950s, the legislature displayed little interest in promoting a proliferation of institutions of higher education or in a substantial increase in public funding for the existing ones. To the contrary, if the legislature hit the gas pedal in 1966, it had ridden the clutch and the brakes in the 1950s. The characteristic ideas of the 1950s sounded more familiar in the 1990s than did those of the 1960s and 1970s that are the focus of this chapter. Legislators before 1966 spoke of how state support for educational costs ought to move down, not up, and they yearned for a time when television's reach might reduce the costs of delivering educational outputs. In the late 1960s, by contrast, the public share went up.

Still, legislators recognized in the 1950s a need for some expansion of opportunities for higher education in Virginia. In 1954, it directed the Virginia Advisory Legislative Council to explore the branch campuses of Virginia state schools VPI, UVA, and William and Mary. The council responded with a report entitled "The Crisis in Higher Education in Virginia and a Solution." It highlighted an imminent crunch between the rising numbers of college-age Virginians and the shortage of facilities to accommodate them. Yet to handle the additional students, it proposed only an increase in two-year extension divisions of the existing schools.

In 1956 the legislature created the State Council of Higher Education for Virginia, a new agency responsible for coordinating the expansion of higher education in the Commonwealth. Whatever else SCHEV did, it was assigned the task of gatekeeping requests by existing institutions to plant new branches or divisions of the sort that William and Mary, UVA, and VPI had been developing during the preceding three decades. Legislators decided that Virginia's institutions of higher education must increasingly "constitute a coordinated system."

The idea of urban two-year facilities grew in favor. Their advantages were immense. They required no student outlays for housing, for students could live at home. They required no investment in dormitory construction, so they were vastly cheaper for the state and the schools. Relatively inexpensive for students and the state alike, they could offer technical courses that prepared some students for immediate employment, and they could offer lower-division courses that prepared other students for transfer to four-year institutions.

A New Social and Political Landscape

The 1950s began the process of re-conceiving the role of the state in fostering higher education for Virginians. The 1960s made greater action both necessary and feasible. The generation of baby boomers, born between 1946 and 1964, began to reach the age of eighteen by the mid-1960s. A reconstructed political system moved public policy into a whole new era.

As had been so often the case in Tech's earlier history, initiatives from the federal government in the 1960s framed developments in higher education in Virginia in the years that followed. Congress and the Supreme Court each played central roles.

A constitutional law case from Virginia, *Davis v. Mann*, was one of a cluster of cases from various states in 1962 in which the Supreme Court mandated reapportionment of both houses of the state legislature to equalize the value of the vote, with the consequence that rural areas lost power. After reapportionment, the cities and suburbs acquired far more power in the legislature than before, and they quickly put it to work. When the newly redistricted legislature met in 1966, it established both a statewide general sales tax and a community college system.

Other forces merged with the reapportionment decision in changing Virginia politics. One was the migration into Virginia of people determined to see the state take a more active role in promoting education at every level. Just as important, within Virginia, people were moving from farm to city and from jobs in agriculture to employment in industry and service. Moreover, in a huge change sweeping across America, the baby boomers were moving through high school and toward college in the 1960s.

A combination of formal amendment and judicial interpretation altered the U.S. Constitution and, as a consequence, the basis for formulating public policy in Virginia. The poll tax, one of the tools employed under the Virginia Constitution of 1902 to curtail voting by most black adults and also many whites, vanished from the political scene in the 1960s. The Twenty-fourth Amendment to the U.S. Constitution, ratified in early 1964, swept the poll tax away in federal elections, and a 1966 Supreme Court decision on a case that arose in Virginia, *Harper v. State Board of Elections*, eliminated it in state elections as well. Together with reapportionment, the end of the poll tax transformed politics in Virginia.

A new day dawned on Virginia politics. In terms of support for education and transportation, Godwin's administration resembled Governor Claude Swanson's sixty years earlier, with the huge distinction that in the late 1960s black Virginians were no longer excluded from the electorate or marginalized in the realm of education. In those respects, the Godwin administration resembled the Readjuster era of the 1880s more than it did the Swanson years.

Rearrangements

The uncoupling of the Blacksburg campus from Radford College in 1964 proved only the first of many rearrangements in higher education in Virginia over the next decade. In a similar change, the uncoupling of UVA and Mary Washington College took place in 1972. UVA had begun, at last, to admit women undergraduates on the Charlottesville campus in 1970, the same year Mary Washington began to admit men. Moreover, Tech let its branch colleges go, those dating from the 1930s and the much more recent ones as well.

Like Mary Washington, the other historically white teachers' colleges for women also became coeducational. Madison College began admitting men in 1966, Radford in 1972, and the last of the four, Longwood College, did so in 1976. Madison College's President G. Tyler Miller counted 164 tax-supported teachers' colleges in the United States, only four of them single-sex, and three of those were in Virginia. Men could take classes as "special" students, but they could not work toward a degree. Miller called throughout the 1950s for full coeducation, but he never got his way on that issue. The vote was sometimes close, even favorable in one house but not the other, but many legislators resisted voting for coeducation, especially when racial integration might be on its way—when some of the new male students to be admitted to a white women's college might turn out to be African American.

Indeed, whichever came first, all of the white women's teachers' colleges soon became both coeducational and multiracial. At Mary Washington College, for example, one black day student enrolled in summer 1962— a decade after the first such attempt—and another in summer 1963. But the school adopted a desegregation policy and admitted its first black resident student, Kaye Estelle Savage, only in 1964. By 1972 Mary Washington's first black graduate, Venus R. Jones '68, had earned an M.D. from UVA, and Savage herself was enrolled in a graduate program at Howard. Radford College admitted young women in the 1950s from Japan, Korea, Taiwan, the Philippines, and also Puerto Rico, but it enrolled its first students recognized as African American only in 1966.

One by one the four teachers' institutes became colleges, and then during the 1970s two became universities. Madison College became James Madison University in 1977, and Radford College, which began offering master's degrees in 1964, became Radford University in 1979.

Meantime, related changes were taking place at Virginia State College. In the 1950s and 1960s, an occasional white student sought enrollment at the Petersburg campus or the Norfolk branch, and the school began admitting white applicants as "special" students, ineligible for degrees. In the 1960s such students could at last be admitted as regular students, candidates for degrees. Similarly, as early as 1950, the school hired some non-black faculty on a part-time, adjunct basis. In 1964, Virginia State began hiring non-blacks as regular faculty. In that sense, something approaching integration came to Virginia State in 1964, as the rules of race changed in Virginia and the school incorporated some students and faculty of European and Asian as well as African ancestry.

By the 1970s, the old arrangements of separate schools by race, by gender, and by curriculum had been, in degree, dismantled. Men and women of every racial identity could attend every school, with the sole exception of male-only VMI. Yet Virginia Tech—largely white, male, and engineering— exemplified how each school carried its history and reflected its origins.

From Branch Colleges to Universities

Beginning in the 1930s, a number of Virginia's institutions of higher education launched distant divisions. Some of those emerged to become separate institutions, even universities with master's and doctoral programs. The College of William and Mary began a Norfolk division in 1930 that became a separate institution in 1962, Old Dominion College, and then Old Dominion University in 1970; future governor Mills Godwin himself began his collegiate studies there in 1931.

Another branch of William and Mary began operations as a two-year college in Newport News in 1960; it became a four-year institution in 1971 named Christopher Newport College, separated from its parent school in 1977, and became Christopher Newport University in 1992. The University of Virginia inaugurated an extension division in Fairfax in 1948 that, by 1972, had emerged as a separate institution, George Mason University.

Virginia Commonwealth University offers another example of these kinds of rearrangements. The Medical College of Virginia, having begun operations in Richmond as a medical department of Hampden-Sydney College, in the 1850s became a separate state-supported institution. Much later, a very different unit, the Richmond School of Social Work and Public Health began operations in 1917. It became the Richmond Division of the College of William and Mary in 1925 and the Richmond Professional Institute of that College in 1939. In 1962, the Richmond Professional Institute became a separate state institution, and in 1968 a merger with the Medical College of Virginia combined the two original pieces of a new entity, Virginia Commonwealth University.

Norfolk State University has its own backstory. It started out in 1935 as a junior college connected with a private black school in Richmond, Virginia Union University. By 1944 it was the Norfolk Division of Virginia State College, and a quarter-century later it became an independent public institution, Norfolk State College. It became Norfolk State University in 1979, the same year Virginia State College took the name Virginia State University.

The Virginia Community College System

The 1966 legislature inaugurated a general sales tax, directed revenues from that source to education at every level, and created a system of community colleges. Some of the community colleges came along only in the 1960s or 1970s, while others, in one incarnation or another, had been around for some years.

Virginia Tech had long maintained two-year programs at locations around the state, particularly Richmond and Norfolk. So, as we have seen, had William and Mary, UVA, and Virginia State. Tech's lower-division extension arrangements with William and Mary in Norfolk and with Bluefield College both ended in 1964, and the arrangement with the Richmond Professional Institute soon ended as well. Some of the various branch schools in Virginia rose to become independent universities, but most two-year programs moved into a new public system of community colleges.

Members of the new system included Blue Ridge Community College, located at Weyer's Cave and established in 1965 as Shenandoah Technical College. Another, located in Dublin, was New River Community College, which originated in 1959 as the New River Vocational and Technical School. What became Dabney S. Lancaster Community College began operations in 1964 as the Clifton Forge-Covington Division of VPI, joined the new system in 1966, and received its new name the next year. Virginia Western Community College resulted from the merger in 1966, of an extension division of UVA that began in 1927 and a more recent school, the Roanoke Technical Institute.

Northern Virginia Community College, which started out in 1965 as the Northern Virginia Technical College, gained its new name when it joined the new system in 1966, and it has since opened new campuses in Northern Virginia. Tidewater Community College was established only in 1968. Like its Northern Virginia counterpart, it developed multiple campuses and enrolled thousands of students.

By the early 1970s, many other schools had joined. Patrick Henry Community College, located in Martinsville, started out in the early 1960s as a branch of UVA and joined the new system in 1971. Eastern Shore Community College first offered classes in 1964, also as a branch of UVA; it, too, became a part of the community college system in 1971.

VPI also shed branches. Wytheville Community College, which first offered classes in 1963 as a two-year branch of VPI, joined the community college system in 1967. Danville Community College combined two existing institutions in 1967, when the Danville Technical Institute, which had originated in 1936, and the Danville Division of VPI, which was established in 1946, came together.

Beginning in the 1920s or 1930s, VPI as well as William and Mary, UVA, and Virginia State—each of Virginia's state-supported institutions of higher education except VMI and the white women's teachers' colleges—had launched one or more branch locations. By the 1970s, nearly every extension school had separated from its parent institution and either emerged as a university itself or joined the community college system.

Additional community colleges were soon authorized as well, among them J. Sergeant Reynolds Community College in Richmond. In the 1970s, a growing number and rising proportion of all the people studying at public institutions of higher education in Virginia were attending community colleges.

Race, Gender, and the Corps of Cadets

While the larger system of public higher education underwent all these rearrangements in the years around 1970, each institution itself made many adjustments. Virginia Tech went far toward completing the transformation of a white men's military school when it incorporated all groups of Virginians regardless of race or sex into every component of the educational system. In 1973, women even entered the Corps of Cadets.

Years before women could join the Corps, Patricia Ann Miller '59 tried, quarter after quarter, to enroll in military classes, but was rebuffed every time. At graduation, though, she was commissioned a second lieutenant in the Army Women's Medical Specialist Corps. Home Economics dean Laura Jane Harper later reported how perhaps every resident of Hillcrest stayed until commencement in order to witness the commissioning.

When the first women students at VPI enrolled in 1921, the conditions of their admission had expressly barred them from the military. The change in policy fifty-two years later reflected conditions both on the Tech campus and in the American military; it anticipated additional changes. After male students' participation in the Corps became voluntary in 1964, the number of cadets dropped sharply, and perhaps the admission of women would reverse the decline. From a broader perspective, Tech was simply offering women a kind of opportunity in ROTC that mirrored the growing opportunities for women in the U.S. military. Then again, the U.S. Naval Academy did not adopt coeducation until 1976, nor did the U.S. Military Academy.

Two women—sophomore Cheryl A. Butler and junior Deborah J. Noss—joined the Virginia Tech Corps of Cadets in 1973, and twenty-three more joined that first year. The Virginia Military Institute and The Citadel, where all students were military, did not have the civilian option that Tech permitted between the 1920s and the 1970s, and both resisted admitting women at all for another two decades and more.

Yet the pioneer female cadets comprised a separate unit, L Squadron, and admission of women into the Corps did not also bring admission into the regimental band, the Highty-Tighties. Back during World War Two, when Tech men were scarce, Radford women had been permitted for a time to play in the band, but that had been long ago. Beginning in 1971, however, even before women joined the Corps, they could join a drill team that marched with the Highty-Tighties. Starting out in 1975, women members of the Corps—Marilyn Helmeyer,

Stephanie Hahn, and others—joined the band itself. In 1979, women cadets were integrated into the previously all-male companies.

Compulsion regarding membership in the Corps of Cadets had vanished. When the first coeds enrolled at Tech in 1921, membership was mandatory for nearly all male undergraduates and banned for all women. The change in 1924 left membership mandatory for a male student's first two years, made it optional after those two years, and left it out of the question for a woman. A subsequent change in 1964 made it optional for all male students while continuing to ban women. Finally, in 1973, every U.S. undergraduate could choose to participate, and none was required to.

The World Comes to Blacksburg

Tech's emergence as a university carried along Blacksburg's development as a much more cosmopolitan community. As the curriculum expanded and the faculty grew, not only did virtually every new faculty member arrive at Tech with doctorate in hand, but the new recruits came from around the world. In the Department of Entomology, Michael Kosztarab began work in 1962 with an undergraduate degree from his native Hungary (which he had fled in 1956 after Soviet tanks rolled in) and a new doctorate from Ohio State. In 1972, Loke T. Kok arrived with degrees from his native Malaysia and the University of Wisconsin. Dr. Kosztarab won one of the three Wine Awards of 1967 for an outstanding teacher at Tech, and Professor Kok won one of the two Alumni Awards for research in 1986.

Similar stories could be found across the university. In 1971, Young-tsu Wong, born in Shanghai, China, began teaching in the history department by way of the National University of Taiwan and the University of Washington. Similarly, Osman Balci joined the computer science department with degrees from his native Turkey and Syracuse University; and Aicha A. Elshabini-Riad joined the electrical engineering department with degrees from her native Egypt and the University of Colorado. Lay Nam Chang, a son of Singapore, joined the physics department in 1978 with degrees from Columbia University and the University of California at Berkeley.

Vet Med

During the 1970s, in a new era of animal science, Virginia Tech drew upon one of its earliest strengths to develop what opened in 1980 as the Virginia–Maryland Regional College of Veterinary Medicine. The effort began during Marshall Hahn's presidency with the appointment in 1974 of Richard B. Talbot as founding dean to explore the possibility, and work toward realization, of a school on the Blacksburg campus to train vets in Virginia.

Despite what seemed like endless obstacles, Virginia governor John N. Dalton and Virginia Tech president William E. Lavery, together with their Maryland counterparts, came to an agreement on a joint venture in early 1980, and the incipient school scrambled to recruit and prepare for an entering class that fall.

Dean Talbot's work to establish and lead the College are honored there at the Richard B. Talbot Educational Resources Center. President Lavery's efforts to bring the vet school to fruition are appropriately commemorated at the William E. Lavery Animal Health Research Center.

Higher Education in Virginia in the 1970s

Tech celebrated its centennial anniversary in 1972. No longer a tiny new school with a curriculum focused on training in agriculture, engineering, and the military, it retained its original major elements but combined them with a very broad range of new curricular offerings. No longer measuring its enrollment by the dozens or the hundreds, it counted students by the thousands. No longer an enclave of white male native Virginians, it included students and faculty alike from across the nation and around the world, though most faculty at the start of Tech's second century continued to be white men from the United States.

By some measures, Tech became Virginia's largest institution of higher education by the 1970s. Its Blacksburg campus enrolled more full-time students than UVA's Charlottesville campus and far more than VMI, Virginia State, William and Mary, or any other Virginia school, though George Mason's total enrollment continued to rocket ahead, as did the aggregate enrollment of the community college system.

Considered in another frame of reference, Tech in the 1970s was only one of a great many state-supported institutions of higher education in the Old Dominion. A century earlier, UVA and VMI were Virginia's only public institutions of higher education, and Virginia Agricultural and Mechanical College became Virginia's third such institution when it joined them in 1872. Virginia State University and Longwood University—to use their twentieth-first-century names—originated in the 1880s. The University of Mary Washington, James Madison University, and Radford University began operations in the years around 1910 as small schools with extremely restricted clientele and curricula.

All these institutions grew in size, expanded their clientele, and broadened their curricula. Together they blanketed the state with a far greater range of educational opportunities than had ever previously been available in Virginia. Between the 1920s and the 1970s, moreover, the major existing schools developed branches. Some branches grew into towering trees: George Mason University in Northern Virginia and Virginia Commonwealth University in the state capital. Displaying substantial if lesser growth were what became Old Dominion University, Norfolk State University, and Christopher Newport University, all near the Chesapeake. Still others, most of very recent origins, developed as members of the new system of community colleges.

In the 1970s—and in the 1980s and 1990s—some observers perceived that the new community colleges were taking over important roles that VPI had once played. The community colleges operated on the basis of open admissions, whereas Tech demanded performance as well as promise and grew increasingly demanding in its entrance requirements. The legislature sought to maintain low tuition costs for the community colleges, lower than four-year institutions could offer. Community colleges therefore better represented innovations in making higher education more accessible than it had previously been. They, more than Tech, offered post-secondary schooling at bargain basement costs, and they, perhaps more than Tech, supplied technical skills with an immediate market in the private economy.

In the 1970s, Virginia Polytechnic Institute and State University embodied its history but permitted no confusion as to whether it was the same school it had been in 1891, when President McBryde took charge of it. The school survived its first twenty years and then forged ahead through its next eighty and more. It became a large school, a university, a research university.,

References

Alvey, *Mary Washington College*, 506–8, 511–14.

Brooks, *Upward: A History of Norfolk State University*, 31–88.

Cox, *Generations of Women Leaders*, 19–20.

Dabney, *Mr. Jefferson's University*, 368–72, 430.

Dabney, *Virginia Commonwealth University*, 222–29.

Eyre, ed., *Virginia–Maryland Regional College of Veterinary Medicine*.

Godson et al., *College of William and Mary*, 2: 814–26, 839, 842–48.

Kneebone and Trani, *Virginia Commonwealth University*.

Kosztarab, *Transylvanian Roots*.

Lewis-Smith, *Radford College*, 109, 116.

Robertson, *Historical Data Book*, 94–96.

Salmon and Campbell, *Hornbook of Virginia History*, 258–71.

Sonner, "Madison College," 53–60.

Sweeney, *Old Dominion University*.

Toppin, *Virginia State University, 1882 to 1992*, 129–31.

Vaughan, *The Community College in America*, 1–24.

Vaughan, *Pursuing the American Dream*, ix–66.

Wallenstein, *Blue Laws and Black Codes*, 184–96.

Wallenstein, "The Morrill Land-Grant College Act of 1862."

Wilkinson, *Harry Byrd*, 285–304.

Chapter 14
1980s: A Research University

David P. Roselle, professor of mathematics in the 1970s, served as dean of the Graduate School and then university provost in the 1980s. During his watch as dean and then provost, the university pushed ahead on becoming a research institution at the same time that it increased its reliance on computer technology. By the time he left to become president of the University of Kentucky, the Virginia Tech community was producing more research than ever before, and thousands of Tech students were using personal computers in their work.

In the 1980s and 1990s, Tech faculty made powerful connections with the world around them. To give one example from 1996, Anthony T. "Terry" Cobb, in Pamplin College's management department, drew on his research and teaching expertise in organizational politics and justice to help two local organizations through the difficulties of effecting a merger. So pleased with the results were the two groups' leaders that they wrote Cobb's dean: "It's people like him that represent the best of how solid research, competent teaching and dedicated public service can benefit the surrounding community." That letter reflected the university's tripartite mission of research, teaching, and service at work in society in the late-twentieth century, and it suggested the connections among the three facets of that mission.

Institutional priorities underwent revision, alterations of various sorts, between the time of Virginia Agricultural and Mechanical College and the time of Virginia Polytechnic

Institute and State University. Research at Tech as an organized function reached its own centennial in 1987. Applied research, at least in agriculture, entered the definition of a land-grant institution of higher education by 1887 with the Hatch Act, and the Adams Act of 1906 effected a partial shift from applied research to pure research. With the Smith-Lever Act in 1914, more than at any previous time, extension, or service, entered the equation—one that from then on had three components, not just one or two.

Yet teaching remained the institution's primary function through Tech's 75th anniversary in 1947 and even beyond. Research in the early years emphasized agriculture. Although agricultural research grew through the twentieth century, a giant wave of research associated with engineering also developed, especially after World War Two. In areas aside from agriculture and engineering, units were long perceived as confined to service roles, their significance restricted to supporting the major mission areas through instruction only. In the 1960s, these units shed their purely service roles and began to grant degrees. By the 1980s, research had become a highly significant part of the entire institution's mission.

From its origins, VPI had a progressive mission, to enhance individuals' life chances and to promote social well-being more generally. That much has always been a given, though its meaning can be a matter of contention. Those twin objectives always animated the teaching of college students. Extension, when it came on-stream, was expressly understood in such terms. Research, too, as it developed, had as a core value the improvement of society. Research might in fact best be understood as itself subsuming a considerable amount of both teaching and service or outreach.

As Virginia Tech's second century emerged ever more fully, that robust pursuit—some combination of exploration, creativity, and publication—could apply as much to the social sciences and the humanities as to science and technology. Nikki Giovanni, poet—wordsmith—extraordinaire, came to Blacksburg in 1987 as a Visiting Commonwealth Scholar in the English department. It was meant as a two-year stint, but then she never left. Appointed to a tenured position as professor in the department in 1989, in 1999 she was named University Distinguished Professor, and perhaps no other member of the university community was as widely known.

The Rise of Research at William and Mary

Well into the twentieth century, an overwhelming emphasis on instruction, not research, was widespread in American higher education, not merely an artifact of the land-grant system. The College of William and Mary provides an instructive example, one that parallels the growth in importance of research at Virginia Tech since the 1950s.

In the late 1940s, the normal teaching load at William and Mary was fifteen hours, five classes. Faculty members urged President John E. Pomfret to cut the standard load from fifteen hours to twelve hours, four courses. Such a move, they argued, would permit William and Mary professors to reallocate a portion of their time, increase their research, and improve their teaching. Better teaching would benefit the students, and more research might bring the school greater visibility and a stronger reputation.

Pomfret refused. Money was scarce, classes must be taught, and research, which Pomfret himself valued, was not a central mission of the College—not a priority claim on faculty time, not a requirement for faculty retention and promotion.

By the 1970s and 1980s, much had changed. In the 1970s, the school used an official figure of twelve hours for the standard teaching load, but in fact the norm had fallen to nine. At the same time, research productivity was climbing in importance with regard to tenure and promotion. Thus the

*William E. Lavery,
president, 1975–1987*

faculty was engaged in far more research than ever before. In the 1980s in the history department, James Axtell—who researched, published, and taught on colonial America—turned out superbly crafted, original essays by the batch and books as often as every year or two. Had a fifteen-hour course load persisted, research productivity like that would have been impossible.

By the 1980s, William and Mary supplied "research assignments" to dozens of faculty for an occasional semester without teaching responsibilities. "Visible scholarship"—research appearing as books and essays—became a priority. Junior faculty knew the terrors as well as the enticements of "publish or perish." A weighting system of evaluating faculty performance assigned equal importance to research and teaching.

Other schools changed in similar ways and at much the same time. At Virginia Commonwealth University, by the 1980s a vast majority of the teaching faculty had doctoral degrees, and the school required annual faculty evaluations that monitored research activities as well as teaching and service.

The same was true at Virginia Tech.

Virginia Tech, Research Institution

Some faculty members hired at Tech in the 1950s never completed a doctoral program. Some of those hired in the 1960s never published a word. By the 1960s, Tech was nonetheless placing increasing emphasis on excellence and productivity in research, and the trend continued through the 1970s and into the 1980s. Expectations had changed. A century had passed since an American school awarded its first Ph.D.— since the time when the highest degree that could be secured, aside from an M.D., was an M.A.

Given the life cycle of individual faculty and, with that, the entire professoriate, by the 1990s few, if any, tenured people with only a master's degree, or with little if any published work to their names, remained at the institution. By the 1960s, the holy trinity of "teaching, research, and extension" had gradually emerged and become the more typical "research, teaching, and service."

Moreover, the expectation of research applied as much to people in history, political science, languages and literature— the new kinds of departments that emerged at Tech then—as to more traditional course areas taught at Tech, like engineering. When Harold C. Livesay was brought in as history department head in 1981, for example, it was with the goal of propelling his new colleagues into still greater research productivity.

Beginning in the 1960s, Tech routinely hired new faculty who had just completed their dissertations. In 1968, for example, Kenneth L. Reifsnider joined the faculty of engineering and science mechanics with a brand new doctorate from Johns Hopkins University, and Thomas J. Adriance did the same in history with a new Ph.D. from Columbia University. In the 1990s, Adriance completed twenty-five years of service as department associate chairman, and Reifsnider was an endowed professor and director of the Center for Composite Materials and Structures.

By the 1980s, research had become a major emphasis in every department across the university. Whether measured in terms of dollars of research grants, publication of books and essays, or the number and percentage of graduate students on campus, it was the hallmark of a research university, and Virginia Tech had become a research university.

No longer could a young faculty member secure tenure and promotion solely on the strength of excellent teaching. Therefore some superb teachers were let go. Departments varied in their assessment of performance in research, but a standard measure in the history department became the publication of a book-length monograph. An assistant professor in history or political science might well be asked, "How is the book coming?" The clock was ticking, and the book must be progressing. For promotion to full professor, the measure of performance—for departments that had required a first book for tenure—included a second book.

To foster research, changes in the operating rules brought teaching loads down. If schools—whether Virginia Tech, William and Mary, or others across the nation—were to get to the point where they gave research and teaching equal weighting in annual evaluations, and if they required substantial research for retention and promotion, then they must do something about the teaching loads.

Four or five courses vanished as a normal requirement or expectation. The new departments that emerged in the 1960s typically demanded a three-course load. A teaching load of two or three courses, or approximately half the previous four- or five-course load, was precisely the kind of adjustment necessary.

Tech displayed another measure of a research university— the number and proportion of graduate students. Tech had supported a small, informal graduate program as early as the beginning of John McBryde's presidency in 1891. Within another fifty years—late in Julian Burruss's presidency, or on the eve of World War Two, many departments in agriculture and engineering were offering master's degrees and some even Ph.D. programs.

In the next half-century, from the 1940s through the 1980s, master's and doctoral programs proliferated, as did the number of students enrolled in them. Ten percent of all Tech students—and then 20 percent and more—were enrolled in graduate programs. For example, the history department graduated its first undergraduate major in 1963; by the

Fralin Biotechnology Center

1970s it was graduating a few students with an M.A., and most such students had researched and written a thesis to satisfy the degree requirements. The rise in research by Tech students rose in tandem with the rise in research by Tech faculty.

What Is a Research University?

The public might have difficulty understanding what a research university was all about. The perception could emerge that faculty members were spending entirely too little of their time and the public's money engaged in the teaching function. What, people might ask, is the utility of this weird research on arcane subjects? What do faculty do with their time and the public's money? Why are they not spending more time in the undergraduate classroom? Is that not where they belong? The answer could be difficult to articulate or demonstrate, unlike a long list of graduates—or a conference championship by the basketball team, a bowl victory for the football team.

A research university could readily be distinguished from a teaching college. Both might demand and reward excellent teaching, and the difference might be one only of degree, a matter of shifts in the mix of teaching and research. A research university, however, had to release faculty from a portion of the instructional load that characterized a teaching school. A faculty member at a research university had to produce what William and Mary's president had called "visible scholarship."

The greater emphasis on research had two implications. One, a research university's reputation is to a great degree a function of its faculty's research visibility. Two, research and teaching should not ideally be entirely separate functions. Rather, students and faculty might well work together in the pursuit of genuine research—and not only at the graduate level. Moreover, the faculty member's research would likely illuminate his or her teaching. If, in fact, the professor was engaged in current research that transformed the ways he or she—and their students—saw the topic under discussion, then lectures could not be simply abstracts or reviews of an assigned textbook. Gone were the nineteenth-century days where instruction might tend to consist of little if anything more than monitoring students as they recited the content of their textbooks.

Undergraduate Research at a Research University

Stories abound of what undergraduate involvement in research might mean. People teaching historical methods, for example, might offer—as an inducement to excellent work, as a means to recruit assistants they had trained—to hire as undergraduate research assistants students who demonstrated superior performance in the course. Regardless of whether students gained such immediate employment and further hands-on experience, they came out of methods courses with enhanced abilities to think through problems; seek out appropriate sources of ideas and information; consider methods of extracting relevant content; and massage their findings into cogent reports. Such strengths should serve them well whatever employment they might pursue.

High-level undergraduate research could be found across the university. Tech inaugurated an annual Research Symposium in 1985, at which students presented their research designs and findings. In 1997, Stephen Bathiche, an electrical engineering major and one of the undergraduate co-winners, worked with a professor in entomology. The other co-winner,

Beth Costine, an animal and poultry science major, worked with a professor to improve the artificial insemination of sheep.

In another project, several undergraduate and graduate students worked with two faculty members in chemistry and biology, Karen J. Brewer and Brenda W. Shirley, on a research project to fight cancer. One of the students presented a paper, co-authored by the entire team, at a meeting of the American Chemical Society in San Francisco in April 1997.

Also in 1997, a replacement bridge over Toms Creek in Blacksburg was constructed of composite materials. Undergraduate classes in engineering science and mechanics, taught by Jack Lesko, worked with real-world problems, not only abstract theory. Lesko's students also worked with faculty members in civil engineering (Thomas E. Cousins) on fiber-reinforced plastic repairs to concrete beams and in chemistry (Judy S. Riffle) on the chemical aspects of resins and adhesives used in the bridge's replacement deck. Students did innovative and interdisciplinary work, learned by doing, and in the process helped repair a bridge so it would more safely carry local traffic.

Robb Wells applied to law school, went for an interview, and found that, quite aside from his generally strong work, one little thing in his letters of recommendation made him stand out. He had worked as an undergraduate research assistant on a professor's project that, when published, acknowledged his contribution in print. Not every applicant had such a credential, and the law school was happy to find a place for him.

It might be considered a western, or a modern, approach to learning—an active approach to creating new knowledge as much as conserving old truths. The world of research universities in the 1980s was not the world of Confucian China or Medieval Europe, where scholars and students might work from the premise—have as their central objective, feel a primary need—that knowledge be conserved, retained, preserved and passed on intact to another generation. Instead, scholars—alone or in teams, in science or the humanities,

Atrium, Pamplin Hall

with high-powered machinery or virtually none at all—worked from the premise that they were seeking new truths, conducting original research, pushing back the boundaries of the known universe, going somehow where no mind had gone before.

Lilliputian Dollars in a Brobdingnagian Budget: Research, Money, Space, and Time

The institution had ways of tilting the playing field, channeling people's energies. Annual evaluations might give greater weight to research and, thus, less to other functions. Promotion committees might demand a published book or published articles in prestigious journals. Faculty committees, when assigned the task of reviewing research proposals for travel money, might decide—or might not—that a faculty member's research proposal offered a legitimate way to spend the taxpayer's money, or the donor's. Departments might—or might not—reward the commitment of time and energy that went into organizing a professional conference. In any number of ways, review groups might—or might not—express pleasure at, direct support for, or offer rewards for the kind of work a faculty member did.

In the 1980s, these and other forces converged, and research caught up with teaching as a major university function. By that time, the seed money that launched the school had long since lost virtually all financial significance, though the Morrill Land-Grant College annuities from 1862 and 1890 continued

into a second century. As
Gulliver might have noted,
had his travels taken him to
the world of the land-grant
schools in the late-twentieth
century or the early-twenty-
first, those Lilliputian dollars
vanished in the school's
Brobdingnagian budget.

In the 1880s, the land-
grant funds typically supplied
the bulk of Tech's income;
in the 1980s, they supplied
a tiny share. The combined
figure from 1900, when Tech
garnered something under

*Robert B. Pamplin Sr. and
Robert B. Pamplin Jr.*

$10,000 from the 1862 fund and another $17,000 from the
1890 fund, might pay the salary of one faculty member but not
cover the operating expenses of a single department.

By the 1980s, new money—and the new technology it
could buy—became essential nutrients for a research university
to grow on. Major grants from Marian Bradley Via endowed
the departments of civil engineering and electrical engineering.
Funds from Tech alumni Robert B. Pamplin Sr. and Robert
B. Pamplin Jr. gave comparable support to the College of
Business. Each of those units adopted the name of its principal
benefactor or benefactors—or, in the case of electrical
engineering, her father, Harry Lynde Bradley.

Especially at the College of Engineering, research was
evaluated in terms of the money it brought into the school
as sponsored research. The university taxed the funds from
research contracts—siphoned off a portion as "overhead,"
which went some distance toward funding other activities. In
this dual manner, corporations and governments helped support
the institution when they funded research, pure or applied,

in everything from polymers to fiber-optics to earthquake-resistant high-rise structures.

In the 1980s, the university's mainframe computer linked perhaps every unit to its computing and word-processing powers. Links to Virginia businesses were fostered at Tech's Corporate Research Center. Tenure even in the social sciences and the humanities hinged as much on productive research efforts as on effective teaching.

The Varieties of Scholarship and Creativity

One of Virginia Tech's outstanding scholars during its fifth quarter-century was Alumni Distinguished Professor James I. Robertson Jr., known across the country for his teaching and research in Civil War history. Perhaps as his contribution to Tech's 125th anniversary year, in 1997 he published a huge biography of Stonewall Jackson that the Book-of-the-Month Club as well as the History Book Club offered as main selections.

A hundred years after agricultural research began to be an important part of Tech's mission, such research continued to produce dividends for Virginia farmers. American farmers grew substantial quantities of soybeans for many years, but to crack major Asian export markets they needed to refine their product. How, for example, to satisfy the demands of Japanese consumers regarding the quality of soybeans used in producing tofu? Researchers at the Eastern Virginia Agricultural Experiment Station worked toward a solution, and funding from the Virginia Center for Innovative Technology assisted the research. Development of the MFS-551 soybean promised Virginia farmers an important new crop for export market.

One way to gauge the variety of research being done at Virginia Tech is to look at one category of awards faculty members have received. Each year, the Virginia Tech Alumni Association recognizes two professors for excellence in research. In 1994, for example, history professor Young-tsu Wong received an alumni research award for his pathbreaking books on the politics and culture of late-nineteenth century China. Richard O. Claus, an endowed professor of electrical engineering, received an award for pathbreaking work on fiber optics conducted at the Fiber and Electro-Optics Research Center at Virginia Tech.

These two professors spanned the range of scholarly inquiry. One scholar, a sole proprietor in the College of Arts and Sciences, lectured, researched, and obtained a readership in various places—China, Taiwan, Australia, the United States—as he reconstructed the origins of twentieth-century patterns in the world's most populous nation and fastest growing economy. The other, in the College of Engineering, taught, researched, and directed a small cooperative colony of professors, technicians, and graduate students who created and applied new technologies for twenty-first century industry and government.

On Founders Day in April 1997, the winners were a math professor, Joseph A. Ball, and a mechanical engineering professor, Christopher R. Fuller. How to set traffic signals to optimize the flow of traffic? How to control noise in airplane cockpits? These were real-world problems that demanded real-world solutions, and engineering answers to such questions required theory married to research. Ball had an international reputation for his innovative work in mathematical theory as well as its application to electrical engineering. Fuller had an international reputation for his work in the field of active noise and vibration control. Among their varied professional activities, Ball worked with the Virginia Tech Center for Transportation Research, and Fuller directed the Vibration and Acoustics Laboratories.

A broadening of scholarship and creativity could be seen in many quarters. The Audubon Quartet was an extraordinary feature associated with the Virginia Tech campus in the 1980s and beyond. Over in the studio arts, David Crane's work in ceramics was a joy to hold or behold. Three professors—Greg Justice in theatre arts, Jack Dudley in sociology, and David

Lux in early-modern French history—combined their talents and passions in the production of a play by Moliere, *Tartuffe*, as well as other works in a series called "Theatre in the Classroom." Thus they mixed creativity and instruction, for example in Dudley's large sociology lecture courses, and they took their ideas and experiences to several professional conferences.

Commercializing Research

Since the inauguration of the agricultural research station in the 1880s, Tech researchers have sought to respond to real-world problems. Over the years, some research has had immediate application, while other research, that of the pure variety, has taken longer to generate benefits, though those benefits, albeit never guaranteed, can bring the greatest returns.

A century into the age of research at Tech, the school sought to institutionalize the process of commercializing new research findings. The sprawling Virginia Tech Corporate Research Center, established in 1985 near the Blacksburg campus, is home to much of the work. Virginia Tech Intellectual Properties Inc., housed at the Corporate Research Center, seeks to facilitate the transfer of technology in multiple ways. VTIP screens the proposals brought to it to determine their potential profit. Given a successful evaluation, VTIP assists in the patenting process and in connecting the innovation with appropriate businesses.

The innovations that have come through VTIP span the kinds of research done at Tech over the past hundred years. One, designed to enhance crop production, produces corn that is resistant to a crop disease, gray leaf spot. Another, designed to reduce pollutants at the same time it enhances efficiency, substitutes a non-toxic alloy for mercury in the switches in applications ranging from automobiles to street lights. Still another attacks cockroaches' reproduction. Others promise, through lightweight headsets, to filter out loud, unwanted noises while letting through necessary sounds; or to manufacture a small antenna, one free from radiation but effecting better sound reception, for use in cellular phones; or, by modifying the genetic composition of pigs, to generate Protein C and reduce the costs of surgery.

Superfluidity and Space Shuttle

A Virginia Tech alumnus shared the 1996 Nobel Prize in physics with two other researchers. Robert C. Richardson graduated from VPI in 1958 and 1959 with B.S. and M.S. degrees in physics and then went on to earn a doctorate

Christopher Columbus Kraft Jr. '44

from Duke. His award-winning work, carried out at Cornell University, related to superfluidity in a helium isotope, helium-3, a cousin of superconductivity in metals. Richardson and his colleagues found that helium-3 could be made to flow without resistance at a temperature barely above absolute zero.

He returned to Tech in April 1997 to give a public lecture as part of the 125th anniversary celebration. If you want to do scientific research, he advised his audience, "look where no one has looked before." Richardson's recommendation could apply to any area of research.

Virginia Tech has left fingerprints all over the National Aeronautics and Space Administration. Christopher C. Kraft Jr., class of 1944, worked in the space program from the 1950s into the 1980s. He gave the Founders Day address in 1974 on "Space in the 1970s," directed flight operations for the Mercury, Gemini, and Apollo programs, worked on the space shuttle, and directed the Lyndon B. Johnson Manned Space Center in Houston from 1972 to 1982. Some years later, in summer 1995, Robert Castle Jr., with degrees from Tech in electrical engineering, directed a shuttle mission that included a docking with the Russian Mir space station.

Roger Crouch, another Hokie who worked for NASA, earned a master's degree at Tech in 1968 and a doctorate in physics in 1971. Beginning in 1985 he was chief scientist for NASA's space and science applications division. Three later Tech graduates in aerospace engineering—Chris Edelin, Eric Hammer, and Greg Oliver—worked together in NASA's Flight Dynamics Group. On Founders Day 1997, their group assisted as Crouch, together with six other crew members, lifted off and Space Shuttle Columbia launched Spacelab on its final scheduled trip in preparation for the International Space Station. The first Hokie in space, Crouch had charge of experiments in microgravity.

References

Cox, *Images and Reflections*, 90–91.

Dabney, *Mr. Jefferson's University*, 430–36.

Dabney, *Virginia Commonwealth University*, 353–68.

Godson et al., *College of William and Mary*, 2: 760, 863, 924.

Graham and Diamond, *The Rise of American Research Universities*.

Kraft, *Flight: My Life in Mission Control*.

Sookhan Ho, "Exemplary Volunteer," *Pamplin* (Spring 1997): 6.

Young, *Virginia Agricultural Experiment Station*, 131–203.

Chapter 15
1990s: Less Public, More High-Tech

Lucinda Roy came to Tech in 1985. In her poetry, she celebrated her Jamaican-born father, her English-born mother, and her childhood in her native England. She brought many gifts, including her wisdom and effervescence, to the English department, the College of Arts and Sciences, Virginia Tech, and Blacksburg. In the 1990s she served for a time in the dean's office, where she promoted, quietly and effectively, all kinds of

Lucinda Roy,
professor of English

initiatives that made for a more inclusive and caring campus and community. In 1998 she gained recognition as an Alumni Distinguished Professor.

Ronnie E. Stephenson attended Tech on an engineering scholarship before deciding he preferred to pursue politics. As a rising sophomore, he was elected president of the class of 1995. A year later he became the first rising junior and the first African American to be elected president of the university's Student Government Association. As SGA president, he fostered enhanced campus security and the re-establishment

Ronnie E. Stephenson '95

of an off-campus student housing office, and he led calls for smaller tuition increases and greater state support for higher education. He majored in political science, connected with the town government, interned in the U.S. Senate, and graduated with honors before heading off to law school.

The institution's past continued to be reflected in the campus population. At the end of the twentieth century, with engineering students still more than 80 percent male, men outnumbered women among Tech's 25,000 students as well as among the faculty. Lucinda Roy sparkled on a faculty that remained largely white and largely male, though the changes since the mid-1960s could be seen as impressive. Ronnie Stephenson accomplished all he did in academics and extracurricular activities on a campus whose student population had not dropped much below 90 percent white, with Asians and Asian-Americans (combined) outnumbering African Americans together with black-identifying people from Africa and the Caribbean.

The Land-Grant Connection

Many of Tech's faculty and administrators continued, much as T. Marshall Hahn had, to spend all or most of their academic careers in the land-grant system. The school's thirteenth and fourteenth presidents offer good examples. James D. McComas earned his undergraduate degree from one land-grant school, West Virginia University, and his graduate degrees from

James D. McComas,
president, 1988–1994

Paul E. Torgersen,
president, 1994–2000

another, Ohio State University. He taught or served as dean of education at New Mexico State University, Kansas State University, and the University of Tennessee. Then he served as president of two universities—one was Mississippi State; the other, his only non-land-grant school, the University of Toledo—before he came to Tech in 1988.

Paul E. Torgersen earned his undergraduate degree from Lehigh University, not a land-grant school, but his M.S. and Ph.D. came from Ohio State University, and he left the faculty at Oklahoma State University to come to Virginia Tech in 1967. When Professor H. L. Manning became an assistant dean in the College of Engineering, Torgersen replaced him as head of the department of industrial engineering. In 1970, the dean of the college, Dr. Willis G. Worcester, died in a plane crash, and Torgersen was appointed dean.

Dr. Torgersen served as interim president between Lavery and McComas, and then he returned to the dean's office in engineering. When President McComas fell seriously ill in 1993, Torgersen agreed to serve once again as interim president. The Board of Visitors soon chose him to succeed McComas, beginning at the start of 1994. A white Mercedes bearing plates that said "TENNIS" accompanied the new president and his wife, Dot, when they moved to the Grove.

History and Virginia Tech

In the 1990s few faculty and fewer students had more than a glimmer of the time when no female student could enroll at Tech, or (for another third of a century) no African American could. Nor did many have any knowledge of the time—a time that continued through the 1960s—when classes met Tuesdays, Thursdays, and Saturdays as well as Mondays, Wednesdays, and Fridays. Fewer could recall when Thanksgiving break— now an entire week—began only after cadets took the train to Roanoke for the annual Thanksgiving football game with VMI. For that matter, few could remember the 1966 legislature that launched higher education in Virginia into a higher orbit—or the Great Depression, when hard times led to large cuts in faculty salaries. History is a story of change as well as continuity.

In the 1990s the great question in the headlines regarding VMI was whether the federal courts would compel the school to enroll women. Farther south, The Citadel found itself in much the same situation. By contrast, William and Mary and UVA, as well as Virginia Tech, had each, years earlier, made the decision or had the decision made for it—whether the change was incremental or pretty much all at once—to incorporate women, at least as students.

Still, even at schools that had been coeducational for what seemed a long time, related issues persisted. At Tech, these took two main forms: few women in senior positions and limited opportunities for women in sports. A new provost appointed in 1989, E. Fred Carlisle, made it a hallmark of his tenure to hire more women in senior faculty and administrative positions, and his successor in 1995 was a woman, Peggy S. Meszaros. In sports, prodding from inside the university and outside it, including a lawsuit filed under Title Nine, led to expanded opportunities for female students in intercollegiate athletics. Women obtained more athletic scholarships, and new teams were organized in soccer, lacrosse, and softball.

Quite aside from questions of race and gender, Tech faced major chronic problems and opportunities in the 1990s. One had to do with the fiscal environment, particularly when a sharp recession, together with political decisions in Richmond, led to cutbacks in state support for higher education. The other related to the microchip revolution as new technologies seemed to offer all kinds of possible new ways to administer, communicate, teach, research, and publish. Virginia Tech took the lead in moving into the world of high-tech higher education, but it found itself unwillingly moving toward an increased reliance on private funding, including higher tuition.

In a quest for greater self-sufficiency and increased resources for all its activities, the university launched an ambitious "Campaign for Virginia Tech" in 1992. It sought $250 million in additional endowment funds from alumni, corporations, and other sources. Acting as co-chairmen of the campaign were T. Marshall Hahn, the former university president and retired CEO of Georgia-Pacific Corporation, and Clifton C. Garvin, class of 1943, who retired as CEO of Exxon in 1986. As Tech reached its 125th birthday, the campaign neared its goal.

A Public School Becomes Less Public

When American states began in the nineteenth century to take on new tasks and help finance such institutions as colleges, mental hospitals, and schools for deaf and blind youngsters, state funds generally supplied only a portion of each facility's needs. Some sort of user fee—sometimes flat-rate, sometimes calibrated to the ability to pay—typically supplied much of the rest. For public institutions of higher education, that could mean that students paid tuition, though in amounts that generally failed to cover the full costs of an education.

Until late in the twentieth century, the dominant direction of change brought the fraction paid out of general funds up, and the user fee's share down. For higher education in Virginia— exemplified by Virginia Tech—that trend underwent a dramatic reversal in the 1990s. The new approach hit out-of-state students first.

Regarding out-of-state students, legislators targeted a politically vulnerable constituency, one with no vote in Virginia elections. Legislators determined that such students should make up smaller fractions of the student populations at Virginia schools and that, if they attended public institutions in Virginia, they should pay full freight. There was some wiggle room here. Students in the 1980s could attend Tech from, for example, Pennsylvania, and pay less in out-of-state expenses than they would have paid as in-state students at home. But imposing a quota or pricing them out carried its own costs.

Virginia schools counted on the higher tuition of out-of-state students to help balance the books. And many faculty members and students welcomed a student mix from various geographical backgrounds. If every state determined to teach only its own residents—not have the taxpayers help out with the costs of students from somewhere else—there could be no net financial gain for anyone, and every campus would be a more insular place. Moreover, schools might accept out-of-state students for the enhanced revenue, and in that fashion force in-state students to go elsewhere and pay out-of-state tuition there.

The bigger change came when tuition costs for in-state students rocketed up. Tuition hikes could not cover the entire shortfall from the state treasury, and many faculty vacancies went unfilled, at least for a time. Things eased in 1993, partly because of political pressures against educational cuts and partly because of a stronger economy. A combination of institutional belt-tightening and higher appropriations made it possible for Tech to hold the line on tuition in the mid-1990s. Still, tuition contributed a larger share of the costs of running the university in the 1990s than had been the case in the 1980s or earlier times. Tech had become much more a "private" school than before—still a "public" institution but with considerably reduced state support.

Fortunately, as Tech became more dependent on private money, other funds besides student families' resources filled some of the void left by the withdrawal of state money. On Founders Day in 1997, for example, Robert Pamplin Sr. and Robert Pamplin Jr. announced a new set of scholarships they were funding for students across the university. Beginning with the high school class of 1998, every high school in Virginia might send one Pamplin scholar to Tech, to major in any college and any subject, with a $1,000 scholarship. To qualify, students had to complete their high school studies in the top 10 percent of their class, compile at least a 3.75 grade point average, and demonstrate leadership and service activities in their school and community.

Other public schools across America shared some of Tech's financial constraints. Yet Virginia dropped in national rankings according to such indicators as public universities' budget percentages derived from state funds, as Virginia's schools experienced greater difficulties than those in many other states.

A High-Tech University

Two of the catch phrases of the 1990s were the "Blacksburg Electronic Village" and the "Smart Road." Blacksburg, Tech, and the Bell Atlantic telephone company joined forces to link the university and the area's citizens, businesses, and local government so that all could communicate online. The

Smart Road was touted for its potential ability to reduce travel time between Blacksburg and Roanoke—though well into the twenty-first century that had not happened yet—while promoting research on highway safety.

In the late 1990s, the university pushed people off the mainframe. This did not constitute a retreat from the computer revolution. Rather, it resulted from a shift to newer technology.

Already in 1984, the university had begun to require that all students in engineering begin their studies as freshmen with their own personal computers. In the 1990s it began a comparable shift when it promoted growing reliance, among faculty and staff, upon personal computers. Most faculty and staff across the university had phone-mail and e-mail as well as "snail mail," and many students were similarly connected.

Comparable to the university's emphasis during much of the 1980s on research was its emphasis in the 1990s on teaching. Regarding the new technology, what this meant was a greater emphasis on new uses of instructional technology. "Faculty Development Institutes" were designed to bring ever more of the faculty into the new regime. Inducements were offered departments and individuals to embrace the new religion. The hope was that it might lead to more "cost-effective" instruction or at least more effective instruction. Faculty members who most fully explored these possibilities reported, in the main, that significant benefits could accrue, but whether such gains offset the investment in time, quite aside from the investment in hardware purchases and maintenance, seemed less clear.

At the lowest end of complexity, the faculty could now more readily receive and respond to communications from their students. At any time, day or night, and without playing phone-tag, students could e-mail a question, and the faculty member could reply. At a higher level of complexity, they might bring in enhanced teaching materials, as classicists did on ancient Greece; construct web pages, where they could post all kinds of materials for their students; or establish chat pages, where their students could discuss among themselves the ideas and materials of the course. Still more advanced were courses that pretty much took place electronically, and not just in STEM areas. Several professors in the English department experimented with online classes, one by a team that included Nancy Metz on Charles Dickens, another by Lucinda Roy on the Civil Rights Movement.

Another innovation—it began in 1996 and became nearly universal in 1997—was the Graduate School's requirement that all graduate theses and dissertations be submitted in electronic form. The Electronic Thesis and Dissertation initiative was expected to save shelving space in the library for the thousands of theses and dissertations completed each year. Proponents hoped it would expand the ways material might be presented; students might incorporate hypertext, videos, and who knew what else into their finished work. Moreover, they intended that the findings of Tech graduate students become radically more accessible to researchers from around the world.

As Tech entered its 125th anniversary year, plans were well advanced to construct a new building, an Advanced Communications and Information Technology Center (ACITC), attached to Newman Library. A proposed Center for Applied Technologies in the Humanities (CATH) looked to connect teaching with research and also high-tech with the humanities. Among the facilities anticipated at the Center was an initiative called "Virginia 1607–2007: A Digital Library," designed to incorporate texts, images, and sounds and promote teaching and research in the history of Virginia as it approached its official 400th anniversary. Conceived by history professor Crandall Shifflett, it drew participants and contributors from libraries and universities across the state, targeted enhanced teaching in Virginia's elementary and secondary schools, and thus projected new meanings for the traditional trilogy of teaching, research, and service.

Global Connections in Teaching and Service

As one indication of Tech's growing population of students from other lands, the Cranwell International Center—for nearly two decades located at 417 South Clay Street, above the tennis courts—was dedicated in 1986. Cranwell operated as clearinghouse and meeting place, where students from other nations could obtain information on such matters as taxes and housing and could relax among other people with international backgrounds or interests. It also hosted such activities as Friday afternoon meetings of the International Club—a new name in the 1980s and 1990s for what had once been the Cosmopolitan Club. International student groups, including the International Club, met there as well as in Squires Student Center.

Each April brought International Week and, with it, the International Street Fair. Whatever might be true of Blacksburg during the rest of the year, the United Nations General Assembly seemed to come to downtown Blacksburg for at least one day every spring. China and India, the planet's two most populous nations, supplied Tech with more students than any other foreign lands, and both had tables at the Street Fair, as did countries from every continent. Malaysians sold sate and curry puffs, and Koreans sold bulgogi. Flags, food, music, and more, from all around the world—Brazil and Bangladesh, Thailand and France, Indonesia and Colombia—came to College Avenue and Draper Road.

One of the buzzwords of Virginia Tech in the 1990s was "globalization." The Department of History offered a course on the Modern World. A consortium of graduate programs created an Area Studies program. Faculty members were encouraged to add more emphasis to the international dimension of their course content. Yet even at the close of the twentieth century Tech had difficulty establishing and maintaining classes in such non-western languages and literatures as Mandarin, Japanese, and Arabic.

Each year, various professors, including Richard E. Wokutch and Philip Y. Huang in management and James E. Littlefield in marketing, took groups of students to East Asia or Eastern Europe. John A. Ballweg, from sociology and Extension, maintained close ties with people and academic programs in the Philippines. Various members of the faculty and staff worked in Albania in the 1990s to help with such matters as computers, libraries,

The 1990s renovation to Squires Student Center reveals the original 1930s façade

agricultural development, and the Agricultural University of Tirana. American professors and students went from Tech to other countries, and faculty and students came to Tech from other countries.

Perhaps the world was becoming a smaller place. Certainly Tech had a larger place in the world. Moreover, a collapsing building in Southeast Asia, like a collapsing political society on one continent or another—such as in Albania—directly affected people in the Tech community who hailed from those places, had worked there, or knew someone there.

The Virginia Tech Foundation acquired a facility in Europe in the 1990s for Tech faculty and students. The Center for European Studies and Architecture (CESA), in Riva San Vitale, Switzerland, rapidly developed into a center for overseas research, teaching, and travel.

In the 1990s, the university established the Service-Learning Center, a unit that facilitated students' exploring a world much closer to home. The Center worked to match students with appropriate organizations so that they would be able to benefit the Montgomery County community at the same time that they obtained hands-on experience related to their academic and professional goals, whether those might be teaching, computing, management, or something else.

One of the Service-Learning Center's initiatives connected Virginia Tech with the Christiansburg Institute Alumni Association. The Christiansburg Institute, established in early 1867 as a Freedmen's Bureau school, had served black residents of Montgomery County, surrounding communities, and even other states throughout the Age of Segregation. In 1966, its doors were closed, as the white public schools finally incorporated black students. Most of its buildings, their purpose of maintaining segregation having been achieved by white interests for as long as possible, were soon obliterated. The school's alumni, however— among them Cora Pack, Jacqueline Eaves, and Elaine Dowe Carter—pursued a dream into the twenty-first century that its remaining buildings, especially the Edgar A. Long Building, might serve as an educational center for Appalachian history, black history, and the history of Montgomery County.

The World of Big College Sports

Virginia Tech's fifth quarter-century saw some athletes excel in major sports in college and go on to do the same in professional sports. In football, Don Strock was one great example with the Miami Dolphins, Bruce Smith another with the Buffalo Bills. In basketball, Dell Curry, Tech's first All-American in that sport, threw in his threes year after year for the Charlotte Hornets.

In college basketball, people who watched would long remember the game at Cassell Coliseum on February 6, 1988, when sophomore Bimbo Coles scored 51 points in a come-from-far-behind, double-overtime, 141–133 victory over the University of Southern Mississippi. Tech's first athlete to participate in the Olympics, Coles played in Seoul, Korea, that summer in the 1988 Games.

College athletics can promote a school's spirit, its visibility, and its resources, as well as some students' physical and leadership development. Yet great seasons on a national stage for whole teams from Tech were something new to the 1990s, though a Tech basketball team had won the NIT in 1973, and Tech students

Charles J. "Jack" Dudley, sociology and University Honors

often excelled in cross-country. In the mid-1990s, Hokies had much to cheer about in the successes of the football team and the men's and women's basketball teams. The football team, nationally ranked, went to the Sugar Bowl in 1995 and defeated Texas and to the Orange Bowl in 1996, though there it lost to defending national champion Nebraska. In basketball, the women went to the NCAA tournament in 1994 and again in 1995, and the men won the NIT in 1995 and went to the NCAA in 1996. Moreover, various other teams, too, went on to NCAA post-season competition. In spring 1997, the baseball team and the men's and women's tennis teams did so.

The World of Big College Academics

Tech attracted and trained outstanding students. Some worked in the more traditional areas of strength at Tech, such as engineering. There, each year, a group of students would embark on building a concrete canoe, for example, or perfecting a solar-powered car. Others flourished in areas much newer to Tech's curriculum, such as theatre arts. Kimberley Sebastian, class of 1985, went with her troupe her senior year to the Kennedy Center in Washington, D.C., to put on an award-winning production of "How I Got That Story."

In the 1990s over in Hillcrest, Charles J. "Jack" Dudley fostered the accomplishments of his brood of Honors students. Dudley had agreed to migrate from the sociology department and take charge of University Honors if he could obtain for his students greater autonomy in putting together their courses of study. Conceded his conditions, he went ahead with an effort to take a good program and make it far better. He knew he had good materials to work with.

The Virginia Tech Foundation inaugurated a program called SEED, for Student-managed Endowment for Educational Development, designed to provide opportunities "to learn by doing" as well as to connect the worlds of business and academe. In February 1993, the university responded to a student initiative by putting the group in charge of investing $1 million of Tech's endowment funds. Three years later, it supplied another $1 million. Keeping pace with the professional managers of Tech's funds, the students, most of them from the Pamplin College of Business, had, by 1997, turned the $2 million into $3 million. It was the nation's third-largest student-managed investment program.

Tech tried out new initiatives to render instruction more effective. "Writing across the curriculum" sought to upgrade students' ability to manipulate the English language, an ancient art thought to be in jeopardy. "Computing across the curriculum," unveiled in 1997, was modeled on the writing program and designed by the computer science department to impart and enhance a very modern skill.

Still another teaching initiative, born about the same time, called for a fuller integration of research and instruction in undergraduate classes, with an emphasis on research skills as much as content. Originating in the new Center for

*Mark Embree '96,
Rhodes Scholar*

Interdisciplinary Studies (CIS), the idea was to expose students to a multiplicity of methods in a single course on a selected topic.

In the 1980s and 1990s, Tech developed a doctoral program in Science and Technology Studies. Students could earn a master's degree or a Ph.D. in an interdisciplinary program that combined such curricular strengths as sociology and the history of science and technology.

Virginia Tech had a second Rhodes Scholar in 1996, the first since 1964. Mark Embree completed his undergraduate studies with majors in computer science and mathematics together with minors in English and history. As an undergraduate, he worked at the Naval Research Laboratory in Washington, D.C., where he wrote computer programs to track satellites and catalog space junk. He wrote poetry, too. "Mathematics and poetry are both modes of discovery," he wrote, and each provides "a language for modeling our environment." Among his varied volunteer activities, he worked with the University Honors Association, which he helped establish to provide Honors students with opportunities for both service and leadership. Embree went from Virginia Tech to Oxford University, where he studied math with a view to working in research with scientific computing. In 2014 Dr. Embree returned to Virginia Tech as a professor.

Research and Teaching Revisited

In the late 1980s and early 1990s, President McComas made a hallmark of his administration a renewed emphasis on undergraduate instruction. With a prodigious memory for names, faces, and details as well as an ability to put people at ease, he became tremendously popular with students. He served as advisor to some, visited with groups in the residence halls, pushed for better food in the dining halls, and maintained an open-door policy in his office.

His administration saw the establishment of a Center for Excellence in Undergraduate Teaching (CEUT) and a higher profile University Honors program. That is what brought Jack Dudley to Hillcrest for an amazing run at directing the Honors program.

In addition, a $1 million bequest from the family of Edward S. Diggs (a 1914 graduate of VPI's two-year agriculture program) led to President McComas's establishment in 1989 of two "endowed professorial chairs," one in the social sciences, the other in the humanities. Appointed to these two positions were Edward Weisband in political science and then Ernest W. Sullivan in English. The Diggs program led also to the establishment of the Diggs Community, comprised of as many as three new Diggs Teaching Scholars each year, all identified as contributing in especially innovative ways to the teaching mission.

McComas's emphasis on undergraduate teaching outlived his time as president. His successor, Paul Torgersen, continued during his presidency, as he had as dean, to teach a course every term in industrial engineering.

A combination of McComas's initiative with a greater force, the relative reduction in public funding, led to a rise in faculty course loads. That meant a partial reversal of the decline from four or five courses per term to three or even two. The course load edged back up toward three and even beyond, though the evaluation formula from the 1980s—research and teaching equally weighted—remained in effect. Even faculty whose primary responsibility was research, not teaching, found themselves teaching more for a time. One science professor observed wryly that his contract previously called for 25 percent teaching, 75 percent research, but now it seemed to demand 75 percent teaching and 75 percent research.

The Multiversity of the 1990s

At the end of Tech's first 125 years, the university consisted of eight colleges in addition to the Graduate School. Some had separated off from earlier homes, while some merged with others. Among them, they displayed the origins of the institution as well as the new directions in which it had grown. The Virginia–Maryland Regional College of Veterinary Medicine built on courses in agriculture that dated back a century, but it constituted the first professional school at a university that had never had a medical school or a law school.

Reflecting the "agricultural" studies in the original mandate were the College of Agriculture and Life Sciences; the College of Veterinary Medicine, which enrolled its first class in 1980; and the College of Forestry and Wildlife Resources, which was even newer. The College of Engineering, Tech's second largest component in the 1990s, carried the school's other original main imperative, a "mechanical" education, as did the College of Architecture and Urban Studies. Subsequent curricular developments were reflected, for one, in the Pamplin College of Business and, for another, in the (combined) College of Human Resources and Education—soon in turn to be merged into the College of Arts and Sciences, which itself would soon be divided.

The College of Arts and Sciences, which originated as a major part of Tech's operations only in the 1960s as the institution became a university, was by the late 1990s the largest college of all, whether measured in faculty, enrollment, or graduates each year. A home to some traditional disciplines at Tech as well as some very recent ones, it contained departments that ranged from physics to psychology, English to geography, Spanish to sociology, political science to computer science, history to chemistry, biology to geology, mathematics to music.

Beginning in the 1930s, Tech offered classes at various off-campus facilities. Over the years, some of those developed into separate community colleges or even full-fledged universities. In the 1990s, the university was still working to take its programs to Virginians wherever they might live, and some branches of the 1980s and 1990s could be seen as reincarnations of those of the 1930s and 1960s. Building on programs that had been in operation for years, Virginia Tech and the University of Virginia jointly operated a Northern Virginia Graduate Center in Falls Church at a new facility that opened in March 1997. Some classes reached from Blacksburg across the state by satellite. And plans were under way to take Tech classes around the planet on the internet.

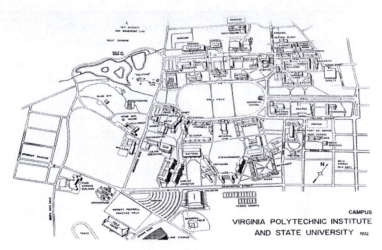

Map of VPI, 1972

References

Cox, *Images and Reflections*, 98–99, 106–7.

Godson et al., *College of William and Mary*, 2: 923–28.

Harris, Sally, "Rhodes Scholar," *Virginia Tech* 18 (Spring 1996): 8–10.

A Model Land-Grant University for the 21st Century

Back at the dawn of the land-grant age in Virginia, when legislators found themselves paralyzed with indecision over how to proceed with the federal funds, William T. Sutherlin and William Henry Ruffner urged the establishment of a new school. It might, Sutherlin allowed, at first be a "purely agricultural and mechanical" institution. Over the longer run, however, it might prove to be "a nucleus around which the accretions of time would gather a really great institution."

Rhetoric and reality alike grew over the years. President Julian A. Burruss spoke often of a "greater VPI." President T. Marshall Hahn Jr. wielded the phrase "land-grant university" from the day he came to campus in 1962 to become Tech's president. By great leadership as well as great timing, Hahn made it so.

Tech's growth and development did not end there, nor did its leadership's aspirations. In the 1990s, President Paul E. Torgersen spoke of making Virginia Tech "a model land-grant university for the twenty-first century."

Gabriel's Horn Sounds Loud, Then Soft: Continuing Struggles for Recognition and Support

The presidents of Tech, like captains of a ship, have fought to make progress, or just prevent capsizing, through heavy political and financial weather. The presidents of the 1880s—

during the time of the struggles to the death between
Readjusters and Funders, Republicans and Democrats—found
themselves swept off the deck even as the ship itself pushed
on. The first two decades—the 1870s and 1880s—supplied the
most treacherous going in Tech's history.

The struggles continued—from McBryde to McComas, from
Burruss to Torgersen—as leadership qualities and good fortune
ebbed and flowed in various patterns. In 1891, President
McBryde inherited a small, scraggly cow college with scant
everything—students, faculty, dollars, physical plant, public
support. In much the longest presidency up to that time—even
now only Burruss exceeds McBryde's tenure, though Newman
nearly matched him—McBryde worked up a foundation on
which succeeding generations built the modern institution.
McBryde benefited from a recovering economy in Virginia as
well as from a considerable increase in federal money, and he
accomplished much with this good fortune.

President Eggleston had a way with words, enormous energy
and commitment, a vision of Tech's promise and a fear of its
collapse. He banged his head against the walls of opposition
and indifference, utterly unable to understand why citizens
and legislators never came around and gave him the support—
never understood the potential benefits, never appropriated the
necessary dollars—he so strongly urged. He advised his faculty
they might have to wait for more resources until "the angel
Gabriel blows his horn"—and some of his successors proved
fortunate enough to hear that horn.

Presidents Burruss and Newman did far more than caretake
the institution through depression, war, and the 1950s. Burruss
brought an end to the era of female exclusion, for example, and
new construction during his presidency transformed the core
campus. Newman laid the basis for Tech's metamorphosis into
a university.

President Hahn placed his indelible stamp upon the place.
Taking a strong institution, he gave it a powerful push toward
greatness. He led it as it approached the ranks of the nation's

leading land-grant schools, a place at which it had never before found itself, a place to which, for much of its history, it could not even aspire.

The presidents of the 1970s, 1980s, and 1990s led the school through an evolution that made it an even stronger and more effective force in the affairs of the community, the state, the nation, and the world. Lavery presided over the school as it became a legitimate research university. McComas tweaked the school's priorities to ensure that research greatness did not come at the cost of dedication to teaching. He strove in varied ways to enhance students' university experience and diversify the faculty—to democratize the institution—though his presidency ran into a financial headwind, and then ill health cut it short.

Paul Torgersen knew the institution and the state as well as any Tech president ever had. He spoke with extraordinary frequency to legislators, alumni, and civic groups. No doubt he sometimes felt as Joseph Eggleston had, in his time, that citizens and legislators failed to give the school the recognition it deserved, the resources that it needed, the dollars that, if supplied, the school had the capacity to multiply in benefits to society. He too fought the good fight.

Generations

Representative families can illuminate something of Virginia Tech's past, its present, and even its future. J. Ambler Johnston enrolled in 1900 and participated in the centennial celebration in 1972. Members of the Hutcheson family, two of them memorialized in Hutcheson Hall, continue to nurture the university. Lucy Lee Lancaster's fifty-four years at VPI, starting with her enrollment in the first cohort of female degree candidates in 1921, followed her father's attendance in 1872 as one of the school's initial cohort of cadets.

Many families no doubt merit mention here, but three more must suffice. Through any one of these three fathers and sons, one can see unfolding a large part of the history of the school.

Each man has contributed in ways that continue to shape the school's growth and development.

One pair is Ellison A. Smyth Jr. and his son of the same name. The elder Smyth migrated to Blacksburg, recruited by a colleague at the University of South Carolina, the new president of VAMC, John McBryde, in 1891. He founded the biology department and chaired it—perhaps one could say constituted it—for the next 34 years, until 1925. He also coached VAMC's first football team, and he formed and coached a gymnastics team.

His son Ellison was born in 1903, grew up in Blacksburg, lived on Faculty Row, and attended VPI, where he joined the track and wrestling teams and graduated in 1925 with a degree in electrical engineering. The younger Ellison Smyth left Blacksburg, worked as an electrical engineer, became a minister, and returned in 1948. As pastor of the Presbyterian Church, he took an active role in community affairs and, in particular, did much to nudge the school and community out of the ways of Jim Crow and into a more equal and less segregated world. In 1993 he published *RetroSpect*, a collection of his memories of such matters as life in Blacksburg and at Tech in the twentieth century's first and third quarters, and in 1997—106 years after his father made his way to Blacksburg— Ellison Smyth the younger brought out another book, *Chips and Shavings*.

William Pamplin grew up in Dinwiddie County and graduated in engineering from VPI in 1928. His younger brother, Robert B. Pamplin Sr., followed him; played intramural baseball, basketball, and volleyball; graduated in 1933 with a degree in business administration; and went on to help build and then head the Georgia-Pacific Corporation. Robert B. Pamplin Jr. attended Tech in the 1960s, class of 1964. Together, father and son run the R. B. Pamplin Corporation in Portland, Oregon. The younger Pamplin, an ordained minister, has said, "Business people have to take the entrepreneurial spirit that they applied to business and apply it to charity."

The two men's philanthropy has included large sums to Tech: millions of dollars to the Pamplin College of Business—money that funded construction of the new edition of Pamplin Hall and that also endowed professorships and supported scholarships—as well as substantial amounts to the Corps of Cadets and the YMCA. In 1997, they endowed hundreds of scholarships for undergraduates from across the state and across the university. Their active participation in Tech's affairs reaches back to the elder Pamplin's enrollment as a freshman cadet in 1929. Together they cover more than half of Tech's first 125 years, and they have done much to influence the school's development. Their work continues to shape the Tech environment.

William H. Daughtrey Sr., from Southampton County, graduated from Tech in 1927 with a degree in agronomy. He began work as assistant county agent and then county agent for the Cooperative Extension Service and, with time out to earn a master's degree in agronomy at Michigan State, spent virtually his entire career associated with VPI and Extension.

In the 1930s Daughtrey administered the Agricultural Adjustment Act in Virginia. After World War Two he promoted marketing education to enhance farmers' ability to adjust to changing technological and economic conditions, and he served as associate director of the Agricultural Extension Service and then, from 1962 until his retirement in 1965, state director of Extension.

William H. Daughtrey Jr. earned a bachelor's degree in physics in 1962 and then a master's in nuclear physics. For his many professional accomplishments, he received the 1997 University Distinguished Achievement Award. In the 1990s, he taught a colloquium in University Honors, and he endowed the Daughtrey Fellowships, which permitted outstanding undergraduates to travel to another country and do creative intellectual work there. By 1997, the two Daughtreys' active involvement in university affairs extended across 74 years, well over half the period since the launching of a fledgling school at Blacksburg in 1872.

Looking Ahead: The Second 125 Years

Tech has outgrown its beginnings as Virginia Agricultural and Mechanical College, yet its origins have not vanished. Making the benefits of education available to a wide cross section of students remains a significant part of the school's mission. So does applying the knowledge generated at the institution to the betterment of social conditions; service to the community remains a significant obligation, as does applied research. The broad categories of teaching, research, and service persist, though their concrete meanings have undergone transformation and continue to undergo scrutiny and rethinking.

Tech's history has never stopped for quarter-century celebrations. The land-grant system reached its first quarter-century marker in 1887, the year Congress passed the Hatch Act and launched the experiment stations with their greater emphasis on research. The system had just marked its first half-century when Congress passed the Smith-Lever Act in 1914. That act fostered the development of institutional extension across each state and lifted service to a status of partnership with instruction and research in the land-grant mission.

Virginia Tech, always ten years younger than the Morrill Act, celebrated its twenty-fifth anniversary in 1897, one year after the school became a "polytechnic institute" and adopted the colors orange and maroon and the motto "Ut Prosim." And it celebrated its fiftieth anniversary in 1922, at the end of the first year of study by Tech's first cohort of women students.

In 1947, the year of Tech's 75th anniversary, the GI Bill brought enrollment to its highest figure ever up to that time,

and civilian students suddenly outnumbered cadets. Though
the numbers of non-Virginians remained relatively small,
never before had so many students come to Tech from foreign
lands. Moreover, the institution was about to embark on a vast
new array of research activities related to the next phase of
industrial development as well as to the Cold War.

Virginia Tech celebrated its centennial in 1972, two years
after it became a university in name. Agriculture and engineering remained core areas of study, but both had developed
world-class graduate programs as well as undergraduate
courses of study, and students came from around the world to
enroll in them. Moreover, Tech had begun graduating students
in English, history, theatre arts, and various other fields in the
humanities and social sciences.

In 1997, on the eve of the twenty-first century, the land-grant
system is alive and well across the nation. It stretches from the
University of Maine at Orono to Washington State University
at Spokane. It embraces the University of Florida, Texas
A&M University, and Virginia Tech, all of them in states that,
at the time the Morrill Act gained passage, were at war with
the United States. In addition, the nation's land-grant schools
include institutions in places that became U.S. territories at
some point after the Morrill Act—not only the University of
Alaska and the University of Hawai'i but also the University
of Puerto Rico, the University of the Virgin Islands, and the
University of Guam. Through the teaching, the research, and
the service that are centered at the many varied land-grant
schools, the system's influence extends around the world.

Justin Morrill's Legacy

Congressman Justin Morrill had great hopes for what might
develop from the seeds his 1862 legislation planted. Senator
Morrill had a still grander vision for the 1890 Act. Even he
would have to be impressed with what, over the years, the
Morrill Land-Grant Acts of 1862 and 1890—combined with

such other measures as the Hatch Act, the Smith-Lever Act, the G.I. Bill, the National Defense Education Act, and the legislation of the Great Society—brought forth.

The man who went to Congress from Vermont in the 1850s took a dream there that he promoted into the 1890s. No matter that he failed most sessions to convince a majority of his colleagues to sign on. He achieved success in 1862 and again in 1890. Other people, including John McLaren McBryde at Virginia Tech beginning in 1891, subsequently shouldered responsibility for perpetuating Morrill's dream and adapting it to the needs and possibilities of changing times.

Look for Justin Morrill's spirit to return for another viewing of the land-grant schools, their mission and their work—perhaps in the year 2012, when the land-grant system turns 150 years old, and again in 2022, when the land-grant institution that started out as Virginia Agricultural and Mechanical College does the same.

References

Sookhan Ho, "The Pamplins," *Virginia Tech Magazine* (Winter 1993), 6–9.

Taylor, John H., "Creative Philanthropy," *Forbes* 400 (Oct. 19, 1994), 64–66.

Appendix A
The Presidents of Virginia Tech 1872–1997

1. Charles Landon Carter Minor (1835–1903), 1872–1879
2. John Lee Buchanan (1831–1922), 1880–1882*
3. Thomas Nelson Conrad (1837–1905), 1882–1886
4. Lindsay Lunsford Lomax (1835–1913), 1886–1891
5. John McLaren McBryde (1841–1923), 1891–1907
6. Paul Brandon Barringer (1857–1941), 1907–1913
7. Joseph Dupuy Eggleston (1867–1953), 1913–1919
8. Julian Ashby Burruss (1876–1947), 1919–1945
9. John Redd Hutcheson (1886–1962), 1945–1947
10. Walter Stephenson Newman (1895–1978), 1947–1962
11. Thomas Marshall Hahn Jr. (1926–2016), 1962–1974
12. William Edward Lavery (1930–2009), 1975–1987
13. James Douglas McComas (1928–1994), 1988–1994
14. Paul Ernest Torgersen (1931–2015), 1994–2000
15. Charles William Steger (1947–2018), 2000–2014
16. Timothy David Sands (1958–), 2014–

* This list supplies the official rendering and numbering of Tech presidents. John Lee Buchanan served as president for three months in 1880 and again for five months in 1881–1882, but he gets only one number. In between those two periods, Scott Ship spent a few days on campus in August 1880 after briefly accepting the presidency, and Professor John Hart served as acting president in 1880–1881.

Federal and State Legislative Foundations of Virginia Tech and the Land-Grant System

The Morrill Land-Grant College Act of 1862

CHAP. CXXX.—An Act donating Public Lands to the Several States and Territories which may provide Colleges for the Benefit of Agriculture and the Mechanic Arts. [37th Cong., Sess. II, ch. 130; approved July 2, 1862; *Statutes at Large*, 12: 503–5.]

Be it enacted by the Senate and House of Representatives of the United States of America in Congress assembled, That there be granted to the several States, for the purposes hereinafter mentioned, an amount of public land, to be apportioned to each State a quantity equal to thirty thousand acres for each senator and representative in Congress to which the States are respectively entitled by the apportionment under the census of eighteen hundred and sixty: *Provided,* That no mineral lands shall be selected or purchased under the provisions of this act.

Sec. 2. And be it further enacted, That the land aforesaid, after being surveyed, shall be apportioned to the several States in sections or subdivisions of sections, not less than one quarter of a section and whenever there are public lands in a State subject to sale at private entry at one dollar and twenty-five cents per acre, the quantity to which said State shall be entitled shall be selected from such lands within the limits of such State, and the Secretary of the Interior is hereby directed to issue to each of the States in which there is not the quantity of public lands subject to sale at private entry at one dollar and twenty-five cents per acre, to which said State may be entitled under the provisions of this act land scrip to the amount in acres for the deficiency of its distributive share: said scrip to be sold by said States and the proceeds thereof applied to the used and purposes prescribed in this act and for no other use or purpose whatsoever: *Provided*, That in no case shall any State to which land scrip may thus be issued be allowed to locate the same within the limits of any other State, or of any Territory of the United States, but their assignees may thus locate said land scrip upon any of the unappropriated lands of the United States subject to sale at private entry at one dollar and twenty five cents, or less, per acre: *And provided, further*, That not more than one million acres shall be located by such assignees in any one of the States: *And provided, further*, That no such location shall be made before one year from the passage of this act.

Sec. 3. And be it further enacted, That all the expenses of management, superintendence, and taxes from date of selection of said lands, previous to their sales, and all expenses incurred in the management and disbursement of the moneys which may be received therefrom, shall be paid by the States to which they may belong, out of the treasury of said States, so that the entire proceeds of the sale of said lands shall be applied without any diminution whatever to the purposes hereinafter mentioned.

Sec. 4. And be it further enacted, That all moneys derived from the sale of the lands aforesaid by the States to which the lands are apportioned, and from the sales of land scrip hereinbefore provided for, shall be invested in stocks of the United States, or of the States, or some other safe stocks, yielding not less than five per centum upon the par value of said stocks; and that the moneys so invested shall constitute a perpetual fund, the capital of which shall remain forever undiminished, (except so far as may be provided in section fifth of this act,) and the interest of which shall be inviolably appropriated, by each State which may take and claim the benefit of this act, to the endowment, support, and maintenance of at least one college where the leading object shall be, without excluding other scientific and classical studies, and including military tactics, to teach such branches of learning as are related to agriculture and the mechanic arts, in such manner as the legislatures of the States may respectively prescribe, in order to promote the liberal and practical education of the industrial classes in the several pursuits and professions in life.

Sec. 5. And be it further enacted, That the grant of land and land scrip hereby authorized shall be made on the following conditions, to which, as well as to the provisions hereinbefore contained, the previous assent of the several States shall be signified by legislative acts:

First. In any portion of the fund invested, as provided by the foregoing section, or any portion of the interest thereon, shall, by any action or contingency, be diminished or lost, it shall be replaced by the State to which it belongs, so that the capital of the fund shall remain forever undiminished; and the annual interest shall be regularly applied without diminution to the purposes mentioned in the fourth section of this act, except that a sum, not exceeding ten per centum upon the amount received by any State under the provisions of this act, may be expended for the purchase of lands for sites or experimental farms whenever authorized by the respective legislatures of said States.

Second. No portion of said fund, nor the interest thereon, shall be applied, directly or indirectly, under any pretense whatever, to the purchase, erection, preservation, or repair of any building or buildings.

Third. Any State which may take and claim the benefit of the provisions of this act shall provide, within five years, at least . . . one college, as described in the fourth section of this act, or the grant to such State shall cease; and said State shall be bound to pay the United States the amount received of any lands previously sold, and that the title to purchasers under the State shall be valid.

Fourth. An annual report shall be made regarding the progress of each college, recording any improvements and experiments made, with their cost and results, and such other matters, including State industrial and economical statistics, as may be supposed useful; one copy of which shall be transmitted by mail free, by each, to all the other colleges which may be endowed under the provisions of this act, and also one copy to the Secretary of the Interior.

Fifth. When lands shall be selected from those which have been raised to double the minimum price, in consequence of railroad grants, they shall be computed to the States at the maximum price, and the number of acres proportionately diminished.

Sixth. No State while in a condition of rebellion or insurrection against the Government of the United States shall be entitled to the benefits of this act.

Seventh. No State shall be entitled to the benefits of this act unless it shall express its acceptance thereof by its legislature within two years from the date of its approval by the President.

Sec. 6. And be it further enacted, That land scrip issued under the provisions of this act shall not be subject to location until after the first day of January, one thousand eight hundred and sixty three.

Sec. 7. And be it further enacted, That the land officers shall receive the same fees for locating land scrip issued under the provisions of this act as in now allowed for the location of military bounty land warrants under existing laws; Provided, their maximum compensation shall not be thereby increased.

Sec. 8. And be it further enacted, That the Governors of the several States to which scrip shall be issued under this act shall be required to report annually to Congress all sales made of such scrip until the whole shall be disposed of, the amount received for the same, and what appropriation has been made of the proceeds.

APPROVED, July 2, 1862.

Congressional Acts and Resolutions, 1864–1869, extending the deadlines and offering the Morrill Act's benefits to Virginia and other states formerly in rebellion

CHAP. LVIII.—An Act extending the Time within which the States and Territories may accept the Grant of Lands made by the [1862 Morrill Act]. [38th Cong., Sess. I, ch. 58; approved April 14, **1864**; *Statutes at Large*, 13: 47.]

Be it enacted by the Senate and House of Representatives of the United States of America in Congress assembled, That any state or territory may accept and shall be entitled to the benefits of the [Morrill Act] by expressing its acceptance thereof as provided in said act, within two years from the date of the approval of this act [therefore by April 1866], subject, however, to the conditions in said act contained.

SEC. 2. *And be it further enacted*, That the benefit of the provisions of this act, and of the [Morrill Act], be, and the same are hereby, extended to the State of West Virginia.

CHAP. CCIX.—An Act to amend the fifth Section of [the 1862 Morrill Act] so as to extend the Time within which the Provisions of said Act shall be accepted and such Colleges stablished. [39th Cong., Sess. I, ch. 209; approved July 23, **1866**; *Statutes at Large*, 14: 208–9.]

Be it enacted by the Senate and House of Representatives of the United States of America in Congress assembled, That the time in which the several States may comply with the provisions of the [1862 Morrill Act] is hereby extended so that the acceptance of the benefits of the said act may be expressed

within three years from the passage of this act [therefore by
July 1869], and the colleges required by the said act may be
provided within five years from the date of the filing of such
acceptance with the commissioners of the general land office:
Provided, That when any Territory shall become a State and be
admitted into the Union, such new State shall be entitled to the
benefits of the said act . . . by expressing the acceptance therein
required within three years from the date of its admission into
the Union, and providing the college or colleges within five
years after such acceptance, as prescribed in this act: *Provided
further*, That any state which has heretofore expressed its
acceptance of the act herein referred to shall have the period
of five years [therefore also extended to July 1869] within
which to provide at least one college, as described in the fourth
section of said act, after the time for providing such college,
according to the [Morrill Act] shall have expired.

Joint Resolution

Extending the benefits of [the 1862 Morrill Act], as
amended by act of [July 23, 1866], to States lately in rebellion
[that is, ten former Confederate states, Tennessee having
already been restored to the Union and provided these benefits].
[40th Cong., Sess. III; S.R. 176; passed by the Senate, July 25,
1868, and by the House of Representatives, February 4, **1869.**]

Whereas under the provisions of [the Morrill Act], and
under the provisions of an act of Congress approved [July 23,
1866] entitled "An act to amend the fifth section of [the Morrill
Act], the several States and Territories became entitled, under
certain conditions, to grants of land or land script; and whereas
by a resolution of the Senate and the House of Representatives
approved [March 29, 1867] the issue or delivery of said
land scrip to any of the States lately in rebellion against the
United States, except the State of Tennessee [which had been
previously approved], was prohibited until said States should
be fully restored to their rights as States by Congress; and

whereas several of said States lately in rebellion have already been fully restored to their rights as States by Congress: Therefore

Be it resolved by the Senate and House of Representatives of the United States of America in Congress assembled, That the issue of the land scrip aforesaid to the States thus fully restored to their rights as States by Congress be hereby now authorized and directed under the conditions and limitations prescribed in the aforesaid acts, and that the authority and direction herein contained be made to apply to States lately in rebellion not yet fully restored to their rights as States by Congress so soon as they shall be thus restored; and all such amount already issued to either of said States are hereby legalized and declared to be a part of the share of such State.

The 1872 Virginia Statute Designating Two Land-Grant Schools

CHAP. 234.—An ACT to Appropriate the Income Arising from the Proceeds of the Land Scrip accruing to Virginia under Act of Congress of July 2, 1862, and the Acts Amendatory Thereof. [*Virginia Acts* (1871–1872), 312–15; approved March 19, 1872.]

1. Be it enacted by the general assembly, That the annual interest accruing from the proceeds of the land scrip donated to the state of Virginia by act of congress of July second, eighteen hundred and sixty-two, and the acts amendatory thereof, shall be appropriated as follows, and on the conditions hereinafter named, that is to say: One-third thereof to the Hampton Normal and Agricultural Institute, in the county of Elizabeth City, and two-thirds thereof to the Preston and Olin Institute, in the county of Montgomery.

2. The said annuity to the Preston and Olin Institute shall be on these express conditions:

First. The name of the said institute shall be changed to the Virginia Agricultural and Mechanical College.

Second. The trustees of the said institute shall transfer, by deed or other proper conveyance, the land, buildings, and other property of said institute, to the Virginia Agricultural and Mechanical College.

Third. The county of Montgomery shall appropriate twenty thousand dollars, to be expended in the erection of additional buildings, or in the purchase of a farm for the use of the said college.

Fourth. A number of students, equal to the number of members of the house of delegates, to be apportioned in the same manner, shall have the privilege of attending said college without charge for tuition, use of laboratories, or public buildings, to be selected by the school trustees of the respective counties, cities and election districts for said delegates, with reference to the highest proficiency and good character, from the white male students of the free schools of their respective counties, cities and election districts, or, in their discretion, from others than those attending said free schools.

Fifth. If at any time the said annuity should be withdrawn from the said Virginia Agricultural and Mechanical College, located at Blacksburg, in the county of Montgomery, the property, real and personal, conveyed and appropriated to its use and benefit by the trustees of the Preston and Olin Institute, and by the county of Montgomery, shall revert to the said trustees and to the said county, respectively, from which it was conveyed and appropriated.

3. The curriculum of the Virginia Agricultural and Mechanical College shall embrace such branches of learning as relate to agriculture and the mechanic arts, without excluding other scientific and classical studies, and including military tactics.

4. The said students, privileged to attend said college without charge for tuition, use of laboratories, or public buildings, shall be selected as soon as may be after the establishment of the said school, and each second year

thereafter: provided, that on the recommendation of the faculty of the said college for more than ordinary diligence and proficiency, any student may be returned by the said trustees for a longer period.

5. As soon after the passage of this act as may be, and on the first day of January, eighteen hundred and seventy-three, and on the same day in every third year thereafter, the governor, by and with the consent of the senate, shall appoint nine persons as visitors of the said college, who shall continue in office until the appointment and acceptance of their successors; and if a vacancy occur in the office of visitor, the governor shall fill the same.

6. If any visitor fail to perform the duties of his office for one year, without good cause shown to the board, the said board shall, at the next meeting after the end of such year, cause the fact of such failure to be recorded in the minutes of their proceedings, and certify the same to the governor, and the office of such visitor shall thereupon be vacant. If so many of such visitors fail to perform their duties that a quorum thereof do not attend for a year, upon a certificate thereof being made to the governor by the rector or any member of the board, or by the chairman of the faculty, the offices of all the visitors failing to attend shall be vacant.

7. The board of visitors shall appoint from their own body a rector, who (or, in his absence, a president pro tempore), shall preside at their meetings. They shall also appoint a clerk to the board.

8. The said board shall meet at Blacksburg, in the country of Montgomery, at least once a year, and at such other times or place as they shall determine, the days of meeting to be fixed by them. Special meetings of the board may be called by the governor, the rector, or any three members. In either of said cases, notice of time and place of meeting shall be given to every other member.

9. The said board shall be charged with the care and preservation of the property belonging to the college. They shall appoint as many professors as they deem proper, and, with the assent of two-thirds of the members of the board, may remove any professor or other officer of the college. They shall prescribe the duties of each professor, and the course and mode of instruction. They shall appoint a president of the college, and may employ such agents or servants as may be necessary; shall regulate the government and discipline of the students; and generally, in respect to the government of the college, may make such regulations as they deem expedient, not contrary to law. Such reasonable expenses as the visitors may incur in the discharge of their duties shall be paid out of the funds of the college.

10. Each professor shall receive a stated salary, to be fixed by the board of visitors; and the board shall fix the fees to be charged for tuition of students other than those allowed under this act to attend the college free of tuition, which shall be a credit to the fund of the college.

11. The trustees of said college shall transfer to the said board of visitors the real estate and buildings, and such other property as they design to be used under this act, with an estimated valuation thereof; and if, in the opinion of the visitors, such valuation should be unjust, appraisers shall be selected and agreed upon by the visitors and trustees, who shall fix such valuation.

12. A portion of said fund, not exceeding ten per centum of the proportion assigned to the Agricultural and Mechanical College and the Hampton Normal and Agricultural Institute, may be expended, in the discretion of the board of visitors of the said respective schools, for the purchase of lands for experimental farms for each of them; and a portion of the accruing interest may be, from time to time, expended by the respective boards of visitors in the purchase of laboratories suitable and appropriate for the said schools.

13. The said appropriation to the Hampton Normal and Agricultural Institute shall be on the following conditions, namely: That the trustees of the same shall, out of the annual interest accruing, as soon as practicable, institute, support and maintain therein, one or more schools or departments wherein the leading object shall be instruction in such branches of learning as relate especially to agriculture and the mechanic arts, and military tactics; and the governor, as soon after the passage of this act as may be, and on the first day of January, eighteen hundred and seventy-three, and on the same day in every fourth year thereafter, shall appoint five persons, three of whom shall be of African descent, citizens of the commonwealth, to be curators of the fund hereby set apart for the use of the said institute, and without the personal presence of a majority of said curators, after a reasonable notice to all of them to be present, recorded in the minutes of the said board of trustees, no action of said board taken under and by virtue of his act shall be valid or lawful.

And the trustees of said college may select not less than one hundred students, with reference to their character and proficiency, from the colored free schools of the state, who shall have the privilege of attending the said institute on the same terms that state students are allowed to attend the Agricultural and Mechanical College under the third section of this act.

14. An annual report shall be made by the proper authorities of each of said institutions, after the close of each collegiate year, of the condition of the institute, and its receipts and disbursements during the preceding year, with the amount of salary paid to each professor, and the amount received in tuition fees from pay students; recording any improvements and experiments made, with their costs and results; and such other matters, including state, industrial and economical statistics, as may be supposed useful—copies of which shall be

delivered to the state superintendent of public instruction, to be laid before the general assembly.

15. The general assembly expressly reserves to itself the right and power, at any time, to repeal or alter this act, and to withdraw from either of said institutions the whole or any part of the appropriations herein granted.

16. This act shall be in force from its passage.

The Morrill Land-Grant Act of 1890

CHAP. 841.—An act to apply a portion of the proceeds of the public lands to the more complete endowment and support of the colleges for the benefit of agriculture and the mechanic arts established under the provisions of an act of Congress approved July second, eighteen hundred and sixty-two. [51st Cong., Sess. I; approved August 30, 1890; *U.S. Statutes at Large*, 26: 417–19.]

Be it enacted by the Senate and House of Representatives of the United States of America in Congress assembled, That there shall be, and hereby is, annually appropriated, out of any money in the Treasury not other wise appropriated, arising from the sale of public lands, to be paid as hereinafter provided, to each State and Territory for the more complete endowment and maintenance of colleges for the benefit of agriculture and the mechanic arts now established, or which may be hereafter established, in accordance with an act of Congress approved July second, eighteen hundred and sixty-two, the sum of fifteen thousand dollars for the year ending June thirtieth, eighteen hundred and ninety, and an annual increase of the amount of such appropriation thereafter for ten years by an additional sum of one thousand dollars over the preceding year, and the annual amount to be paid thereafter to each State and Territory shall be twenty-five thousand dollars to be applied only to instruction in agriculture, the mechanic arts, mathematical, physical, natural and economic science, with special reference to their applications in the industries of life, and to the facilities for such instruction: *Provided*, That no money shall be paid out under this act to any State or Territory for the support and maintenance of a college where a distinction of race or color is made in the admission of students, but the establishment and maintenance of such colleges separately for white and colored students shall be held to be a compliance with the provisions of this act if the funds received in such State or Territory be equitably divided as hereinafter set forth: *Provided*, That in any state in which there has been one established in pursuance of the act of July second, eighteen hundred and sixty-two, and also in which an educational institution of like character has been established, or may hereafter be established, and is now aided by such State from its own revenue, for the education of colored students in agriculture and the mechanic arts, however named or styled, or whether or not it has received money heretofore under the act to which this act is an amendment, the legislature of such State may propose and report to the Secretary of the Interior a just and equitable division of the fund to be received under this act between one college for white students and one institution for colored students established as aforesaid, which shall be divided into two parts and paid accordingly, and thereupon such institution for colored students shall be entitled to the benefits of this act and subject to its provisions, as much as it would have been if it had been included under the act of eighteen hundred and sixty-two, and the fulfillment of the foregoing provisions shall be taken as a compliance with the provision in reference to separate colleges for white and colored students.

Sec. 2. That the sums hereby appropriated to the States and Territories for the further endowment and support of colleges shall be annually paid on or before the thirty-first day of July of each year, by the Secretary of the Treasury, upon the

warrant of the Secretary of the Interior, out of the Treasury
of the United States, to the State or territorial treasurer, or to
such officer as shall be designated by the laws of such State
or Territory to receive the same, who shall, upon the order
of the trustees of the college, or the institution for colored
students, immediately pay over such sums to the treasurers of
the respective colleges or other institutions entitled to receive
the same, and such treasurers, shall be required to report to the
Secretary of Agriculture and to the Secretary of the Interior
on or before the first day of September of each year, a detailed
statement of the amount so received and of its disbursement.
The grants of moneys authorized by this act are made subject
to the legislative assent of the several States and Territories to
the purpose of such grants: *Provided*, That payments of such
installments of the appropriation herein made shall become due
to any State before the adjournment of the regular session of
legislature meeting next after the passage of this act shall be
made upon the assent of the governor thereof, duly certified to
the Secretary of the Treasury.

Sec. 3. That if any portion of the moneys received by the
designated officer of the State or Territory for the further and
more complete endowment, support, and maintenance of
colleges, or of institutions for colored students, as provided
in this act, shall, by any action or contingency, be diminished
or lost, or be misapplied, it shall be replaced by the State
or territory to which it belongs, and until so replaced no
subsequent appropriation shall be apportioned or paid to such
State or territory; and no portion of such moneys shall be
applied, directly or indirectly, under any pretense whatever, to
the purchase, erection, preservation, or repair of any building
or buildings. An annual report by the president of each of said
colleges shall be made to the Secretary of Agriculture, as well
as to the Secretary of the Interior, regarding the condition and
progress of each college, including statistical information in

relation to its receipts and expenditures, its library, the number of its students and professors, and also as to any improvements and experiments made under the direction of the experiment stations attached to said colleges, with their cost and results, and such other industrial and economical statistics as may be regarded as useful, one copy of which shall be transmitted by mail free to all other colleges further endowed under this act.

Sec. 4. That on or before the first day of July in each year, after the passage of this act, the Secretary of the Interior shall ascertain and certify to the Secretary of the Treasury as to each State and Territory whether it is entitled to receive its share of the annual appropriation for colleges, or for institutions for colored students, under this act, and the amount which thereupon each is entitled, respectively, to receive. If the Secretary of the Interior shall withhold a certificate from any State or territory of its appropriation the facts and reasons therefor shall be reported to the President, and the amount involved shall be kept separate in the Treasury until the close of the next Congress, in order that the State or Territory may, if it should so desire, appeal to Congress from the determination of the Secretary of the Interior. If the next Congress shall not direct such sum to be paid it shall be covered into the Treasury. And the Secretary of the Interior is hereby charged with the proper administration of this law.

Sec. 5. That the Secretary of the Interior shall annually report to Congress the disbursements which have been made in all the States and Territories, and also whether the appropriation of any State or territory has been withheld, and if so, the reasons therefor.

Sec. 6. Congress may at any time amend, suspend, or repeal any or all of the provisions of this act.

Approved, August 30, 1890.

Appendix C
Enrollment at Virginia Tech, 1872–1997

Notes: Through academic year 1967–1968, figures include all students enrolled during the year (except for Accelerated War Program [AWP] figures for winter, spring, and summer 1944).

1872–73	132	1895–96	335	1918–19	477
1873–74	197	1896–97	336	1919–20	757
1874–75	222	1897–98	333	1920–21	798
1875–76	255	1898–99	303	1921–22	975
1876–77	224	1899–00	343	1922–23	977
1877–78	186	1900–01	386	1923–24	1,110
1878–79	160	1901–02	472	1924–25	1,191
1879–80	50	1902–03	627	1925–26	1,205
1880–81	78	1903–04	727	1926–27	1,224
1881–82	148	1904–05	728	1927–28	1,300
1882–83	163	1905–06	619	1928–29	1,392
1883–84	190	1906–07	577	1929–30	1,495
1884–85	132	1907–08	546	1930–31	1,659
1885–86	98	1908–09	565	1931–32	1,810
1886–87	110	1909–10	509	1932–33	1,817
1887–88	152	1910–11	471	1933–34	1,561
1888–89	127	1911–12	463	1934–35	1,694
1889–90	139	1912–13	471	1935–36	1,836
1890–91	150	1913–14	527	1936–37	2,115
1891–92	135	1914–15	490	1937–38	2,376
1892–93	177	1915–16	505	1938–39	2,780
1893–94	236	1916–17	533	1939–40	3,119
1894–95	325	1917–18	519	1940–41	3,243

1941–42	3,382	1949–50	4,857	1960–61	5,747
1942–43	3,582	1950–51	3,948	1961–62	5,827
1943–44	1,559	1951–52	3,259	1962–63	6,358
		1952–53	3,215	1963–64	6,555
1944 (AWP)	982	1953–54	3,322	1964–65	7,305
		1954–55	3,747	1965–66	7,711
1944–45	738	1955–56	4,420	1966–67	9,064
1945–46	2,331	1956–57	4,786	1967–68	10,254
1946–47	4,971	1957–58	5,138		
1947–48	5,458	1958–59	5,318		
1948–49	5,689	1959–60	5,496		

Figures for Fall Term only (quarter or semester):

Fall 1968	10,289	Fall 1978	20,261	Fall 1988	22,361
Fall 1969	11,028	Fall 1979	20,780	Fall 1989	22,922
Fall 1970	12,043	Fall 1980	21,069	Fall 1990	23,365
Fall 1971	13,282	Fall 1981	21,584	Fall 1991	23,912
Fall 1972	14,471	Fall 1982	21,510	Fall 1992	23,637
Fall 1973	16,367	Fall 1983	21,357	Fall 1993	23,865
Fall 1974	17,470	Fall 1984	21,454	Fall 1994	23,873
Fall 1975	18,477	Fall 1985	22,044	Fall 1995	23,674
Fall 1976	18,238	Fall 1986	22,345	Fall 1996	24,812
Fall 1977	19,648	Fall 1987	22,702		

Appendix D
Graduation from Virginia Tech, 1872–1997

Notes: Some students completed a 3-year program during VAMC's first decade, but the first four-year degrees were granted only in 1883. Associate degrees are not compiled here. The first Ph.D. was awarded in 1942; figures beginning with 1984 include the new Doctor of Veterinary Medicine degree.

	Bachelor's	Master's	Doctorates
1883	2		
1884	4		
1885	1		
1886	3		
1887	2		
1888	1		
1889	4		
1890			
1891	1		
1892	5	1	
1893	7	2	
1894	9	3	
1895	18	3	
1896	19	6	
1897	19	5	
1898	17	3	
1899	25	4	
1900	25	11	

	Bachelor's	Master's	Doctorates
1901	35	6	
1902	44	9	
1903	35	17	
1904	58	14	
1905	77	19	
1906	65	13	
1907	70	13	
1908	42	17	
1909	45	14	
1910	48	15	
1911	69	9	
1912	44	15	
1913	47	13	
1914	52	7	
1915	60	13	
1916	77	15	
1917	67	12	
1918	29	3	
1919	36	8	
1920	79	7	
1921	75	8	
1922	117	17	
1923	112	12	
1924	113	11	
1925	141	10	
1926	133	15	
1927	149	14	
1928	180	14	
1929	178	17	
1930	208	19	
1931	213	28	
1932	227	55	
1933	280	64	
1934	274	41	
1935	280	35	

	Bachelor's	Master's	Doctorates
1936	257	39	
1937	275	62	
1938	311	48	
1939	378	65	
1940	440	74	
1941	464	65	
1942	467	46	1
1943	523	34	3
1944	184	10	
1945	102	8	1
1946	97	18	1
1947	535	58	
1948	673	87	1
1949	1,042	80	4
1950	1,341	97	5
1951	1,004	113	5
1952	727	98	5
1953	620	120	7
1954	504	90	5
1955	470	113	7
1956	549	90	13
1957	710	99	10
1958	911	127	16
1959	858	131	12
1960	896	122	18
1961	881	162	20
1962	954	186	25
1963	1,032	205	22
1964	1,008	194	24
1965	1,087	173	52
1966	1,064	208	64
1967	1,170	247	128
1968	1,348	250	86
1969	1,766	241	90
1970	2,068	234	107

	Bachelor's	Master's	Doctorates
1971	2,117	295	128
1972	2,182	385	114
1973	2,297	634	102
1974	2,660	767	132
1975	2,999	870	156
1976	3,034	861	186
1977	3,211	1,027	167
1978	3,250	834	178
1979	3,373	866	193
1980	3,521	898	194
1981	3,436	938	211
1982	3,639	963	227
1983	3,680	914	246
1984	3,851	1,003	333
1985	3,757	812	332
1986	3,690	835	354
1987	3,581	1,002	375
1988	3,877	1,072	366
1989	3,612	1,194	380
1990	3,669	1,095	419

Figures after 1990 are on an academic year basis.

1991–92	4,066	1,264	442
1992–93	3,904	1.266	445
1993–94	3,939	1,416	454
1994–95	4,336	1,467	438
1995–96	4,031	1,375	454
1996–97	3,838	1,373	490

Bibliography

In part, this book is based on primary sources, the raw materials of history, whether interviews and newspaper articles or college catalogs and yearbooks. References at the end of some chapters specify such sources, particularly where one is quoted. Yearbooks include *The Bugle* (the Virginia Tech yearbook, starting in 1895), *The Tin Horn* (four issues published by VPI women, the first in 1925), and *Corks and Curls* (the University of Virginia yearbook). Newspapers include the Tech student paper (first named *The Virginia Tech*, subsequently *The Collegiate Times*) as well as the *Roanoke Times*, the *Richmond Times-Dispatch*, and the *New York Times*.

Oral histories are available in a great many collections of interviews listed under Oral History @ VT: Oral History Collections, https://guides.lib.vt.edu/c.hp?g=989141&p=7155036, including the ongoing VT Stories Oral History Project, initiated in 2015 and directed by Professor Katrina Powell.

In part, too, of course, this book has relied on secondary sources—published books and essays and unpublished theses and dissertations. What follows is a list of items that supplied material for this book or that represent places a reader might forage for further exploration. Emphasized here are such topics on higher education beyond Virginia Tech as women and higher education, racial segregation and desegregation, other institutions in Virginia, and schools throughout the land-grant system.

Items followed by an asterisk have been added since the 1997 edition.

Alcott, Pouneh Moghadam. "Women at The Ohio State University in the First Four Decades, 1873-1912." Ph.D. diss., Ohio State University, 1979.*

Alvey, Edward, Jr. *History of Mary Washington College, 1908–1972.* Charlottesville: University Press of Virginia, 1974.

Anderson, James D. *The Education of Blacks in the South, 1860–1935.* Chapel Hill: University of North Carolina Press, 1988.

Andrew, Rod, Jr. *Long Gray Lines: The Southern Military School Tradition, 1839–1915.* Chapel Hill: University of North Carolina Press, 2001.*

Bartley, Numan V. *The New South, 1945–1980.* Baton Rouge: Louisiana State University Press, 1995.

Beamer, Frank, with Jeff Snook. *Let Me Be Frank: My Life at Virginia Tech.* Chicago: Triumph Books, 2013.*

Bettersworth, John K. *People's University: The Centennial History of Mississippi State.* Jackson: University Press of Mississippi, 1980.

Billings, Roger D. "The Homestead Act, Pacific Railroad Act and Morrill Act." *Northern Kentucky Law Review* 39 (2012): 699–736.*

Bishop, Morris. *A History of Cornell.* Ithaca: Cornell University Press, 1962.

Bitter, Andy. *100 Things Virginia Tech Fans Should Know and Do before They Die.* Chicago: Triumph Books, 2019.*

Bloss, F. Donald. *WWII, Mineralogy, and Me: A Memoir.* Chantilly, VA: Mineralogical Society of America, 2012.*

Bounds, Stuart Murray. "Environmental and Political Correlates of Appropriations for Higher Education in Virginia, 1950–1972." Ed.D. diss., College of William and Mary, 1974.*

Bradshaw, Herbert Clarence. *History of Hampden-Sydney College,* vol. 1, *From the Beginnings to the Year 1856.* Durham, NC, 1976.*

Breaux, Richard Melvin. "'We Must Fight Prejudice Even More Vigorously in the North': Black Higher Education in America's Heartland, 1900–1940." Ph.D. diss., University of Iowa, 2003.*

Brickman, William W., and Stanley Lehrer, eds. *A Century of Higher Education: Classical Citadel to Collegiate Colossus.* Westport, CT: Greenwood Press, 1962.

Brinkley, John Luster. *On This Hill: A Narrative History of Hampden-Sydney College, 1774–1994.* [Farmville, VA: Hampden-Sydney], 1994.

Brint, Steven, and Jerome Karabel. *The Diverted Dream: Community Colleges and the Promise of Educational Opportunity in America, 1900–1985.* New York: Oxford University Press, 1989.

Brodie, Laura Fairchild. *Breaking Out: VMI and the Coming of Women.* New York: Pantheon Books, 2000.*

Brooks, Lyman Beecher. *Upward: A History of Norfolk State University, 1935 to 1975.* Washington, DC: Howard University Press, 1983.

Brown, Ellen A. *From Jamestown to Blacksburg: The Path to the College of Natural Resources at Virginia Tech.* Blacksburg: College of Natural Resources, 2007.*

Bruce, Philip Alexander. *History of the University of Virginia, 1819–1919: The Lengthened Shadow of One Man.* 5 vols.; New York: Macmillan, 1920–1922.

Buck, J. L. Blair. *The Development of Public Schools in Virginia, 1607–1952.* Richmond: State Board of Education, 1952.

Bullock, Henry Allen. *A History of Negro Education in the South, from 1619 to the Present.* Cambridge, MA: Harvard University Press, 1967.

Callcott, George H. *A History of the University of Maryland.* Baltimore: Maryland Historical Society, 1966.

Campbell, Hugh C. *The Blacksburg Drama: A History of Blacksburg in Three Acts.* np: McNaughton and Gunn, 2019.*

Capps, Marian P. "The Virginia Out-of-State Graduate Aid Program, 1936-1950." Ph.D. diss., Columbia University Teachers College, 1954.

Carey, James C. *Kansas State University: The Quest for Identity.* Lawrence: Regents Press of Kansas, 1977.

Cato, William Hall. "The Development of Higher Education for Women in Virginia." Ph.D. diss., University of Virginia, 1941.

Caver, Joseph D. *From Marion to Montgomery: The Early Years of Alabama State University, 1867–1925*. Montgomery, AL: NewSouth Books, 2020.*

Chait, Richard Paul. "The Desegregation of Higher Education: A Legal History." Ph.D. diss., University of Wisconsin, 1972.

Chapman, Jill Lee. "Early Veterinary Activities at Virginia Polytechnic Institute, 1870s–1920s: The Rise and Fall of Virginia's State-Controlled Veterinary Complex." M.S. thesis, Science and Technology Studies, 2006.*

Cheek, William, and Aimee Lee Cheek. "John Mercer Langston: Principle and Politics." In *Black Leaders of the Nineteenth Century*, ed. Leon Litwack and August Meier, 103–26. Urbana: University of Illinois Press, 1988.

Cheek, William, and Aimee Lee Cheek. *John Mercer Langston and the Fight for Black Freedom, 1829–1865*. Urbana: University of Illinois Press, 1989.

Cherry, Lindsay. *Walk by Faith, Not by Sight: The Life of Lindsay Cherry*. Meadville, PA: Christian Faith Publishing, 2019.*

China Institute in America. *A Survey of Chinese Students in American Universities and Colleges in the Past One Hundred Years*. New York, 1954.*

Chittenden, Russell H. *History of the Sheffield Scientific School of Yale University, 1846–1922*. 2 vols.; New Haven: Yale University Press, 1928.

Clark, E. Culpepper. *The Schoolhouse Door: Segregation's Last Stand at the University of Alabama*. New York: Oxford University Press, 1993.

Clark, Thomas D. *Indiana University, Midwestern Pioneer*, vol. 1, *The Early Years*. Bloomington: Indiana University Press, 1970.

Cochran, John Perry. "The Virginia Agricultural and Mechanical College: The Formative Half Century, 1872–1919, of the

Virginia Polytechnic Institute." Ph.D. diss., University of Alabama, 1961.

Cohen, Michael David. *Reconstructing the Campus: Higher Education and the American Civil War*. Charlottesville: University of Virginia Press, 2012.*

Cohill, Andrew Michael, and Andrea L. Kavanaugh, eds. *Community Networks: Lessons from Blacksburg, Virginia*. Boston: Artech House, 1997.

Cohodas, Nadine. *The Band Played Dixie: Race and the Liberal Conscience at Ole Miss*. New York: Free Press, 1997.

Cole, Eddie R. *The Campus Color Line: College Presidents and the Struggle for Black Freedom*. Princeton: Princeton University Press, 2020.*

Connell, Raewyn. *The Good University: What Universities Actually Do and Why It's Time for Radical Change*. London: Zed Books, 2019.*

Cope, Alexis. *History of the Ohio State University*, Vol. 1, *1870–1910*, ed. Thomas C. Mendenhall. Columbus: Ohio State University Press, 1920.*

Couper, William. *Claudius Crozet: Soldier—Scholar—Educator—Engineer, 1789–1864. Southern Sketches*, No. 8; Charlottesville: Historical Publishing Co., 1936.

Couper, William. *One Hundred Years at V.M.I.* 4 vols.; Richmond: Garrett and Massie, 1939.

Cox, Clara B. *Generations of Women Leaders at Virginia Tech, 1921–1996*. Blacksburg, 1996.

Cox, Clara B. *Images and Reflections: Virginia Tech, 1872–1997*. Louisville: Harmony House, 1997.

Cox, Clara B. "The Life and Times of William Addison Caldwell, Virginia Tech's First Student." *Smithfield Review* 24 (2020): 21–57.*

Cox, Clara B. "Olin and Preston Institute and Preston and Olin Institute: The Early Years of Virginia Polytechnic Institute and State University, Part I." *Smithfield Review* 19 (2015): 61–76.*

Cox, Clara B. "Olin and Preston Institute and Preston and Olin Institute: The Early Years of Virginia Polytechnic Institute and State University, Part II." *Smithfield Review* 20 (2016): 1–26.*

Crawley, William B., Jr. *University of Mary Washington: A Centennial History, 1908–2008*. Fredericksburg: University of Mary Washington, 2008.*

Cremin, Lawrence A. *American Education: The Metropolitan Experience, 1876–1980*. New York: Harper and Row, 1988.

Cristo, Anthony Bandeira. "The Development of the Community College System in Virginia to 1972." Ph.D. diss., Duke University, 1973.

Cronin, Paul, ed. *A Time to Stir: Columbia '68*. New York: Columbia University Press, 2018.*

Cross, Coy F., II. *Justin Smith Morrill, Father of the Land-Grant Colleges*. East Lansing: Michigan State University Press, 1999.*

Crow, Jeffrey J., Paul D. Escott, and Flora J. Hatley. *A History of African Americans in North Carolina*. Raleigh: Division of Archives and History, 1992.

Cummins, Cedric. *The University of South Dakota, 1862–1966*. Vermillion, SD: Dakota Press, 1975.*

Curry, Leonard P. *Blueprint for Modern America: Nonmilitary Legislation of the First Civil War Congress*. Nashville: Vanderbilt University Press, 1968.

Curti, Merle, and Vernon Carstensen. *The University of Wisconsin: A History, 1848–1925*. 2 vols.; Madison: University of Wisconsin Press, 1949.

Dabney, Virginius. *Mr. Jefferson's University*. Charlottesville: University Press of Virginia, 1981.

Dabney, Virginius. *Virginia Commonwealth University: A Sesquicentennial History*. Charlottesville: University Press of Virginia, 1987.

Dailey, Jane. *Before Jim Crow: The Politics of Race in Postemancipation Virginia*. Chapel Hill: University of North Carolina Press, 2000.*

Daniels, Maurice C. *Ground Crew: The Fight to End Segregation at Georgia State.* Athens: University of Georgia Press, 2019.*

Deel, Anthony Blaine. "Virginia's Minimal Resistance: The Desegregation of Public Graduate and Professional Education, 1935–1955." M.A. thesis, Virginia Polytechnic Institute and State University, 1990.

Dennis, Michael. *Lessons in Progress: State Universities and Progressivism in the New South, 1880–1920.* Urbana: University of Illinois Press, 2001.*

Dethloff, Henry C. *A Centennial History of Texas A&M University, 1876–1976.* 2 vols.; College Station: Texas A&M University Press, 1975.

DiCroce, Deborah M. "*Ut Prosim*—The Balance of Liberal and Useful Education in the American Land-Grant University: A Case Study of Virginia Tech." Ed.D. diss., College of William and Mary, 1984.*

Dingledine, Raymond C., Jr. *Madison College: The First Fifty Years, 1908–1958.* Harrisonburg: Madison College, 1959.

Doherty, William T., Jr., and Festus P. Summers. *West Virginia University: Symbol of Unity in a Sectionalized State.* Morgantown: West Virginia University Press, 1982.

Domer, Dennis, and Barbara Watkins, eds. *Embattled Lawrence: Conflict and Community* [University of Kansas]. Lawrence: University of Kansas Continuing Education, 2001.*

Duderstadt, James J., and Farris W. Womack. *Beyond the Crossroads: The Future of the Public University in America.* Baltimore: Johns Hopkins University Press, 2003.*

Dyer, Thomas G. *The University of Georgia: A Bicentennial History, 1785–1985.* Athens: University of Georgia Press, 1985.

Eagles, Charles W. *The Price of Defiance: James Meredith and the Integration of Ole Miss.* Chapel Hill: University of North Carolina Press, 2009.*

Ehrlich, Thomas, with Juliet Frey. *The Courage to Inquire: Ideals and Realities in Higher Education.* Bloomington: Indiana University Press, 1995.

Eisenmann, Linda. *Higher Education for Women in Postwar America, 1945–1965*. Baltimore: Johns Hopkins University Press, 2006.*

Ely, James W., Jr. *The Crisis of Conservative Virginia: The Byrd Organization and the Politics of Massive Resistance*. Knoxville: University of Tennessee Press, 1976.

Emerson, Bruce. "A History of the Relationships between the State of Virginia and Its Public Normal Schools, 1869–1930." Ed.D., College of William and Mary, 1973.

Endersby, James W., and William T. Horner. *Lloyd Gaines and the Fight to End Segregation*. Columbia: University of Missouri Press, 2016.*

Engs, Robert Francis. *Freedom's First Generation: Black Hampton, Virginia, 1861–1890*. Philadelphia: University of Pennsylvania Press, 1979.

Eschenbacher, Herman F. *The University of Rhode Island: A History of Land-Grant Education in Rhode Island*. New York: Appleton-Century-Crofts, 1967.

Eyre, Peter, ed. *Breaking New Ground: A History of the Virginia–Maryland Regional College of Veterinary Medicine*. 2005.*

Faragher, John Mack, and Florence Howe, eds. *Women and Higher Education in American History*. New York: Norton, 1988.

Farnham, Christie Anne. *The Education of the Southern Belle: Higher Education and Student Socialization in the Antebellum South*. New York: New York University Press, 1994.

Favors, Jelani M. *Shelter in a Time of Storm: How Black Colleges Fostered Generations of Leadership and Activism*. Chapel Hill: University of North Carolina Press, 2019.*

Ferrell, Henry C., Jr. *Claude A. Swanson of Virginia: A Political Biography*. Lexington: University Press of Kentucky, 1985.

Fishel, Andrew, and Janice Pottker. *National Politics and Sex Discrimination in Education*. Lexington, MA: Lexington Books, 1977.*

Fisher, Ada Lois Sipuel, with Danney Goble. *A Matter of Black and White: The Autobiography of Ada Lois Sipuel Fisher*. Norman: University of Oklahoma Press, 1996.

Fisher, Regina Bowles. "Coeducation at the University of Virginia, 1920–1940." M.A. thesis, University of Virginia, 1942.

Fite, Robert C. *A History of Oklahoma State University Extension and Outreach*. Stillwater: Oklahoma State University, 1988.*

Fleming, Walter L. *Louisiana State University, 1860–1896*. Baton Rouge: Louisiana State University Press, 1936.

Fraser, James W., and Lauren Lefty. *Teaching Teachers: Changing Paths and Enduring Debates*. Baltimore: Johns Hopkins University Press, 2018.*

Fraser, Walter J., Jr. "William Henry Ruffner: A Liberal in the Old and New South." Ph.D. diss., University of Tennessee, 1970.*

Fraser, Walter J., Jr. "William Henry Ruffner and the Establishment of Virginia's Public School System." *Virginia Magazine of History and Biography* 79:3 (July 1971): 259–79.

Frykman, George A. *Creating the People's University: Washington State University, 1890–1990*. Pullman: Washington State University Press, 1990.

Gadell, John. "Charles Allen Prosser: His Work in Vocational and General Education." Ph.D. diss., Washington University, 1972.*

Geiger, Roger L. *To Advance Knowledge: The Growth of American Research Universities, 1900–1940*. New York: Oxford University Press, 1986.*

Geiger, Roger L., and Nathan M. Sorber, eds. *The Land-Grant Colleges and the Reshaping of American Higher Education. Perspectives on the History of Higher Education* 30 (2013).*

Gelber, Scott M. *The University and the People: Envisioning American Higher Education in an Era of Populist Revolt*. Madison: University of Wisconsin Press, 2011.*

Gittleman, Sol. *An Entrepreneurial University: The Transformation of Tufts, 1976–2002*. Medford, MA: Tufts University Press, 2004.*

Givens, Lula Porterfield. *Christiansburg, Montgomery County, Virginia, in the Heart of the Alleghanies*. Pulaski, VA, 1981.

Godson, Susan H., et al. *The College of William and Mary: A History*. 2 vols.; Williamsburg: King and Queen Press, 1993.

Goldstone, Dwonna. *Integrating the 40 Acres: The 50-Year Struggle for Racial Equality at the University of Texas*. Athens: University of Georgia Press, 2006.*

Gordon, Lynn D. *Gender and Higher Education in the Progressive Era*. New Haven: Yale University Press, 1990.

Goree, Cathryn T. "Steps toward Redefinition: Coeducation at Mississippi State College, 1930–1945." Ph.D. diss., Mississippi State University, 1993.

Graham, Hugh Davis. *The Uncertain Triumph: Federal Education Policy in the Kennedy and Johnson Years*. Chapel Hill: University of North Carolina Press, 1984.

Graham, Hugh Davis, and Nancy Diamond. *The Rise of American Research Universities: Elites and Challengers in the Postwar Era*. Baltimore: Johns Hopkins University Press, 1997.*

Grundy, Pamela, and Susan Shackelford. *Shattering the Glass: The Remarkable History of Women's Basketball*. Chapel Hill: University of North Carolina Press, 2005.*

Hamilton, Phillip. *Serving the Old Dominion: A History of Christopher Newport University, 1958–2011*. Macon, GA: Mercer University Press, 2011.*

Hantman, Jeffrey L. *Monacan Millennium: A Collaborative Archaeology and History of a Virginia Indian People*. Charlottesville: University of Virginia Press, 2018.*

Hardin, John A. *The Pursuit of Excellence: Kentucky State University, 1886–1920*. Charlotte, NC: Information Age Publishing, 2021.*

Harlan, Louis R. *Separate and Unequal: Public School Campaigns and Racism in the Southern Seaboard States, 1901–1915*. Chapel Hill: University of North Carolina Press, 1958.

Harper, Laura Jane, and W. Charlene Howery. "History of Home Economics at V.P.I." Unpublished manuscript, 1985.*

Harris, Adam. *The State Must Provide: Why America's Colleges Have Always Been Unequal—And How to Set Them Right.* New York: HarperCollins, 2021.*

Harris, Leslie M., James T. Campbell, and Alfred L. Brophy, eds. *Slavery and the University: Histories and Legacies.* Athens: University of Georgia Press, 2019.

Hawkins, Hugh. *A History of the Johns Hopkins University, 1874–1889.* Ithaca: Cornell University Press, 1960.*

Hawkins, Hugh. *Banding Together: The Rise of National Associations in American Higher Education, 1887–1950.* Baltimore: Johns Hopkins University Press, 1992.*

Hill, Lena M., and Michael D. Hill, eds. *Invisible Hawkeyes: African Americans at the University of Iowa during the Long Civil Rights Era.* Iowa City: University of Iowa Press, 2016.*

Hine, Darlene Clark. *Black Women in White: Racial Conflict and Cooperation in the Nursing Profession, 1890–1950.* Bloomington: Indiana University Press, 1989.*

Hine, William C. *South Carolina State University: A Black Land-Grant College in Jim Crow America.* Columbia: University of South Carolina Press, 2018.*

Hofer, Stefanie. "Lockout: Spacing Trauma and Recovery in the Aftermath of the Virginia Tech Shootings." *American Imago* 72:3 (2015): 231–83.*

Hoffer, Williamjames Hull. *To Enlarge the Machinery of Government: Congressional Debates and the Growth of the American State, 1858–1891.* Baltimore: Johns Hopkins University Press, 2007.*

Hofstadter, Richard, and C. DeWitt Hardy. *The Development and Scope of Higher Education in the United States.* New York: Columbia University Press, 1952.

Hollars, B. J. *Opening the Doors: The Desegregation of the University of Alabama and the Fight for Civil Rights in Tuscaloosa.* Tuscaloosa: University of Alabama Press, 2013.*

Hollis, Daniel Walker. *University of South Carolina*. 2 vols.; Columbia: University of South Carolina Press, 1951–1956.

Hooper, William T., Jr. "Governor Edmund J. Davis, Ezra Cornell, and the A&M College of Texas." *Southwestern Historical Quarterly* 78:3 (January 1975): 307–12.*

Hopkins, James F. *The University of Kentucky: Origins and Early Years*. Lexington: University of Kentucky Press, 1951.

Hoyer, Randal Leigh. "The Gentleman from Vermont: The Career of Justin S. Morrill in the United States House of Representatives." Ph.D. diss., Michigan State University, 1974.*

Hulse, James W. *The University of Nevada: A Centennial History*. Reno: University of Nevada Press, 1974.

Humes, Edward. *Over Here: How the G.I. Bill Transformed the American Dream*. Orlando: Harcourt, 2006.*

Hyman, Harold M. *American Singularity: The 1787 Northwest Ordinance, the 1862 Homestead and Morrill Acts, and the 1944 G.I. Bill*. Athens: University of Georgia Press, 1986.

Jacobs, Barry. *Across the Line: Profiles in basketball Courage— Tales of the First Black Players in the ACC and SEC*. Gilford, CT: Lyons Press, 2008.*

Johnson, Eldon L. "Misconceptions about Early Land-Grant Colleges." *Journal of Higher Education* 52:4 (July–August 1981): 333–51.*

Jones, Nancy Bondurant. *Rooted on Blue Stone Hill: A History of James Madison University*. Santa Fe: Center for American Places, distributed by University of Virginia Press, 2004.*

Kao, Hsin-Yi Sandy. "Chinese/Chinese American Students at the University of Mississippi from 1946 to 1975." Ph.D. diss., University of Mississippi, 2012.*

Kapsidelus, Thomas P. *After Virginia Tech: Guns, Safety, and Healing in the Era of Mass Shootings*. Charlottesville: University of Virginia Press, 2019.*

Karman, Thomas A. *A History of Oklahoma State University College of Education*. Stillwater: Oklahoma State University, 1989.*

Kay, Bryan. "The History of Desegregation of the University of Virginia, 1950–1969." Senior thesis, Department of History, University of Virginia, 1979.

Kean, Melissa. *Desegregating Private Higher Education in the South: Duke, Emory, Rice, Tulane, and Vanderbilt*. Baton Rouge: Louisiana State University Press, 2008.*

Kerr, Norwood Allen. *The Legacy: A Centennial History of the State Agricultural Experiment Stations, 1887–1987*. Columbia: Missouri Agricultural Experiment Station, 1987.*

Kinnear, Duncan Lyle. "A History of Agricultural Education in Virginia with Special Emphasis on the Secondary School Level." Ph.D. diss., Ohio State University, 1952.

Kinnear, Duncan Lyle. *The First 100 Years: A History of Virginia Polytechnic Institute and State University*. Blacksburg: Virginia Polytechnic Institute Educational Foundation, 1972.

Kluger, Richard. *Simple Justice: The History of* Brown v. Board of Education *and Black America's Struggle for Equality*. New York: Random House, 1974.

Kneebone, John T., and Eugene P. Trani. *Fulfilling the Promise: Virginia Commonwealth University and the City of Richmond, 1968–2009*. Charlottesville: University of Virginia Press, 2020.*

Knoll, Robert E. *Prairie University: A History of the University of Nebraska*. Lincoln: University of Nebraska Press, 1995.

Kopecky, Pauline W. *A History of Equal Opportunity at Oklahoma State University*. Stillwater: Oklahoma State University, 1990.*

Kraft, Christopher C. *Flight: My Life in Mission Control*. New York: Dutton, 2001.*

Kraybill, Donald B. *Eastern Mennonite University: A Century of Countercultural Education*. University Park: Pennsylvania State University Press, 2017.*

Kuhn, Madison. *Michigan State: The First Hundred Years, 1855–1955*. East Lansing: Michigan State University Press, 1955.

Lamon, Lester C. "The Tennessee Agricultural and Industrial Normal School: Public Education for Black Tennesseans." *Tennessee Historical Quarterly* 32:1 (March 1973): 42–58.*

Langston, John Mercer. *From the Virginia Plantation to the National Capitol, or The First and Only Negro Representative in Congress from the Old Dominion.* Hartford, CT: American Publishing Company, 1894.*

Larsen, William E. *Montague of Virginia: The Making of a Southern Progressive.* Baton Rouge: Louisiana State University Press, 1965.

Lavergne, Gary M. *Before* Brown: *Heman Marion Sweatt, Thurgood Marshall, and the Long Road to Justice.* Austin: University of Texas Press, 2010.*

Lazenby, Roland, ed. *April 16th: Virginia Tech Remembers.* New York: Plume, 2007.*

Lebsock, Suzanne. *Virginia Women, 1600–1945: "A Share of Honour."* Richmond: Virginia State Library, 1987.

Lee-aphon, Gigi. *Cato Lee: Pioneer of the Lee-aphon Clan.* Advance, NC: Lotus Seed Press, 2017.*

Lee, Robert. "How We Investigated the Land-Grant University System." *High Country News* (30 March 2020).*

Lee, Robert, and Tristan Ahtone. "Land-Grab Universities: Expropriated Indigenous Land Is the Foundation of the Land-Grant University System." *High Country News* (30 March 2020).*

Lesesne, Henry H. *A History of the University of South Carolina, 1940–2000.* Columbia; University of South Carolina Press, 2001.*

Levine, Arthur, ed. *Higher Learning in America, 1980–2000.* Baltimore: Johns Hopkins University Press, 1993.

Levy, David W. *Breaking Down Barriers: George McLaurin and the Struggle to End Segregated Education.* Norman: University of Oklahoma Press, 2020.*

Levy, David W. "The Rise and Fall and Rise and Fall of Edwin ('Daddy') DeBarr." *Chronicles of Oklahoma* 88:3 (2010): 288–315.*

Lewis, Ronald L. *Aspiring to Greatness: West Virginia University since World War II.* Morgantown: West Virginia University Press, 2013.*

Lewis-Smith, Lanora Geissler. *Radford College: A Sentimental Chronicle through Its First Half-Century.* 1971.

Lindon, Mary Elizabeth, ed. *Virginia's Montgomery County.* Christiansburg: Montgomery Museum and Lewis Miller Regional Art Center, 2009.*

Link, William A. *A Hard Country and a Lonely Place: Schooling, Society, and Reform in Rural Virginia, 1870–1920.* Chapel Hill: University of North Carolina Press, 1986.

Link, William A. *William Friday: Power, Purpose, and American Higher Education.* Chapel Hill: University of North Carolina Press, 1995.

Littlejohn, Jeffrey L., and Charles H. Ford. *Elusive Equality: Desegregation and Resegregation in Norfolk's Public Schools.* Charlottesville: University of Virginia Press, 2012.*

Lockmiller, David A. *History of the North Carolina State College of Agriculture and Engineering of the University of North Carolina, 1889–1939.* Raleigh, 1939.

Logan, Frenise A. "The Movement in North Carolina to Establish a State Supported College for Negroes." *North Carolina Historical Review* 35 (April 1958): 167–80.

Loss, Christopher P. *Between Citizens and the State: The Politics of American Higher Education in the 20th Century.* Princeton: Princeton University Press, 2012.*

Lowe, Richard. *Republicans and Reconstruction in Virginia, 1856–70.* Charlottesville: University Press of Virginia, 1991.

Lucas, Marion B. *A History of Blacks in Kentucky*, vol. 1, *From Slavery to Segregation, 1760–1891.* Kentucky Historical Society, 1992.

Maddex, Jack P. "Virginia: The Persistence of Centrist Hegemony," in *Reconstruction and Redemption in the South*, ed. Otto H. Olsen, 113–55. Baton Rouge: Louisiana State University Press, 1980.

Manegold, Catherine S. *In Glory's Shadow: Shannon Faulkner, The Citadel, and a Changing America.* New York: Knopf, 2000.*

Manley, Robert N. *Centennial History of the University of Nebraska.* 2 vols.; Lincoln: University of Nebraska Press, 1969.*

Maraniss, Andrew. *Strong Inside: Perry Wallace and the Collision of Race and Sports In the South.* Nashville: Vanderbilt University Press, 2014.*

Marcus, Alan I, ed. *Service as Mandate: How American Land-Grant Universities Shaped the Modern World, 1920–2015.* Tuscaloosa: University of Alabama Press, 2015.*

Martin, Charles H. *Benching Jim Crow: The Rise and Fall of the Color Line in Southern College Sports, 1890–1980.* Urbana: University of Illinois Press, 2010.*

Martin, Charles H. "The Color Line in Midwestern College Sports, 1890–1960." *Indiana Magazine of History* 98:2 (June 2002): 85–112.*

Martin, Tracy. "Black Education in Montgomery County, Virginia, 1939–1966." M.A. thesis, Virginia Polytechnic Institute and State University, 1996.

Mathews, Kimberly A., and Raymond Pierre Hylton. *The Richmond 34 and the Civil Rights Movement.* Charleston, SC: Arcadia Publishing, 2020.*

McCandless, Amy Thompson. *The Past in the Present: Women's Higher Education in the Twentieth-Century American South.* Tuscaloosa: University of Alabama Press, 1999.*

McCaughey, Robert A. *A College of Her Own: A History of Barnard.* New York: Columbia University Press, 2020.*

McCaughey, Robert A. *A Lever Long Enough: A History of Columbia's School of Engineering and Applied Science since 1864.* New York: Columbia University Press, 2014.*

McCaughey, Robert A. *Stand, Columbia: A History of Columbia University in the City of New York, 1754–2004.* New York: Columbia University Press, 2003.*

McCormick, Richard P. *Rutgers: A Bicentennial History*. New Brunswick, NJ: Rutgers University Press, 1966.

McInnis, Maurie D., and Louis P. Nelson, eds. *Educated in Tyranny: Slavery at Thomas Jefferson's University*. Charlottesville: University of Virginia Press, 2019.*

McMath, Robert C., Jr., et al. *Engineering the New South: Georgia Tech, 1885–1985*. Athens: University of Georgia Press, 1985.

Meagher, Hugh A. "Charles A. Vawter and Representations of Progressive Education." Ph.D. diss., University of Virginia, 2017.*

Miles, Saranette D. "A Fighter to the End: The Remarkable Life and Career of Laura Jane Harper." M.A.Ed. thesis, Educational Leadership and Policy Studies, Virginia Tech, 1999.*

Miller-Bernal, Leslie, ed. *Separate by Degree: Women Students' Experiences in Single-Sex and Coeducational Colleges*. New York: Peter Lang, 2000.*

Miller-Bernal, Leslie, and Susan L. Poulson, eds. *Challenged by Coeducation: Women's Colleges since the 1960s*. Nashville: Vanderbilt University Press, 2006.*

Miller, Mark F. *"Dear Old Roanoke": A Sesquicentennial Portrait, 1842–1992*. Macon, GA: Mercer University Press, 1992.

Mohr, Clarence L., and Joseph E. Gordon. *Tulane: The Emergence of a Modern University, 1945–1980*. Baton Rouge: Louisiana State University Press, 2001.*

Montgomery, James Riley, Stanley J. Folmsbee, and Lee Seifert Greene. *To Foster Knowledge: A History of the University of Tennessee, 1794–1970*. Knoxville: University of Tennessee Press, 1984.

Moore, James Tice. *Two Paths to a New South: The Virginia Debt Controversy, 1870–1883*. Lexington: University Press of Kentucky, 1974.

Morris, Robert C. "Educational Reconstruction," in *The Facts of Reconstruction: Essays in Honor of John Hope Franklin*, ed.

Eric Anderson and Alfred A. Moss Jr., 141–66. Baton Rouge: Louisiana State University Press, 1991.

National Association of State Universities and Land-Grant Colleges. *Serving the World: The People and Ideas of America's State and Land-Grant Universities*. Washington, DC: National Association of State Universities and Land-Grant Colleges, 1987.

Nevins, Allan. *The State Universities and Democracy*. Urbana: University of Illinois Press, 1962.

Newcomb, Daniel C. "'Living in a New World': World War One and the Decline of Military Tradition at Virginia Polytechnic Institute, 1916–1923." *Smithfield Review* 22 (2018): 29–52.*

Neyland, Leedell W. *Historically Black Land-Grant Institutions and the Development of Agriculture and Home Economics, 1890–1990*. Tallahassee: Florida A&M University Foundation, 1990.

Neyland, Leedell W., and John W. Riley. *The History of Florida Agricultural and Mechanical University*. Gainesville: University of Florida Press, 1963.

Nieman, Donald G. *Promises to Keep: African-Americans and the Constitutional Order, 1776 to the Present*. New York: Oxford University Press, 1991.

Norberg, John. *Ever True: 150 Years of Giant Leaps at Purdue University*. West Lafayette: Purdue University Press, 2019.*

Norrell, Robert J. *A Promising Field: Engineering at Alabama, 1837–1987*. Tuscaloosa: University of Alabama Press, 1990.*

Ogren, Christine A. *The American State Normal School: "An Instrument of Great Good."* New York: Palgrave Macmillan, 2005.*

Overton, Edward Franklin. "A Study of the Life and Work of Joseph Dupuy Eggleston, Junior." Ph.D. diss., University of Virginia, 1943.*

Pacheco, Josephine F. "Margaret Douglass," in *Three Who Dared: Prudence Crandall, Margaret Douglass, Myrtilla*

Miner—Champions of Antebellum Black Education, ed. Philip S. Foner and Josephine F. Pacheco, 55–95. Westport, CT: Greenwood Press, 1984.

Parker, William Belmont. *The Life and Public Services of Justin Smith Morrill*. Boston: Houghton Mifflin Company, 1924.

Patel, Leigh. *No Study without Struggle: Confronting Settler Colonialism in Higher Education*. Boston: Beacon Press, 2021.*

Patterson, Zella J. Black, with Lynette L. Wert. *Langston University: A History*. 2 vols.; Norman: University of Oklahoma Press, 1979.

Pezzoni, J. Daniel. "Our Native Stone: Architecture and Identity at Virginia Polytechnic Institute, 1872–1922." *Smithfield Review* 1 (1997): 37-52.

Phillips, Sarah T. "Antebellum Agricultural Reform, Republican Ideology, and Sectional Tension." *Agricultural History* 74:4 (Fall 2000): 799–822.*

Pollard, James E. *History of the Ohio State University: The Story of the First Seventy-Five Years, 1873–1948*. Columbus: Ohio State University Press, 1952.

Poulton, Bruce R. *North Carolina State University: The Quest for Excellence*. New York: Newcomen Society of the United States, 1987.

Pratt, Robert A. *The Color of Their Skin: Education and Race in Richmond, Virginia, 1954–89*. Charlottesville: University Press of Virginia, 1992.

Pratt, Robert A. *We Shall Not Be Moved: The Desegregation of the University of Georgia*. Athens: University of Georgia Press, 2002.*

Pritchard, Pamela. "The Negro Experience at the Ohio State University in the First Sixty-Five Years, 1873–1938: With Special Emphasis on Negroes in the College of Education." Ph.D. diss., Ohio State University, 1982.*

Proctor, Samuel, and Wright Langley. *Gator History: A Pictorial History of the University of Florida*. Gainesville: South Star Publishing Co., 1986.

Rabby, Glenda Alice. *The Pain and the Promise: The Struggle for Civil Rights in Tallahassee, Florida*. Athens: University of Georgia Press, 1999.*

Radke-Moss, Andrea G. *Bright Epoch: Women and Coeducation in the American West*. Lincoln: University of Nebraska Press, 2008.*

Ragosta, John A., Peter S. Onuf, and Andrew J. O'Shaughnessy, eds. *The Founding of Thomas Jefferson's University*. Charlottesville: University of Virginia Press, 2019.

Rainsford, George N. *Congress and Higher Education in the Nineteenth Century*. Knoxville: University of Tennessee Press, 1972.

Rainville, Lynn. *Invisible Founders: How Two Centuries of African American Families Transformed a Plantation into a College* [Sweet Briar College]. New York: Berghahn, 2019.*

Range, Willard. *The Rise and Progress of Negro Colleges in Georgia, 1865–1949*. Athens: University of Georgia Press, 1951.

Richardson, Heather Cox. *The Greatest Nation of the Earth: Republican Economic Policies during the Civil War*. Cambridge, MA: Harvard University Press, 1997.*

Richardson, Joe M. *A History of Fisk University, 1865-1946*. [Tuscaloosa]: University of Alabama Press, 1980.*

Risen, Clay. *The Bill of the Century: The Epic Battle for the Civil Rights Act*. New York: Bloomsbury Press, 2014.*

Rivers, Larry Eugene, and Canter Brown Jr. "'A Monument to the Progress of the Race': The Intellectual and Political Origins of the Florida Agricultural and Mechanical University, 1865–1887." *Florida Historical Quarterly* 85:1 (July 2006): 1–41.*

Robertson, Jenkins Mikell, comp. *Historical Data Book: Centennial Edition*. Blacksburg, 1972.

Roebuck, Julian B., and Komanduri S. Murty. *Historically Black Colleges and Universities: Their Place in American Higher Education*. Westport, CT: Praeger, 1993.

Rogers, William Warren. "The Founding of Alabama's Land-Grant College at Auburn." *Alabama Review* 40:1 (January 1987): 14–37.*

Ross, Earle D. *Democracy's College: The Land-Grant Movement in the Formative Stage*. Ames: Iowa State College Press, 1942.

Roy, Lucinda. *No Right to Remain Silent: The Tragedy at Virginia Tech*. New York: Harmony Books, 2009.*

Rudolph, Frederick. *The American College and University: A History*. New York: Alfred A. Knopf, 1962.

Rudy, Willis. *Building America's Schools and Colleges: The Federal Contribution*. Cranbury, NJ: Cornwall Books, 2003.*

Rulon, Philip Reed. *Oklahoma State University—since 1890*. Stillwater: Oklahoma State University Press, 1975.

Sackett, Everett B. *New Hampshire's University: The Story of a New England Land-Grant College*. Somersworth, NH: New Hampshire Publishing Company, 1974.*

Salmon, Emily J., and Edward D. C. Campbell, Jr., eds. *The Hornbook of Virginia History*. 4th ed.; Richmond: Library of Virginia, 1994.

Sanford, James K., ed. *Sight and Insight: The Story of Paul N. Derring at Virginia Tech*. Richmond: Dietz, 1968.*

Sansing, David G. *Making Haste Slowly: The Troubled History of Higher Education in Mississippi*. Jackson: University Press of Mississippi, 1990.

Saunt, Claudio. *Unworthy Republic: The Dispossession of Native Americans and the Road to Indian Territory*. New York: Norton, 2020.*

Sawyer, William E. "The Evolution of the Morrill Act of 1862." Ph.D. diss., Boston University, 1948.

Scanlon, Edward James. *Randolph-Macon College: A Southern History, 1825–1967*. Charlottesville: University Press of Virginia, 1983.

Schall, Keith L. *Stony the Road: Chapters in the History of Hampton Institute*. Charlottesville: University Press of Virginia, 1977.*

Schneller, Robert J., Jr. *Breaking the Color Barrier: The U.S. Naval Academy's First Black Midshipman and the Struggle for Racial Equality*. New York: New York University Press, 2005.*

Schor, Joel. *Agriculture in the Black Land-Grant System to 1930*. Tallahassee, 1982.

Schrum, Ethan. *The Instrumental University: Education in Service of the National Agenda after World War II*. Ithaca: Cornell University Press, 2019.*

Shabazz, Amilcar. *Advancing Democracy: African Americans and the Struggle for Access and Equity in Higher Education in Texas*. Chapel Hill: University of North Carolina Press, 2004.*

Sherer, Robert G. *Subordination or Liberation? The Development and Conflicting Theories of Black Education in Nineteenth Century Alabama*. [Tuscaloosa]: University of Alabama Press, 1977.

Simon, John Y. "The Politics of the Morrill Act." *Agricultural History* 37:2 (Spring 1963): 103–11.*

Skiles, Faith. "Change amidst Tradition: The First Two Years of the Burruss Administration at VPI." *Smithfield Review* 20 (2016): 27–45.*

Smith, Christi M. *Reparation and Reconciliation: The Rise and Fall of Integrated Higher Education* [c. 1840–1910]. Chapel Hill: University of North Carolina Press, 2016.*

Smith, David C. *The First Century: A History of the University of Maine, 1865–1965*. Orono: University of Maine at Orono Press, 1979.

Smyth, Ellison A. *RetroSpect, or Growing up in Blacksburg and Other Tales through a Long Life*. Blacksburg: Pocahontas Press, 1993.

Solberg, Winton U. *The University of Illinois, 1867–1894: An Intellectual and Cultural History*. Urbana: University of Illinois Press, 1968.

Sonner, Ray Vincent. "Madison College: The Miller Years, 1949–1970." Ed.D. diss., University of Virginia, 1974.

Sorber, Nathan M. "Farmers, Scientists, and Officers of Industry: The Formation and Reformation of Land-Grant Colleges in the Northeastern United States, 1862–1906." Ph.D. diss., Pennsylvania State University, 2011.*

Stadtman, Verne A. *The University of California, 1868–1968.* New York: McGraw-Hill, 1970.

Stadtmueller, Scott. "Early Science at the University of Virginia and the Pursuit of Land Grant Status." np, 1996? Special Collections, Virginia Tech.

Stephens, Frank F. *A History of the University of Missouri.* Columbia: University of Missouri Press, 1962.

Steward, Tyran Kai. "Time Not Ripe: Black Women's Quest for Citizenship and the Battle for Full Inclusion at Ohio State University." *Ohio History* 121 (2014): 4–34.*

Stiles, Lindley J. "Publish-or-Perish Policies in Perspective." *Journal of Teacher Education* 17:4 (Winter 1966): 464–67.*

Stimson, William L. *Going to Washington State: A Century of Student Life.* Pullman: Washington State University Press, 1989.*

Strother, Warren H., and Peter Wallenstein. *From VPI to State University: President T. Marshall Hahn Jr. and the Transformation of Virginia Tech, 1962–1974.* Macon, GA: Mercer University Press, 2004.*

Strum, Philippa. *Women in the Barracks: The VMI Case and Equal Rights.* Lawrence: University Press of Kansas, 2002.*

Summerville, James. *Educating Black Doctors: A History of Meharry Medical College.* [Tuscaloosa]: University of Alabama Press, 1983.*

Sutphin, Cathy M., and John Hillison. "History of Extension Work in Virginia Prior to Smith-Lever." *Journal of Extension* 37:6 (December 1999).*

Sutphin, Cathy McNeely. "History of Virginia Congressional District Agricultural High Schools." Ph.D. diss., Virginia Tech, 1999.*

Swain, Ann Scott. "Christiansburg Institute: From Freedmen's Bureau Enterprise to Public High School." M.A. thesis, Radford College, 1975.

Sweeney, James R. *Old Dominion University: A Half Century of Service*. Norfolk, 1980.

Synnott, Marcia Graham. *The Half-Opened Door: Discrimination and Admissions at Harvard, Yale, and Princeton, 1900–1970*. Westport, CT: Greenwood Press, 1979.

Temple, Harry Downing. *The Bugle's Echo: A Chronicle of Cadet Life*, vol. 1, *1872–1900*, through vol. 6, *1930–1934*. Blacksburg: Virginia Tech Corps of Cadets, 1996.*

Thelin, John R. *Going to College in the 1960s*. Baltimore: Johns Hopkins University Press, 2018.*

Thorp, Daniel B. *Facing Freedom: An African American Community in Virginia* [Montgomery County] *from Reconstruction to Jim Crow*. Charlottesville: University of Virginia Press, 2017.*

Tillar, Thomas C., Jr., ed. *Tech Triumph: A Pictorial History of Virginia Tech*. Blacksburg: Virginia Tech Alumni Association, 1984.

Toppin, Edgar. *Loyal Sons and Daughters: Virginia State University, 1882 to 1992*. Norfolk: Pictorial Heritage Publishing Company, 1992.

Topping, Robert W. *A Century and Beyond: The History of Purdue University*. West Lafayette, IN: Purdue University Press, 1988.

Trelease, Allen W. *Making North Carolina Literate: The University of North Carolina at Greensboro, from Normal School to Metropolitan University*. Durham: Carolina Academic Press, 2004.*

Trillin, Calvin. *An Education in Georgia: Charlayne Hunter, Hamilton Holmes, and the Integration of the University of*

Georgia. 1964; reprint Athens: University of Georgia Press, 1991.

Tucker, Rob, ed. *Radford University: Investing in Lifetimes*. Radford, VA: Radford University Foundation Press, 2006.*

Tushnet, Mark V. *The NAACP's Legal Strategy against Segregated Education, 1925–1950*. Chapel Hill: University of North Carolina Press, 1987.

Urban, Wayne J. *More Than Science and Sputnik: The National Defense Education Act of 1958*. Tuscaloosa: University of Alabama Press, 2010.*

Vaughan, George B. *The Community College in America: A Short History*. Washington, DC: American Association of Community and Junior Colleges National Center for Higher Education, rev. 1985.

Vaughan, George B. *Pursuing the American Dream: A History of the Virginia Community College System*. Richmond: Virginia Community College System, 1987.

Veysey, Laurence R. *The Emergence of the American University*. Chicago: University of Chicago Press, 1965.

Vines, Karen A., and John Hillison, eds. *One Hundred Years of Agricultural Education at Virginia Tech*. Blacksburg: Virginia Tech Publishing, 2018.*

Wallenstein, Peter. *Blue Laws and Black Codes: Conflict, Courts, and Change in Twentieth-Century Virginia*. Charlottesville: University of Virginia Press, 2004.*

Wallenstein, Peter. "*Brown v. Board of Education* and Segregated Universities: From Kluger to Klarman—Toward Creating a Literature on Federal Courts and Undergraduate Admissions." *Virginia Social Science Journal* 50 (2015): 13–23.*

Wallenstein, Peter, comp. *Essays on the History of Virginia Tech: The 125th Anniversary, Fall 1997*. Blacksburg: Virginia Tech, 1997.*

Wallenstein, Peter, comp. *Essays on the History of Virginia Tech: The 125th Anniversary, Honors Colloquium, Spring 1998*. Blacksburg: Virginia Tech, 1998.*

Wallenstein, Peter, comp. *Essays on the History of Virginia Tech: Fall 1998.* Blacksburg: Virginia Tech, 1998.*

Wallenstein, Peter. *From Slave South to New South: Public Policy in Nineteenth-Century Georgia.* Chapel Hill: University of North Carolina Press, 1987.

Wallenstein, Peter. "Higher Education and the Civil Rights Movement: Desegregating the University of North Carolina." In *Warm Ashes: Issues in Southern History at the Dawn of the Twenty-First Century,* ed. Winfred B. Moore Jr., Kyle S. Sinisi, and David H. White Jr., 280–300. Columbia: University of South Carolina Press, 2003.*

Wallenstein, Peter, ed. *Higher Education and the Civil Rights Movement: White Supremacy, Black Southerners, and College Campuses.* Gainesville: University Press of Florida, 2008.*

Wallenstein, Peter. "Higher Education in Civil War Virginia." In *Virginia at War, 1864,* ed. William C. Davis and James I. Robertson Jr., 99–119. Lexington: University Press of Kentucky, 2009.*

Wallenstein, Peter. "The Morrill Land-Grant College Act of 1862: Seedbed of the American System of Public Universities." In *Civil War Congress and the Creation of Modern America: A Revolution on the Home Front,* ed. Paul Finkelman and Donald R. Kennon, 82–117. Athens: Ohio University Press, 2018.*

Wallenstein, Peter. "Reintegrating the American Past: Revisiting the West, Frederick Jackson Turner, and the Early Republic." *Virginia Social Science Journal* 47 (2012): 86–102.*

Wallenstein, Peter. "'These New and Strange Beings': Women in the Legal Profession in Virginia, 1890–1990." *Virginia Magazine of History and Biography* 101 (April 1993): 193–226.

Walsh, Mary Roth. *Doctors Wanted, No Women Need Apply: Sexual Barriers in the Medical Profession, 1835–1975.* New Haven: Yale University Press, 1977.

Walton, Dennis, ed. *Radford University: Celebrating the Century, Forging the Future.* Virginia Beach, VA: Donning Company, 2011.*

Wattley, Cheryl Elizabeth Brown. *A Step toward* Brown v. Board of Education: *Ada Lois Sipuel Fisher and Her Fight to End Segregation*. Norman: University of Oklahoma Press, 2014.*

Waugh, Lillian J., and Judith G. Stitzel. "'Anything but Cordial': Coeducation and West Virginia University's Early Women." *West Virginia History* 49 (March 1990): 68–80.*

Webster, Sandy, ed. *I Remember Paul: A Collection of Letters from Alumni of Virginia Tech and Friends of Paul Derring*. Blacksburg: Young Men's Christian Association of Virginia Tech, 1993.

Wells, Thomas Learned. "The Legislative Consequences of Urban Growth: The Case of Virginia, 1966." Ph.D. diss., University of Virginia, 1968.

Wennersten, John R., and Ruth Ellen Wennersten. "Separate and Unequal: The Evolution of a Black Land Grant College in Maryland, 1890–1930." *Maryland Historical Magazine* 72:1 (Spring 1977): 110–17.*

Whipple, Chris. *The Gatekeepers: How the White House Chiefs of Staff Define Every Presidency*. New York: Crown, 2017.*

White, Derrick E. *Blood, Sweat, and Tears: Jake Gaither, Florida A&M, and the History of Black College Football*. Chapel Hill: University of North Carolina Press, 2019.*

White, Derrick E. "From Desegregation to Integration: Race, Football, and 'Dixie' at the University of Florida." *Florida Historical Quarterly* 88 (Spring 2010): 469–96.*

Wildes, Karl L., and Nilo A. Lindgren. *A Century of Electrical Engineering and Computer Science at MIT, 1882–1982*. Cambridge, MA: MIT Press, 1985.

Wilkinson, J. Harvie III. *Harry Byrd and the Changing Face of Virginia Politics, 1945–1966*. Charlottesville: University Press of Virginia, 1968.

Williams, Clarence G. *Technology and the Dream: Reflections on the Black Experience at MIT, 1941–1999*. Cambridge, MA: MIT Press, 2001.*

Williams, Leslie Ogg. "Access and Inclusion: Women Students at VPI, 1914–1964." M.A. thesis, History, Virginia Tech, 2006.*

Williams, Roger L. *The Origins of Federal Support for Higher Education: George W. Atherton and the Land-Grant College Movement.* University Park: Pennsylvania State University Press, 1991.*

Wills, Brian Steel. *No Ordinary College: A History of the University of Virginia's College at Wise.* Charlottesville: University of Virginia Press, 2004.*

Wise, Henry A. *Drawing out the Man: The VMI Story.* Charlottesville: University Press of Virginia, 1978.

Wright, George C. *A History of Blacks in Kentucky,* vol. 2, *In Pursuit of Equality, 1890–1980.* Kentucky Historical Society, 1992.*

Wynes, Charles E. *Race Relations in Virginia, 1870–1902.* Charlottesville: University of Virginia Press, 1961.

Young, Harold N. *The Virginia Agricultural Experiment Station, 1886–1966.* Charlottesville: University Press of Virginia, 1975.

Index

An *italicized page number* indicates an image.